The PROTECTION of
FOREIGN INVESTMENT

Six Procedural Studies

THE PROCEDURAL ASPECTS OF
INTERNATIONAL LAW SERIES

RICHARD B. LILLICH, *editor*

International Claims: Their Adjudication by
National Commissions
RICHARD B. LILLICH (1962)

International Claims: Their Preparation
and Presentation
RICHARD B. LILLICH and GORDON A. CHRISTENSON (1962)

The Role of Domestic Courts in the
International Legal Order
RICHARD A. FALK (1964)

The Use of Experts by International
Tribunals
GILLIAN M. WHITE (1965)

The Protection of Foreign Investment
Six Procedural Studies
RICHARD B. LILLICH (1965)

The PROTECTION of FOREIGN INVESTMENT

Six Procedural Studies

RICHARD B. LILLICH

SYRACUSE UNIVERSITY PRESS

Library of Congress Catalog Card: 65-15855

Manufactured in the United States of America
by The Heffernan Press of Worcester, Massachusetts
and Vail-Ballou Press of Binghamton, New York

To Eleanor G. Lillich

PREFACE

During the past half-dozen years I have worked on procedural aspects of the law of international claims. Since most such claims today arise from the nationalization of foreign property, much of my research has overlapped the topic of this volume. However, in the two works which I have prepared, the latter written in collaboration with Gordon A. Christenson, it was assumed that the United States had concluded a lump sum settlement of claims with the foreign country. Therefore, no attempt was made to discuss means of achieving better settlements, nor were other remedial or preventive measures that might be taken to cushion a foreign property owner against possible loss considered.

The main purpose of this volume, which is intended to serve as a bridge between the above two works and a future treatise on lump sum settlements, is to discuss and evaluate various procedures whereby foreign investment may receive a greater measure of protection. A large body of literature on this topic, much of it special pleading, has poured forth in recent years. Most of it has centered on two methods of protecting investments abroad: (1) the use of bilateral Friendship, Commerce and Navigation treaties under which the United States and the foreign country agree to compensate each other's nationals for any taking of their property; and (2) the promulgation of a multilateral investment convention under which capital-importing countries would agree to pay just compensation should they take foreign property. Both these approaches have been so thoroughly discussed and leave so much to be desired that they are not covered in this work which, as its title indicates, does not purport to be a definitive treatment of the subject.

Instead, this volume contains six interrelated studies examining and evaluating several more promising approaches to the problem. Three studies, covering somewhat familiar material, are necessitated by important recent developments (the *Rich* case, the *Sabbatino* controversy and the payment of the first claims under the IGP). The other three studies are based upon new material which has not been considered elsewhere. The over-all thesis of the six studies is that existing protective measures are generally inadequate and often inconsistent, and that an expanded and integrated program is needed to protect the property of Americans who have been and are being urged by their government to invest abroad. This program should assure just compensation to persons whose property is taken, while at the same time minimizing the taking's effect on broader foreign policy objectives of the United States.

I wish to thank the Editors of the Iowa, Rutgers, University of Pennsylvania, and Villanova *Law Reviews* for their permission to use portions of articles originally appearing in these periodicals. I also would like to express my appreciation to the Ford Foundation for financial assistance under a Law Faculty Fellowship and through a grant from the International Organization Research Program of Syracuse University which made the completion of this volume possible. Among my students and former students who participated in the preparation of these studies the following deserve mention: Barton C. Green, Thomas R. Kennedy, Mark Kessel, and Leslie G. Lewis. Special thanks should go to Mr. Kessel for reading proof and preparing the index while I was abroad. Finally, my thanks go once again to various academic, government, and practicing lawyers, too numerous to mention, for reading and commenting upon various preliminary drafts. The final product, for which I am solely responsible, constitutes the fifth volume in the Procedural Aspects of International Law Series prepared under the auspices of the Syracuse University College of Law International Legal Studies Program and published by Syracuse University Press.

RICHARD B. LILLICH

Syracuse University
May, 1965

CONTENTS

Part Three. Protection for the Future

Part One

PROTECTION IN MUNICIPAL COURTS

In the past both the international law rule of sovereign immunity and the Anglo-American act of state doctrine have combined to bar Americans whose foreign properties have been nationalized from obtaining relief in those rare instances when they have been able to hail the foreign country before municipal courts. Following the Department of State's adoption of the restrictive theory of sovereign immunity in 1952 and the American Law Institute's tentative acceptance of an "international law" exception to the act of state doctrine in 1960, it appeared for a time that municipal courts might come to play an important part in the application and development of this body of international law. The decisions in the Rich *and* Sabbatino *cases put an end to this great expectation. The two Chapters in this Part criticize the rationale of these cases and argue that municipal courts, under congressional mandate if need be, should assume a more active role in cases involving questions of international law.*

I.

Sovereign Immunity

The Origin and Development of the Doctrine

THE ORIGIN of the international law rule of sovereign immunity remains shrouded in semantics. One school of thought maintains that "the immunity from the jurisdiction of local courts enjoyed by foreign states . . . is usually based on the mutual equality and independence of states."[1] According to this theory, "the purely practical argument that to permit process to issue would 'vex the peace of nations' " has generated a rule of customary international law which bestows upon all states immunity from the jurisdiction of another state's courts.[2] A second school contends that "it is very difficult to give any more substantial rationalization for the doctrine of sovereign immunity than the reference to international comity."[3] This school takes the view that, while many states have granted jurisdictional immunities to foreign states, no rule of international law compels them to do so.[4] Hackworth takes the middle ground by concluding that the doctrine, having its origin in comity, gradually ripened into a rule of customary international law.[5]

For present purposes the rule's origin is important only because debate thereon often has obscured the fact that the rule is grounded upon practical considerations rather than abstract conceptualism. True, the Anglo-American municipal law concept of sovereign immunity, derived from the belief that "the king can do no wrong,"[6] undoubtedly contributed to the development of its international

[1] ALLEN, THE POSITION OF FOREIGN STATES BEFORE NATIONAL COURTS 4 (1933).

[2] Angell, *Sovereign Immunity—The Modern Trend*, 35 YALE L.J. 150, 152-53 (1925).

[3] Riesenfeld, *Sovereign Immunity of Foreign Vessels in Anglo-American Law: The Evolution of a Legal Doctrine*, 25 MINN. L. REV. 1, 3 n.12 (1940).

[4] H. Lauterpacht, *The Problem of Jurisdictional Immunities of Foreign States*, 28 BRIT. YB. INT'L L. 220, 228 (1951).

[5] 2 HACKWORTH, DIGEST OF INTERNATIONAL LAW 393 (1941).

[6] See Borchard, *Government Liability in Tort*, 34 YALE L.J. 1, 2 (1924).

law counterpart.[7] However, the impact of Austin's analytical jurisprudence in the United States, which reached its zenith when
Holmes stated in *The Western Maid* that "the authority that makes
the law is itself superior to it,"[8] had not been felt when Marshall
wrote his opinion in *The Schooner Exchange*[9]—the landmark case
granting immunity to a warship of a friendly foreign power. This
opinion, devoid of conceptualism, shows conclusively that, in contrast to the basis of the local sovereign's immunity, "the immunity
of a foreign sovereign flows from considerations of comity and practical expediency in friendly international intercourse."[10] As Frank-
furter pointed out 143 years later in *National City Bank v. Republic
of China*, "the nonsuability of the United States without its consent
is likewise derived from considerations of policy. But these are of
a different order from those that give a foreign nation such immunity."[11]

The enormous impact which *The Schooner Exchange* has had on
the law of sovereign immunity stems in part from the fact that the
case often is regarded as simply declarative of "one of the oldest-
established principles of international law."[12] While the decision,
unlike Athena, did not spring full blown from the brow of Zeus,
nevertheless "Marshall was not prepared to say that the doctrine
of sovereign immunity was already 'part of the fabric of our law'
when he decided *The Schooner Exchange* in 1812."[13] Indeed, he
prefaced his opinion with the following admission: "*In exploring*

[7] BRIGGS, THE LAW OF NATIONS 442 (2d ed. 1952).

[8] The Western Maid, 257 U.S. 419, 432 (1922). See also Kawananakoa v.
Polyblank, 205 U.S. 349, 353 (1907): "Some doubts have been expressed as to
the source of the immunity of a sovereign power from suit without its own
permission, but the answer has been public property since before the days of
Hobbes. (Leviathan, c. 26, 2.) A sovereign is exempt from suit, not because of
any formal conception or obsolete theory, but on the logical and practical ground
that there can be no legal right as against the authority that makes the law on
which the right depends."

[9] 11 U.S. (7 Cranch) 116 (1812).

[10] Hervey, *The Immunity of Foreign States When Engaged in Commercial
Enterprises: A Proposed Solution*, 27 MICH. L. REV. 751, 761 (1929). Counsel
for the libelant in *The Schooner Exchange* refuted the argument that "it is to
be presumed, that he [the foreign sovereign] will never do wrong. Such a presumption, contrary to the fact, may be calculated to give him weight at home,
but can be of no use abroad." 11 U.S. (7 Cranch) at 128.

[11] 348 U.S. 356, 359 (1955).

[12] U.N. CONFERENCE ON THE LAW OF THE SEA, OFF. REC., Second Committee,
Doc. No. A/Conf. 13/40 at 69 (1958) (U.S.S.R.).

[13] JESSUP, THE USE OF INTERNATIONAL LAW 75 (1959).

an unbeaten path, with few, if any, aids from precedents or written law, the court has found it necessary to rely much on general principles, and on a train of reasoning, founded on cases in some degree analogous to this."[14] Only after reviewing the reasons for granting immunity to foreign sovereigns, their diplomats and their armies in transit did he deem it "to be a principle of public law, that national ships of war, entering the port of a friendly power, open for their reception, are to be considered as exempted by the consent of that power from its jurisdiction."[15] Thus, the decision, while compatible with "the usages and received obligations of the civilized world,"[16] used these old precedents to justify placing the judicial imprimatur upon a new class of immunity case. Immunity was bestowed upon foreign warships, then, not because some theoretical conception of the status of sovereigns in international law required it, but because the same practical considerations which warranted immunity in three analogous situations also were found to exist in this context.

Unfortunately, subsequent Anglo-American cases extended the application of the rule in *The Schooner Exchange* to situations where these same practical considerations were not present, or if present existed to a lesser degree. The above case was decided at a time when the "sovereign" activities of a state encompassed far less than they do today, and when the idea that a sovereign state might engage in ordinary commerce was alien to international lawyers.[17] Therefore, it is highly unlikely that Marshall intended to formulate a principle broad enough to bestow immunity upon acts not then envisaged as properly performable by a sovereign. Indeed, the United States Attorney in *The Schooner Exchange,* while arguing that immunity was warranted under the facts of the case, admitted that "if a sovereign descend from the throne and become a merchant, he submits to the laws of the country."[18] Specific dictum in the case makes it plain that Marshall himself

[14] 11 U.S. (7 Cranch) at 136. (Emphasis added.) Ziegler suggests that Marshall's reference to lack of precedents constituted a reflection upon the quality of argument by counsel. ZIEGLER, THE INTERNATIONAL LAW OF JOHN MARSHALL 84-87 (1939). Considering the counsel, however, this argument seems specious.

[15] *Id.* at 145-46.

[16] *Id.* at 137.

[17] Fensterwald, *Sovereign Immunity and Soviet State Trading,* 63 HARV. L. REV. 614 (1950).

[18] 11 U.S. (7 Cranch) at 123.

meant to limit sovereign immunity to public armed ships in the service of foreign sovereigns.[19] In short, if anything is to be read into his opinion, it is that government-owned commercial vessels would not be entitled to the same immunity.[20]

Sixty-six years later, in *The Parlement Belge*,[21] the first noteworthy case involving the immunity of a foreign state-owned ship engaged in commerce, the holding in *The Schooner Exchange* was extended to accord immunity to a nonwarship of a foreign country. Acknowledging that Marshall's "decision applies, in fact, only to the case of a ship of war,"[22] the British court held that a Belgian mail packet, secondarily engaged in transporting merchandise and passengers, was entitled to immunity. Sovereign immunity, based upon "international comity" and the Austinian concept of the "absolute independence of every sovereign authority," was said to clothe "the public property of any state which is destined to its public use. . . ."[23] Furthermore, "the mere fact of the ship being used subordinately and partially for trading purposes does not take away the general immunity."[24] While the holding represented an extension of *The Schooner Exchange*, the rationale of the American case did give some support to the decision, since a public function of a foreign sovereign was involved.[25]

---

[19] "Without indicating any opinion on this question, it may safely be affirmed, that there is a manifest distinction between the private property of the person who happens to be a prince, and that military force which supports the sovereign power, and maintains the dignity and the independence of a nation. A prince, by acquiring private property in a foreign country, may possibly be considered as subjecting that property to the territorial jurisdiction; he may be considered as so far laying down the prince, and assuming the character of a private individual; but this he cannot be presumed to do, with respect to any portion of that armed force, which upholds his crown, and the nation he is intrusted to govern." *Id.* at 145.

[20] This probability is strengthened by Marshall's language in Bank of the United States v. Planters' Bank of Georgia, 22 U.S. (9 Wheat.) 904, 906 (1824).

[21] 5 P.D. 197 (1878).

[22] *Id.* at 208.

[23] *Id.* at 217.

[24] *Id.* at 220. "The question decided there was whether *The Parlement Belge*, which carried the mails, had or had not, by reason of its private trading, lost its character as a public ship." Mighell v. Sultan of Johore, [1894] 1 Q.B. 149, 152.

[25] It is worth noting that, in a memorandum of July 5, 1881 on *Foreign Ships Carrying Mails*, one F. S. Reilly opposed a bill to clothe mail packets with the immunity of foreign ships of war on the ground that international law, *The Parlement Belge* notwithstanding, did not require such immunity.

Although, as a notewriter has concluded, "it was clearly not intended by the court to treat state-owned ships, engaged solely in rendering freight and passenger service to the general public, as ships serving 'a public purpose,' "[26] a British court in *The Porto Alexandre*[27] so interpreted *The Parlement Belge*. Rejecting the argument that the earlier case was not "authority for the proposition that a foreign state-owned merchant ship engaged on an ordinary mercantile voyage is immune from the process of arrest,"[28] the court in 1920 granted immunity to a Portuguese merchantman, stating that "there are no limits to the immunity which he enjoys. ... It has been held . . . in *The Parlement Belge* that trading on the part of a sovereign does not subject him to any liability to the jurisdiction."[29] Acknowledging the fact that "in the days when the early decisions were given, no doubt what were called Government vessels were confined almost entirely, if not exclusively, to vessels of war,"[30] the court nevertheless stretched these decisions to grant immunity to government-owned commercial vessels.

If international comity was the rationale behind the granting of sovereign immunity to foreign warships, and indeed foreign public ships in general, surely, to quote counsel in *The Porto Alexandre*, "international comity does not extend the same immunity to the property of states unless employed in the public service."[31] The effect of the court's decision, however, was to place all government ships in the "public service" class without regard to whether comity necessitated such a broad grant of immunity. Indeed, the interests of comity might well have been better served had the court refused to allow immunity on the ground that "hard core" sovereign

---

Fourthly, I think it questionable whether Parliament would ever approve of a measure, protecting against responsibility for collision in British waters, a foreign vessel, really a trading vessel, under the pretext of her being a foreign ship of war, especially as the Queen's own ships do not enjoy immunity in this respect. Parliament would, I should expect, refuse to import this fiction into our statute law, when it is clear that there is no warrant for it in the common international law of the world. . . .

See Conf. No. 4507, p. 2, on file at the Public Record Office, London. See generally 1 McNAIR, INTERNATIONAL LAW OPINIONS 95-96 (1956).

[26] Note, 39 COLUM. L. REV. 510, 511 (1939).
[27] [1920] P. 30.
[28] *Id.* at 32.
[29] *Id.* at 36-37.
[30] *Id.* at 34.
[31] *Id.* at 32.

functions were not involved.[32] As Judge Mack wrote the following year:

> Where the application of the doctrine is not clear, a solution is not to be found by reference to strict Austinian theory which assumes, by mere definition, that the sovereign is not subject to his own laws. Nor is it to be found by uncritical reference to historical origins. The reasons which in the past led to the exemption of the sovereign from suit may or may not justify the extension of the principle in modern law.[33]

This reasoned approach to the sovereign immunity issue was ignored by the Supreme Court when it decided *Berizzi Bros. Co. v. S.S. Pesaro*,[34] a 1926 case correctly called "one of the most unfortunate decisions ever made by the Supreme Court."[35] Rejecting the Department of State's opinion in the "Hughes Letter" that where foreign government-owned vessels were engaged in commercial pursuits they should be treated like privately owned ships,[36] the Court, reviewing *The Schooner Exchange* and the above British cases, concluded that

> the principles are applicable alike to all ships held and used by a government for a public purpose, and that when, for the purpose of advancing the trade of its people or providing revenue for its treasury, a government acquires, mans and operates ships in the carrying trades, they are public ships in the same sense that war ships are. We know of no international usage which regards the maintenance

[32] "Indeed, it would seem that foreign relations are much less likely to be disturbed if the rights and obligations of foreign states growing out of their ordinary civil transactions were dealt with by the established rules of law, than if they were made a matter of diplomatic concern." The Pesaro, 277 Fed. 473, 485 (S.D.N.Y. 1921). See McDougal & Burke, The Public Order of the Oceans 155 (1962). After writing the sentence in the text, this writer came across a similar use of the term "hard core" in an excellent article by Friedmann, *Some Impacts of Social Organization on International Law*, 50 Am. J. Int'l L. 475, 480 (1956).

[33] 277 Fed. at 475.

[34] 271 U.S. 562 (1926).

[35] Sanborn, *The Immunity of Government-Owned Merchant Vessels*, 39 Am. J. Int'l L. 794 (1945).

[36] 2 Hackworth, *op. cit. supra* note 5, at 437. In light of subsequent developments, it should be noted that the Secretary of State then took the position that "the questions involved are particularly suitable for determination by Courts, rather than by political departments of the Government." *Id.* at 429. See text at note 129 *infra*.

and advancement of the economic welfare of a people in time of peace as any less a public purpose than the maintenance and training of a naval force.[37]

True and enlightened as the final sentence above may be, the Court's opinion "begs the question as to whether it is expedient, under modern conditions, to extend to these 'public' business activities of governments the immunity which . . . [had] been granted only to their public administrative activities."[38] The Court, reasoning syllogistically that public ships were entitled to immunity, that government-owned merchant vessels were public ships, and that hence such merchant ships might claim immunity, failed to give sufficient consideration to the fact that the doctrine of sovereign immunity "grew up in an age when the operation of merchant vessels by the state was unknown, and when all state-owned or operated ships were in a real sense public vessels, and when there was some excuse for the immunities which were accorded them."[39] The result was the complete acceptance of the "absolute" immunity concept in Anglo-American, if not customary international, law.

THE RISE AND PREDOMINANCE OF THE RESTRICTIVE THEORY

By the time sovereign immunity reached its high-water mark in the United States, however, an undertow already had commenced. As a consequence of World War I, many nations acquired commercial fleets and went into the maritime carrying business.[40] Stated succinctly by Dickinson, the problem then became: "Should they be permitted to take their immunities with them?"[41] Uniformly the

---

[37] 271 U.S. at 574.

[38] Sanborn, *The Immunity of Merchant Vessels When Owned by Foreign Governments*, 1 ST. JOHN'S L. REV. 5, 21 (1926). *Cf.* MCDOUGAL & BURKE, *op. cit. supra* note 32, at 146 n.165.

[39] Garner, *Legal Status of Government Ships Employed in Commerce*, 20 AM. J. INT'L L. 759, 766-67 (1926). The Court related that when *The Schooner Exchange* was decided "merchant ships were operated only by private owners and there was little thought of governments engaging in such operations. That came much later." 271 U.S. 573. However, it failed to see the implications of its own observation.

[40] The emergence of the Soviet Union, with its state-conducted foreign trade monopoly, also posed the same problem. Fox, *Competence of Courts in Regard to "Non-Sovereign" Acts of Foreign States*, 35 AM. J. INT'L L. 632 (1941).

[41] Dickinson, *The Immunity of Public Ships Employed in Trade*, 21 AM. J. INT'L L. 108 (1927).

commentators answered this rhetorical question in the negative.[42] Synthesizing their views, they favored dividing government vessels into two groups, "public" ships and "private" ships (meaning state-owned ships engaged in commerce), and restricting immunity from jurisdiction to the former. In making the classification, the actual use to which the ship was being put was to be the determining factor.[43] This criterion was adopted by the drafters of the Brussels Convention of 1926,[44] which retained immunity only for ships of war, government yachts, patrol vessels, hospital ships, auxiliary vessels, supply ships, and other craft owned or operated by a state and used exclusively in government and noncommercial service. The main drawback with the convention, aside from the fact that only twelve states ratified it, was its limited scope, excluding as it did many state trading activities. Nevertheless, even among countries which were not parties to the convention, there began a steady swing to the policy of "restrictive" immunity. By 1955 Lauterpacht was able to conclude that "there are now only a few States which adhere without qualification to the practice of conceding jurisdictional immunities to State-owned ships engaged in commerce."[45]

While the United States did not join the Brussels Convention, its adherence to the absolute immunity theory was questioned a dozen years later in *Compania Espanola v. Navemar*,[46] a case which also injected the Department of State into the immunity picture. In this 1938 Supreme Court decision, a Spanish corporation sued to recover possession of a merchant vessel. The Spanish ambassador appeared, claimed the ship was the property of Spain by virtue of a presidential decree, and questioned the jurisdiction of the court on the ground that the ship, a public vessel of Spain, was immune from the court's jurisdiction. The Department of State refused to act upon the Spanish claim of ownership and possession of the vessel.

---

[42] See, *e.g.*, MATSUNAMI, IMMUNITY OF STATE SHIPS 55 (1924). See also Fairman, *Some Disputed Applications of the Principle of State Immunity*, 22 AM. J. INT'L L. 566, 588-89 (1928), and Garner, *Immunities of State-Owned Ships Employed in Commerce*, 6 BRIT. YB. INT'L L. 128, 143 (1925).

[43] Hayes, *Private Claims Against Foreign Sovereigns*, 38 HARV. L. REV. 599, 617 (1925).

[44] 176 L.N.T.S. 199 (1937). The Convention is discussed in Franck, *The New Law for the Seas*, 42 L.Q. REV. 308 (1926).

[45] 1 OPPENHEIM, INTERNATIONAL LAW 857 (8th ed., Lauterpacht 1955).

[46] 303 U.S. 68 (1938).

Chief Justice Stone, after restating the *Pesaro* rule,[47] indicated in dictum the Court's willingness to bestow immunity in all cases where the claim had been "recognized and allowed" by the executive branch.[48] Since the Department of State had not forwarded such a suggestion, however, the Court thought itself not bound to accept the ambassador's claim of immunity as conclusive and, as there was no evidence that the ship actually was in the possession of Spain, the Court denied immunity.[49] The decision, while paying lip service to the *Pesaro*, shows both the Court's awareness of the broad statements contained therein and its intention to construe the holding as strictly as possible. Possession, listed as a prerequisite of immunity in the *Pesaro*, being absent, immunity was not allowed.

Ex parte Peru,[50] arising from a libel against a Peruvian steamship for its failure to carry a cargo of sugar from Peru to New York, afforded the Court an excellent opportunity to reconsider the *Pesaro*. Instead, Stone converted his *Navemar* dictum into holding by stating that the Department of State's suggestion of immunity, apparently made in an attempt to follow the decision in *Pesaro*,[51] "must be accepted by the courts as a conclusive determination by the political arm of the Government that the continued retention of the vessel interferes with the proper conduct of our foreign relations."[52] The rationale behind this relinquishment of jurisdiction was the desire not "to embarrass the executive arm of the Government in conducting foreign relations."[53] Presumably this embarrassment would have occurred had the Court denied immunity and Peru then claimed that such denial violated its

[47] 303 U.S. at 74.

[48] "If the claim is recognized and allowed by the executive branch of the government, it is then the duty of the courts to release the vessel upon appropriate suggestion by the Attorney General of the United States, or other officer acting under his direction." *Id.* at 74. In the *Pesaro*, it will be recalled, the Court had not believed itself bound by a suggestion to deny immunity. See text at note 36 *supra*.

[49] *Id.* at 75.

[50] 318 U.S. 578 (1943).

[51] RESTATEMENT, FOREIGN RELATIONS § 72, Reporters' Note (1)(b) at 233-34 (Proposed Official Draft 1962). See also RESTATEMENT, FOREIGN RELATIONS § 75, Reporters' Note at 248-49 (Proposed Official Draft 1962).

[52] 318 U.S. at 589.

[53] *Id.* at 588.

rights under international law.[54] Although international law no longer requires immunity in such a case,[55] thus eliminating this possible source of embarrassment, the argument still is used by advocates of executive supremacy in sovereign immunity matters.[56]

The last in the trio of immunity cases decided by the Court since *Pesaro, Mexico v. Hoffman,*[57] also involved a libel in rem, this time filed by the owner of an American fishing vessel against a ship owned by the Mexican government, but leased to a private Mexican corporation, for damages from a collision. The Mexican ambassador filed a suggestion of immunity with the Court, stating that the ship was owned and possessed by Mexico, while the libelant, on the other hand, denied that the vessel was in the government's possession, public service, or use. The Department of State, showing "courteous neutrality,"[58] submitted a note accepting as true the ambassador's statement regarding the vessel's ownership but expressing no opinion about the asserted immunity. Stone, once again writing for the Supreme Court, declined to grant immunity since such action had not been requested by the Department of State and since the vessel had not been in Mexico's possession at the time of the collision. Thus the holding represents a reaffirmation of the strict construction of *Pesaro* found in the *Navemar.*[59]

The case is more important, however, as an illustration of the role played by the Department of State in the determination of immunity. In the prior two cases, Stone indicated a willingness to be bound by the Department's affirmative suggestion of immunity, believing that the question of immunity was an appropriate subject for judicial injuiry only in the absence of such a suggestion. In *Mexico v. Hoffman* Stone reiterated the view that, "in the absence of recognition of the claimed immunity by the political branch of the government, the courts may decide for themselves whether all the

[54] RESTATEMENT, FOREIGN RELATIONS § 72, Reporters' Note (1)(e) at 238 (Proposed Official Draft 1962).

[55] *Ibid.* See text at notes 45 *supra* and 70 *infra.* See also SWEENEY, THE INTERNATIONAL LAW OF SOVEREIGN IMMUNITY iv (1963).

[56] METZGER, INTERNATIONAL LAW IN NATIONAL COURTS, PROCEEDINGS OF THE THIRD SUMMER CONFERENCE ON INTERNATIONAL LAW 12 (1960) [hereinafter cited as PROCEEDINGS].

[57] 324 U.S. 30 (1945).

[58] Ulen & Co. v. Bank Gospodarstwa Krajowego, 261 App. Div. 1, 4, 24 N.Y.S.2d 201, 204 (2d Dep't 1940).

[59] See text following note 49 *supra.*

requisites of immunity exist."[60] Unfortunately, he then clouded the issue by adding that "it is therefore not for the courts to deny an immunity which our government has seen fit to allow, or to allow an immunity on new grounds which the government has not seen fit to recognize."[61] This language indicates a complete "judicial abdication"[62] in the process of determining and applying the international law rule of sovereign immunity.[63]

Calling the decision "a converse illustration of judicial deference," a notewriter has concluded that "the Court held that the recognition of sovereign immunity by the courts when the State Department has refused to suggest it may be equally embarrassing to the conduct of foreign affairs, thus accepting as binding on the courts the refusal by the State Department to suggest sovereign immunity."[64] Whether the Department's silence or courteous neutrality is to be treated as a "binding" determination of no immunity is not quite so certain.[65] The Supreme Court has not yet clarified its views on the question, although it did remark in a 1955 dictum that the Department's "failure or refusal to suggest such immunity has been accorded significant weight by this Court."[66] Lower courts, although

[60] 324 U.S. at 34-35. Footnote text supports the view that the Court considered itself free to determine the immunity question when the Department of State was silent on the subject. *Id.* at 35 n.1.

[61] *Id.* at 35.

[62] Jessup, *Has the Supreme Court Abdicated One of Its Functions?*, 40 AM. J. INT'L L. 168 (1946).

[63] Insofar as it suggests that the Court will not grant immunity where the Department of State has refused to suggest it, the opinion also represents a departure from the *Pesaro*. See text at and accompanying note 66 *infra*.

[64] Comment, *The Sovereign's Immunity and Private Property: A Due Process Problem*, 50 GEO. L.J. 284, 290-91 (1961).

[65] See text at note 60 *supra*. See Note, *Procedural Aspects of a Claim of Sovereign Immunity by a Foreign State*, 20 U. PITT. L. REV. 126, 134-35 (1958).

[66] National City Bank v. Republic of China, 348 U.S. 356, 360 (1955). The Supreme Court has recently declined to clarify the question. See Comisaria General de Abastecimientos y Transportes v. Victory Transport Inc., 336 F.2d 354 (2d Cir. 1964), *petition for cert. filed*, 33 U.S.L. WEEK 3255 (U.S. Jan. 7, 1965) (No. 815), where the court of appeals, while refusing "to say that the courts will never grant immunity unless the State Department specifically requests it," took the position "that the courts should deny immunity where the State Department has indicated, either directly or indirectly, that immunity need not be accorded." 336 F.2d at 358. Citing the *National City Bank* case, the court of appeals considered itself bound "to deny a claim of sovereign immunity that has not been 'recognized and allowed' by the State Department unless it is plain that the activity in question falls within one of the categories of strictly

considering themselves "free to determine the matter in the exercise of judicial responsibility"[67] when the Department has not acted affirmatively, uniformly deny immunity in such cases.[68] The Department itself cautiously concluded that "the courts are less likely to allow a plea of sovereign immunity where the executive has declined to do so."[69]

The rôle of the executive in immunity cases took on added importance in 1952 when the Department of State, concluding that international law no longer required adherence to the absolute theory of sovereign immunity, issued the so-called Tate Letter indicating its willingness "to follow the restrictive theory of sovereign immunity in the consideration of requests of foreign governments for a grant of sovereign immunity."[70] While the Department "realized that a shift in policy by the executive cannot control the courts," in a fine display of understatement it also perceived "indications that at least some justices of the Supreme Court feel that in this matter courts should follow the branch of the Government charged with responsibility for the conduct of foreign relations."[71]

---

political or public acts about which sovereigns have traditionally been quite sensitive." *Id.* at 360. The Supreme Court, after inviting the Solicitor General to file a brief expressing the views of the United States, 85 Sup. Ct. 939 (1965), denied certiorari. 33 U.S.L. WEEK 3388 (U.S. June 1, 1965) (No. 815). See Note, 53 GEO. L.J. 837 (1965); Note, 17 STAN. L. REV. 501 (1965).

[67] Et Ve Balik Kurumu v. B.N.S. Corp., 25 Misc.2d 299, 301, 204 N.Y.S.2d 971, 975 (Sup. Ct. 1960), 12 SYRACUSE L. REV. 270 (1960).

[68] *Cf. In re* Grand Jury Investigation of the Shipping Industry, 186 F. Supp. 298 (D.D.C. 1960), where the Department of State refused to recognize or allow the Philippine government's claim of immunity for the Philippine National Lines because it was engaged in commercial activities. Government counsel, citing *Mexico v. Hoffman,* maintained that "since the State Department has denied immunity here, the Court must also refuse to recognize the Philippine National Lines' claim of sovereign immunity." *Id.* at 319. Counsel for the lines, on the other hand, contended that "the State Department's refusal to recognize its claim of sovereign immunity is not in any way binding on this Court. . . ." *Ibid.* The Court, impliedly rejecting the government's argument, reserved its views as to the issuance of a subpoena pending a showing by the government, among other things, that the lines' activities were substantially, if not entirely, commercial, and hence not immune. *Id.* at 319-20.

[69] 26 DEP'T STATE BULL. 984, 985 (1952).

[70] *Ibid.* See Bishop, *New United States Policy Limiting Sovereign Immunity,* 47 AM. J. INT'L L. 93, 94 (1953).

[71] 26 DEP'T STATE BULL. 984, 985 (1952).

"The practical effect of the Tate letter," as a leading practitioner notes, "has been to make the *Pesaro* decision a dead letter,"[72] a fact recognized in 1958 by the Reporters of the Restatement of Foreign Relations Law when they adopted a rule denying immunity to the commercial activities of foreign countries.[73] This "bright dawn of the doctrine of relative immunity"[74] was highlighted further when the Department of State fought hard and successfully for the inclusion of the restrictive rule in the 1958 Geneva Convention on the Territorial Sea and the Contiguous Zone.[75] Numerous lower court cases citing the Tate Letter attest to the rejection of the absolute sovereign immunity theory by the United States.[76]

THE ROLE OF THE DEPARTMENT OF STATE IN SOVEREIGN IMMUNITY CASES UNDER THE RESTRICTIVE THEORY

Ironically, while the shift in executive policy was designed to free the courts to adjudicate actions against foreign sovereigns, it also has had the effect of making the judiciary even more dependent upon suggestions by the Department of State. With no backlog of experience in determining what fact patterns warranted immunity under the new test, they have followed the lead of the Supreme Court and have treated the Department's pronouncements as determinative, despite Jessup's observation that "an abundant jurisprudence in many countries as well as the position of the State Department

[72] Timberg, *Expropriation Measures and State Trading*, 55 A.S.I.L. PROCEEDINGS 113, 114 (1961).

[73] RESTATEMENT, FOREIGN RELATIONS § 55 (Tent. Draft No. 2, 1958). The Restatement retained this rule in its final draft. See RESTATEMENT, FOREIGN RELATIONS § 72 (Proposed Official Draft 1962).

[74] Timberg, *Sovereign Immunity, State Trading, Socialism and Self-Deception*, in ESSAYS ON INTERNATIONAL JURISDICTION 40, 46 (1961).

[75] U.N. DOC. No. A/Conf. 13/L. 52 (1958), reprinted in 52 AM. J. INT'L L. 834 (1958). See Lillich, *The Geneva Conference on the Law of the Sea and the Immunity of Foreign State-Owned Commercial Vessels*, 28 GEO. WASH. L. REV. 408 (1960). The United States ratified this Convention on March 24, 1961, and it has now received the necessary ratifications to come into force.

[76] Most of these cases are gathered in a student Comment, *International Law: Sovereign Immunity: The First Decade of the Tate Letter Policy*, 60 MICH. L. REV. 1142 (1962). Important oversights include Harris & Co. Advertising, Inc. v. Republic of Cuba, 127 So. 2d 687 (Dist. Ct. App. Fla. 1961) (contract to promote tourism nongovernmental function), and Rich v. Naviera Vacuba, S.A., text at notes 91-102 *infra*. See also Note, *The American Law of Sovereign Immunity Since the Tate Letter*, 4 VA. J. INT'L L. 75 (1964).

itself, attests the validity of the conclusion that the granting or withholding of immunity is a legal question."[77] Although the Restatement construes the trio of Supreme Court cases to require only that "great weight" be accorded an executive suggestion,[78] in recent years lower courts have decided that the Department's views were "conclusive" upon them,[79] that once the Department had spoken the "court was without further jurisdiction of the case . . . ,"[80] and that "the filing of the suggestion . . . effectively terminated the power and jurisdiction of the trial court with reference to matters contained in the suggestion."[81] Whether the Supreme Court decisions require automatic judicial acceptance of executive suggestions or not,[82] "the fact is that statements of policy in this area have had almost absolute control over the outcome of the cases, for never has a court failed to grant immunity in the face of a positive suggestion of immunity by the Department of State."[83] In Falk's blunt words, "with respect to immunities the court agrees to play dead whenever the executive chooses to act."[84]

This concept of judicial acquiescence to executive domination has been criticized for twenty-five years.[85] Some writers have argued that the theory of separation of powers is being violated, since the determination of immunity by the executive requires the exer-

[77] JESSUP, *op. cit. supra* note 13, at 83. See text accompanying note 36 *supra*.
[78] RESTATEMENT, FOREIGN RELATIONS § 75(2) (Proposed Official Draft 1962).
[79] Et Ve Balik Kurumu v. B.N.S. Corp., 25 Misc. 2d 299, 301, 204 N.Y.S.2d 971, 974 (Sup. Ct. 1960), 12 SYRACUSE L. REV. 270 (1960).
[80] Republic of Cuba v. Dixie Paint & Varnish Co., 104 Ga. App. 854, 123 S.E.2d 198 (1961).
[81] State v. Dekle, 137 So. 2d 581, 583 (Dist. Ct. App. Fla. 1962).
[82] This question will be discussed later in this Chapter. See text at notes 103-33 *infra*.
[83] M. H. Cardozo, *Judicial Deference to State Department Suggestions: Recognition of Prerogative or Abdication to Usurper?*, 48 CORNELL L.Q. 461, 473 (1963) [hereinafter cited as Cardozo]. Compare Stephen v. Zivnostenska Banka, 12 N.Y.2d 781, 186 N.E.2d 676, 235 N.Y.S.2d 1 (1962), *affirming* 15 App. Div. 2d 111, 222 N.Y.S.2d 128 (1st Dep't 1961).
[84] FALK, THE ROLE OF DOMESTIC COURTS IN THE INTERNATIONAL LEGAL ORDER 160 (1964).
[85] See, *e.g.*, Jessup, note 62 *supra*; Kuhn, *The Extension of Sovereignty to Government-Owned Commercial Corporations*, 39 AM. J. INT'L L. 772, 775 (1945); Note, 97 U. PA. L. REV. 79, 91-92 (1948). But see Dickinson & Andrews, *A Decade of Admiralty in the Supreme Court of the United States*, 36 CALIF. L. REV. 169, 215 (1948); Note, 50 YALE L.J. 1088, 1093 (1941).

cise of powers that belong to the judiciary.[86] Others believe that the Department of State's ex parte determination of sovereign immunity constitutes a denial of due process,[87] which opens the door to frivolous claims of immunity.[88] Still others assert that the procedure works to deprive a private party of his day in court.[89] Jessup, for instance, contends:

> The State Department is totally unequipped to handle such questions. If attorneys for a private plaintiff ask the Department to inform the Court that a certain defendant government is not entitled to immunity, attorneys for the defendant are not given a hearing in the Department. If the Department shares the view of the plaintiff, and notifies the court that the immunity is not "recognized and allowed," and if the court, following Chief Justice Stone, so orders, the decision has been completely *ex parte* and the foreign state could quite properly assert that it had been denied justice. On the other hand, if a defendant government persuades the Department to "allow" the immunity, the plaintiff is completely denied his day in court.[90]

Such criticism generally has a twofold thrust, condemning the propriety of the judiciary's excessive reliance upon executive suggestions as well as the informal procedures by which the Department of State reaches its conclusions in such cases. The validity of both points of criticism was illustrated most graphically in *Rich v. Naviera Vacuba, S.A.*,[91] a case which bids fair to become one of the international legal monstrosities of American courts for the 1960's. In this case the courts considered themselves bound by precedent to fol-

---

[86] Déak, *The Plea of Sovereign Immunity and the New York Court of Appeals*, 40 COLUM. L. REV. 453, 461 (1940).

[87] Timberg, *op. cit. supra* note 74, at 57-60.

[88] Déak, *supra* note 86, at 464.

[89] M. H. Cardozo, *Sovereign Immunity: The Plaintiff Deserves a Day in Court*, 67 HARV. L. REV. 608 (1954).

[90] JESSUP, *op. cit. supra* note 13, at 83.

[91] 295 F.2d 24 (4th Cir. 1961), *affirming* 197 F. Supp. 710 (E.D. Va. 1961), 13 SYRACUSE L. REV. 492 (1962). The Supreme Court denied applications for a stay on September 11, 12 and 14, 1961. "The Chief Justice, in denying the applications for a stay as to the libellants other than United Fruit Sugar Company, relied on the classic sovereign immunity decisions of this Court, endorsing on the papers 'Application for stay denied. See *Ex Parte Peru*, 318 U.S. 578, and *Republic of Mexico v. Hoffman*, 324 U.S. 30.' " Petition for Writ of Certiorari, p. 19, Banco Nacional de Cuba v. Sabbatino, 376 U.S. 398 (1964).

low, without question, an executive suggestion clearly contrary both to international law and the principles enunciated in the Tate Letter—a suggestion, moreover, made with no semblance of due process whatsoever.

The facts in *Rich,* for present purposes, may be stated briefly. On August 8, 1961, the "Bahia de Nipe," a vessel formerly owned by Naviera Vacuba, S.A., and now operated by the Republic of Cuba, sailed from Cuba with a cargo of 5,000 bags of sugar. Nine days later, when the ship was on the high seas destined for a Russian port, she was seized by her master and ten crewmen and brought in to anchor off Lynnhaven, Virginia, remaining thereafter within the three-mile limit. On August 18, 1961, a libel was filed against the vessel by two longshoremen who previously had recovered judgments against the Republic of Cuba and Naviera Vacuba, S.A., in federal court. In rapid succession similar libels were filed, one seeking recovery of a judgment rendered against the Republic of Cuba by a state court. A libel against the cargo of sugar also was filed by the United Fruit Sugar Company, alleging that the sugar had originated from its properties which had been nationalized by Cuba in July, 1960.

At a hearing before the federal district court on August 19, 1961, the United States Attorney advised the court that a communication would be forthcoming from the Department of State. This communication, which consisted of a brief letter from the Secretary of State to the Attorney General, was read to the court over the telephone and admitted in evidence without objection. In it the Secretary stated simply that "the release of this vessel would avoid further disturbance to our international relations in the premises."[92] The hearing having been adjourned until August 21, 1961, a second such letter, dated the previous day, was admitted in evidence over the objections of libelants. The Secretary this time stated his understanding that the vessel "is owned by the Government of Cuba and is employed in the carriage for the Government of Cuba of a cargo of sugar which is the property of the Government of Cuba," and concluded again that, "in the circumstances, it is my opinion that the prompt release of the vessel is necessary to secure the observance of the rights and obligations of the United States."[93] It will be noted

[92] 197 F. Supp. at 714.
[93] *Id.* at 714-15.

that the Secretary made no claim that international law required immunity.

The district court, citing *Ex parte Peru* and *Mexico v. Hoffman,* held that "whenever a claim of sovereign immunity is recognized and allowed by the Department of State, the courts are no longer permitted to inquire into the sufficiency of the suggestion."[94] Admitting that "the certification by the State Deparment leaves much to be desired, and adopts qualifying language with respect to ownership of the vessel and cargo," it nevertheless concluded that "the acceptance of these facts as true is conclusive upon the court. . . ."[95] Certainly this represents a complete abdication of judicial responsibility. To the argument that the Department of State's position in the case was inconsistent with its policy established in the Tate Letter,[96] the court replied that "the short answer to these contentions is that no policy with respect to international relations is so fixed that it cannot be varied in the wisdom of the Executive. Flexibility, not uniformity, must be the controlling factor in times of strained international relations."[97] Thus the executive's interposition can stunt the application and development of international law and deny relief to those persons, among others, who had their property taken by Cuba without the payment of just compensation.[98]

On appeal to the Court of Appeals for the Fourth Circuit, "the libellants argue[d] that before sovereign immunity may be granted

[94] *Id.* at 726.

[95] *Ibid.*

[96] See text at notes 70-76 *supra.*

[97] *Id.* at 724. "In one final word we must recognize that rapidly changing events in the world of today compel the Executive to take action involving international affairs which, in the eyes of the public, may seem a bit strange. However that may be, while the doctrine of sovereign immunity may, in a particular case, operate to the benefit of the foreign sovereign, the invocation of such a doctrine is undoubtedly of great concern to our own country. Since the President, in his wisdom, has seen fit to recognize and allow the claim of Cuba, it is the duty of this Court to give judicial support to that decision." *Id.* at 726.

[98] "It is conceded that United Fruit Sugar Company had valuable properties taken from it by the expropriation decree and, of course, no compensation has been paid for such taking. Under our system of laws, the Court would, if permitted to do so, find that the title to the cargo of sugar remains in the United Fruit Sugar Company. Unfortunately, this is not sufficient as the decided cases tend to the view that vessels and cargo expropriated by, and in possession of, a foreign sovereign are immune from suit upon a suggestion of immunity." *Id.* at 724.

they should be heard by the court on whether the foreign government is in fact the owner and possessor of the property in question and, as to the ship, whether she was operated by that government not commercially but in a public capacity."[99] Furthermore, the United Fruit Sugar Company "asserted that release of the cargo under the doctrine of sovereign immunity, upon the mere certificate of the State Department without opportunity for further inquiry, would deprive it of its property without due process of law in violation of the Fifth Amendment."[100] The court, pausing only to note that the communications from the executive were "infelicitously expressed,"[101] summarily held that "the certificate and grant of immunity issued by the Department of State should be accepted by the court without further inquiry. . . . We think that the doctrine of the separation of powers under our Constitution requires us to assume that all pertinent considerations have been taken into account by the Secretary of State in reaching his conclusion."[102]

The *Rich* case, then, serves as an excellent background for a critical discussion of the two points mentioned above: (1) the basis for the executive's intervention in sovereign immunity cases before the courts, including the weight to be accorded its "suggestions"; and (2) the due process questions raised by the Department of State's decision-making process, including the problem of whether an affirmative suggestion of immunity in a case where international law would deny immunity constitutes a taking of property under the Fifth Amendment.

THE BASIS AND WEIGHT OF DEPARTMENT OF STATE SUGGESTIONS OF IMMUNITY

Clearly the executive branch has a role to play in sovereign immunity cases. The courts quite properly look to the Department of State for guidance in such cases, just as they do in cases involving the interpretation of a treaty.[103] The question, rather, is whether its "suggestions" should be just that—suggestions entitled to great

[99] 295 F.2d at 25.

[100] *Id.* at 26.

[101] *Id.* at 25.

[102] *Id.* at 26. The court of appeals cited only the three Supreme Court cases discussed above. The Supreme Court relied on these cases in denying applications for a stay. See note 91 *supra*.

[103] RESTATEMENT, FOREIGN RELATIONS § 155 (Proposed Official Draft 1962).

weight but not conclusive—or whether they should be binding on the courts, either under a self-imposed court rule or on constitutional grounds. As noted above, the Restatement interprets the Supreme Court cases as requiring "great weight" to be given these suggestions.[104] "Such a suggestion," it adds, "is conclusive as to issues of fact or law which relate to matters within the exclusive competence of the executive branch of the government *but is not conclusive as to other issues*."[105] The Reporters thus construe the Supreme Court's broad language about the binding effect of Department of State suggestions[106] "to be applicable, literally, only to those questions which it considered to be within the exclusive competence of the executive branch."[107] Examples of such questions are "whether the government is recognized, whether the ambassador is accredited and whether the foreign political entity is one with which the United States conducts diplomatic relations directly or one which the United States treats as a political subdivision of another state."[108] An example of a question where the Department's determination is not binding is "whether a bank holds certain funds as a financial agent for a foreign government or as an agent for the bondholders of such government. . . ."[109] Although such a suggestion "will be given weight, it will not preclude a finding by the court, on the basis of proof, as to the status of the funds."[110]

The Restatement's analysis, under which the degree of weight to be accorded executive pronouncements depends upon the character of the issue pronounced upon, is a good one, but it appears to over-clarify existing case law.[111] Certainly the distinction between a con-

---

[104] See text at note 78 *supra.*

[105] RESTATEMENT, FOREIGN RELATIONS § 75(2) (Proposed Official Draft 1962). (Emphasis added.) See also RESTATEMENT, FOREIGN RELATIONS § 75, comment *b* at 247 (Proposed Official Draft 1962).

[106] See text accompanying note 48 and at notes 50-53 *supra.*

[107] RESTATEMENT, FOREIGN RELATIONS § 75, Reporter's Note at 250 (Proposed Official Draft 1962).

[108] *Ibid.*

[109] *Ibid.*

[110] RESTATEMENT, FOREIGN RELATIONS § 75, comment *b*, illustration 3, at 248 (Proposed Official Draft 1962). *Cf.* Stephen v. Zivnostenska Banka, note 83 *supra.*

[111] "Although the extent to which State Department suggestions of immunity are conclusive on the courts has often been debated by legal scholars, it has never been adequately delineated by the courts." Note, 61 MICH. L. REV. 396, 400 (1962).

clusive suggestion about the status of a foreign government and a persuasive determination that title to contested property resides in a foreign sovereign represents a sensible allocation of functions between the two branches of government. Even assuming that the Department's determination of title to property before a court would not violate the separation of powers doctrine, "the State Department is, for practical reasons, a poor forum in which to determine the traditionally legal question of title to property, lacking, as it does, the necessary machinery for conducting an adversary proceeding."[112] This view finds support in the assertion by an Assistant Legal Adviser of the Department of State that "when there is a controversy about particular property, with respect to which a question of sovereign immunity is raised, the State Department does not make a suggestion of immunity, because the very basis on which the suggestion would be made would be uncertain."[113] As Franck concludes, "the State Department ought to be confined to determining matters of international law that affect the national interest. The question of who is lawfully in possession of a ship is, on its face, not such a matter."[114]

Unfortunately, the dictum in *Compania Espanola v. Navemar*[115] and the holding in *Ex parte Peru*[116] appear not to support the Restatement's gloss on these cases. Moreover, in the *Rich* case, where one of the main issues was whether Cuba owned and possessed the property in question, the Secretary of State concluded that the ship and its cargo were owned by the government of Cuba,[117] a determination which the court believed should be accepted without further inquiry.[118] This decision, contrary to the Restatement and not mentioned by it, squarely holds that an executive suggestion of immunity will be treated as conclusive by the courts right across the board.[119]

[112] Comment, *supra* note 64, at 291.

[113] PROCEEDINGS 11 (Yingling).

[114] Franck, *The Courts, the State Department and National Policy: A Criterion for Judicial Abdication*, 44 MINN. L. REV. 1101, 1117 (1960).

[115] See text at and accompanying note 48 *supra*.

[116] See text at notes 51-52 *supra*.

[117] See text at note 93 *supra*.

[118] See text at note 102 *supra*.

[119] See Note, 50 CALIF. L. REV. 559, 562-63 (1962). This attitude "is in sharp contrast with the English practice. Though the English courts continue to recognize the doctrine of sovereign immunity, they accept the Foreign Office certifica-

The holding that the suggestion should be treated as conclusive even with respect to determinations of title has been commended[120] and condemned,[121] but it apparently reflects the state of the law on the matter.[122]

If the above analysis is correct, then another matter also is clarified by the broad holding in *Rich*: the weight to be accorded the Department of State's determination that the activities of the foreign sovereign are or are not entitled to immunity under international law. This aspect of the immunity problem, which only became important with the issuance of the Tate Letter in 1952,[123] has not been passed upon by the Supreme Court,[124] and the Restatement,

---

tion of immunity as conclusive only on the question whether the particular government is a sovereign entitled to immunity and not on question of law." Comment, *supra* note 64, at 297-98, citing Brandon, *Sovereign Immunity of Government-Owned Corporations and Ships,* 39 CORNELL L.Q. 425, 445 (1954).

[120] "In the first place, the result of refusing a suggestion in the face of a dispute of ownership is to force the foreign sovereign into a domestic court to protect its asserted right. This is the affront that is supposed to be avoided by the immunity doctrine. It is naturally to be hoped that foreign governments will often be willing to litigate this issue in our courts, recognizing that arguing the point before judicial officers is probably no more undignified than arguing before diplomats. But, they will sometimes be unwilling to do this, as would probably be the case if the United States were asked to do the same thing abroad. The question of title then must be determined by the State Department before it can decide whether or not to make a suggestion of immunity." Cardozo 475.

[121] "It is submitted, however, that when the litigant asserts a claim of ownership to property before the court, and the court recognizes its constitutional duty, effect will be given to the State Department suggestion of immunity only insofar as the sovereign establishes its title to the property. To do otherwise, that is, to accept a suggestion as conclusive without a prior determination that the foreign sovereign is the titleholder to contested property, is to deprive the plaintiff of any forum in which a right to assert a claim exists, and this, it is submitted, is a deprivation of substantive due process." Comment, *supra* note 64, at 309.

[122] The decision in *Rich* is distinguished in Stephen v. Zivnostenska Banka, 12 N.Y.2d 781, 186 N.E.2d 676, 235 N.Y.S.2d 1 (1962), *affirming on opinion below* 15 App. Div. 2d 111, 120, 222 N.Y.S.2d 128, 137-38 (1st Dep't 1961). See also text accompanying note 91 *supra*.

[123] Before then all such activities warranted immunity and hence no executive determination of this question was required. *Cf.* Timberg, *op. cit. supra* note 74, at 48.

[124] The Court referred to "this chilly feeling against sovereign immunity" in National City Bank v. Republic of China, 348 U.S. 356, 359 (1955), but it did not question its earlier decisions indicating a willingness to be bound by Department of State suggestions generally. See text accompanying note 66 *supra*.

having originally deemed this aspect of an executive suggestion merely persuasive,[125] eventually straddled this essentially legal question.[126] *Rich* makes quite clear that the Department's suggestion on this question is binding, despite its inconsistency with the restrictive theory of sovereign immunity advocated by the Tate Letter. Thus the Department's determinations on all issues of law and fact in a suggestion of immunity are conclusive on the courts.[127] "One can summarize the situation of immunity claims in United States courts," concludes Falk, "by observing that the subject is governed by executive decision."[128]

While the courts may have believed themselves bound by Department of State pronouncements, until *Rich* there had been no intimation that under the separation of powers doctrine they considered themselves constitutionally required to follow the Department's advice. In 1960, however, a representative of the Department of State had advanced this interpretation of the Supreme Court cases.

> These decisions are made by the State Department under its conception of international law. I think, from the domestic law standpoint and from the Constitutional law standpoint, that the courts consider this to be a political or a policy decision by the branch of the government which is charged, under the Constitution,

[125] "A decision by a court on this issue stands, on no different footing from a decision of the Court on the interpretation of a treaty, where the interest of a foreign government is asserted. The entire system of separation and balance of powers requires recognition that the executive branch of the government, while it is the only branch of the government which can conduct foreign relations, must rely on its ability to persuade, rather than to command, in order to perform this function." RESTATEMENT, FOREIGN RELATIONS § 59, Reporter's Note at 206 (Tent. Draft. No. 2, 1958).

[126] In its proposed official draft, the second sentence from the tentative draft, note 125 *supra*, was omitted. RESTATEMENT, FOREIGN RELATIONS § 75, Reporter's Note at 250 (Proposed Official Draft 1962).

[127] See text at notes 78-84 *supra*. Compare the pre-*Rich* opinion of Judge Fahy, who believed that an executive suggestion "isn't conclusive. It isn't a question of taking away jurisdiction. It is comity. It is a statement of views emanating as it does, in the field of international competence, in the State Department, that is entitled to great consideration and deference on the part of the courts." PROCEEDINGS 136. Contrast this approach with that of a Florida appellate court decision holding that a Cuban governmental agency was entitled to a writ of mandamus compelling a lower court judge to perform his "clear legal duty to enter an order recognizing the suggestion to sovereign immunity. . . ." State v. Dekle, 137 So. 2d 581, 583 (Dist. Ct. App. Fla. 1962).

[128] FALK, *op. cit. supra* note 84, at 164.

with deciding that kind of policy. I think they feel that they are not free to disregard the State Department's determinations in these cases. The State Department, of course, is speaking for the President.

I feel that it is not, as some people have suggested, a voluntary limitation by the courts of a jurisdiction which they, at their discretion, are free to exercise or not; but it is a finding by the courts of a legal situation where the executive, and not they, has the power and, therefore, where they are bound by what the executive does.[129]

This interpretation was rejected promptly at the time,[130] but it received some judicial support in *Rich* when the court of appeals held that the Department's abrupt turnabout "should be accepted by the court without further inquiry. . . . We think that the doctrine of the separation of powers requires us to assume that all pertinent considerations have been taken into account by the Secretary of State in reaching this conclusion."[131] While this language is not unambiguous, it has been construed to support the pseudoconstitutional argument.[132] Should the question ever reach the Supreme Court, however, it is unlikely that the Court would read the Constitution to require judicial deference in immunity cases. Probably it would hold, as it did with respect to the act of state doctrine in *Banco Nacional de Cuba v. Sabbatino,* that the concept of deference developed by the courts does have " 'constitutional' underpinnings."[133] This approach would leave it free to clarify the respective roles of the two branches of government on a case-by-case basis.

A proper rationale for executive intervention in immunity cases must start from the premise that the doctrine of sovereign immunity, while it sprang from and is based upon comity, is nevertheless a rule of international law. Moreover, as the 1952 Tate Letter,[134] the

[129] PROCEEDINGS 4 (Yingling). Compare the 1918 opinion of the Department of State in the text accompanying note 36 *supra.*

[130] "*Mr. Dillard*: And I submit Mr. Yingling was wrong on the constitutional idea that under the separation of powers doctrine, it was a constitutional prerogative of the State Department." *Id.* at 136.

[131] 295 F.2d at 26. See Note, 13 SYRACUSE L. REV. 492, 494 (1962).

[132] "The court . . . [held] that the granting of sovereign immunity falls entirely within the executive's constitutional power to regulate the conduct of foreign relations." Comment, *The Castro Government in American Courts: Sovereign Immunity and the Act of State Doctrine*, 75 HARV. L. REV. 1607, 1611 (1962).

[133] 376 U.S. 398, 423 (1964).

[134] See note 69 *supra.*

1958 Geneva Convention[135] and the 1963 Department of State study show,[136] it is a rule of some definiteness which is accepted and applied by courts throughout the world.[137] Thus, while the courts should look to the Department of State for guidance on issues arising from sovereign immunity cases and treat such suggestions as binding when they involve issues, such as whether a foreign government is recognized, falling within the exclusive competence of the executive branch under the Constitution, they should accord determinations of issues outside such competence as entitled only to "great weight" or whatever respect the issue may require. "Particularly, the court should restrict the tendency of the executive to take over, in proceedings which lack procedural safeguards, the determination of an entire case merely because the case happens to have an international law element."[138]

The argument most often advanced to justify extreme deference by the courts to the executive, even on the key question of the application of the international law rule to the facts of a given case, is that an independent judicial decision might embarrass the executive in its conduct of foreign relations.[139] It is one of the most overrated arguments in the annals of American legal history.[140] The content and application of the doctrine of sovereign immunity, like the question of whether a foreign act of state violates international law, is a juridical issue, and "the duty of the courts to render a decision on the merits should not be subordinated to political considerations on no more solid grounds than exaggerated apprehension of national prejudice to the conduct of the United States foreign relations."[141] Indeed, it can be argued that allowing the courts to adjudicate on international questions without executive intervention actually lessens possible international tensions and resultant embarrassment to

---

[135] See note 75 *supra*.

[136] See generally SWEENEY, note 55 *supra*.

[137] See text at note 77 *supra*.

[138] Franck, *supra* note 114, at 1123.

[139] See text at notes 53-56 *supra*.

[140] "Stan Metzger presented the viewpoint of 'embarrassing the executive department by a court decision.' Can you give me a single case, in the whole history of the United States, where the government was embarrassed by a court decision? They are embarrassed by many other things." PROCEEDINGS 15 (Domke). See McDOUGAL & BURKE, *op. cit. supra* note 32, at 141-42.

[141] COMM. ON INT'L LAW, N.Y.C.B.A., A RECONSIDERATION OF THE ACT OF STATE DOCTRINE IN UNITED STATES COURTS 11 (1959).

the executive.[142] Moreover, judicial independence reaffirms the commitment by the United States to international law as a basis for dispute settlement. The concept of judicial deference, on the other hand, which reached its zenith in the *Rich* case, "sounds like a notion developed by men who are skeptical about the role of law as a regulator of international matters, for what could be more embarrassing to the development of the habits of law than a bland endorsement of an inconsistent pattern of disposition?"[143]

Until recently, most commentators have rejected the embarrassment argument, agreeing with Jessup that the Supreme Court "has allowed itself to become wedded to a proposition which has never been proved or even expounded in detail."[144] Following the *Rich* decision, however, a lengthy article by Cardozo appeared advancing the thesis "that the executive branch has a duty to make its voice heard in many international cases before the courts and that the judges usually must, without question, give heed to what is said."[145] Arguing that "where comity is the wellspring of the rule of international law,"[146] as in the case of sovereign immunity, then "the nation's foreign policy qualifies the way the rule of law applies to the case,"[147] he justified the *Rich* decision as a proper application of "the rule of law that provides for sovereign immunity when required in the interest of comity and denies the immunity when it would not serve that interest."[148] Furthermore, the decision did not constitute an

> "abdication" of the judicial function because it is not for the courts
> to evaluate the demands of comity in foreign relations. This is a func-

---

[142] As Stevenson notes, "we have been too concerned in many aspects of this question with the extent to which judicial decisions could embarrass the executive. I think that in many of these areas . . . if you can find that what has previously been called a political question is a judicial question, and let the courts handle it, that, far from increasing international tension and embarrassing the executive, it will actually reduce international tension." PROCEEDINGS 72.

[143] FALK, *op. cit. supra* note 84, at 161.

[144] JESSUP, *op. cit. supra* note 13, at 82.

[145] Cardozo 462.

[146] *Id.* at 469.

[147] *Id.* at 468.

[148] *Id.* at 471. "The courts rightly accepted the Department's determination as impelling them to grant the immunity as a matter of law, because the rule says that a recognized foreign sovereign is immune to jurisdiction in our courts when the comity of nations calls for it." *Id.* at 474.

tion that belongs to the department of our government charged with the conduct of our foreign relations. That department is not then deciding the basic legal principle governing the immunity, but only the presence or absence of a factual situation that invokes the immunity.[149]

To disregard an executive determination on the issue, especially one shaped by the "aims of foreign policy,"[150] might allow a decision disturbing to international relations. Thus the courts should follow such determinations without equivocation. "The voices of the judges, when they pass over the water's edge, must harmonize with the executive's."[151]

Cardozo's article contains the best rationalization advanced to date for giving the executive "almost absolute control" over sovereign immunity cases. By resurrecting the concept of comity, by redefining it in foreign relations terms, by making the application of the doctrine of sovereign immunity turn on its presence or absence, and finally by deeming the Department of State the sole body competent to decide this key issue, he has produced a consistent argument for executive intervention which sidesteps the charge of "judicial abdication"[152] and justifies such deviations from the policy of the Tate Letter as took place in *Rich*.[153] Indeed, as mentioned above, he considers that the courts there "properly applied *the rule of law* that provides for sovereign immunity when required in the interest of comity and denies the immunity when it would not serve that interest."[154]

[149] *Id.* at 471-72.

[150] *Id.* at 473.

[151] *Id.* at 498.

[152] Indeed, arguing for executive intervention in immunity cases, he admonishes the Department of State that "it cannot escape its responsibility by abdicating it to the courts." *Id.* at 474.

[153] "Surely carrying sugar across the seas in commerce is the kind of activity that the Tate Letter was intended to cover. But the State Department nonetheless suggested immunity, obviously because the *general* principle that comity does not require immunity in such cases had to give way to the particular fact that in *this* case it was required. The courts rightly accepted the Department's determination as impelling them to grant the immunity as a matter of law, because the rule says that a recognized foreign sovereign is immune to jurisdiction in our courts when the comity of nations calls for it." *Ibid.*

[154] *Id.* at 471. (Emphasis added.) See text at note 148 *supra*.

This argument is extremely sophisticated and at the same time somewhat sophistic. What "rule of law" decided *Rich*? Surely not international law, for under the restrictive theory now prevalent no immunity was required.[155] No other country has defined the international law rule of sovereign immunity to require the granting of immunity when its executive, for reasons of "comity," deems it diplomatically desirable. Such a definition, while it may offer a plausible explanation for inconsistent decisions by American courts, would render the outcome of immunity cases completely unpredictable.[156] Transposed to the world arena, it would deprive the rule of any substantive content and turn it into a mere "policy instrument in the conduct of foreign relations."[157] The result would be a mass of inconsistent decisions based upon similar fact patterns. In turn, divergent decisions in different countries would fragmentize international law on a point where a meaningful consensus is in sight.[158] Ultimately there would evolve the "American Doctrine of Sovereign Immunity," the "Canadian Doctrine of Sovereign Immunity," and the like.[159] Certainly a stable sovereign immunity doctrine is rendered virtually impossible if the rule is redefined to turn upon a prior political determination. Thus Cardozo's approach to sovereign immunity, in addition to being without international precedent, cannot be supported on its merits.

If the "rule of law" which decided *Rich* is not one of international law, is it instead one of the "foreign relations law of the United States"?[160] Here Cardozo, while still unconvincing, would be on firmer ground. *Ex parte Peru,* after all, justifies executive intervention on the ground "that the continued retention of the vessel inter-

---

[155] See text at notes 70-77 and 134-37 *supra.*

[156] Compare the *Rich* case with *In re* Grand Jury Investigation of the Shipping Industry, 186 F. Supp. 298, 318-20 (D.D.C. 1960). See note 68 *supra.*

[157] FALK, *op. cit. supra* note 84, at 142.

[158] See text at notes 74-75 *supra.* See generally SWEENEY, note 55 *supra.*

[159] That this possibility is not a *reductio ad absurdum*, see Flota Maritima Browning de Cuba v. Motor Vessel Ciudad, 218 F. Supp. 938, 942-43 (D. Md. 1963), aff'd, 335 F.2d 619 (4th Cir. 1964) (2-1). See Note, 53 GEO. L.J. 841 (1965).

[160] The Restatement defines this phrase to include international law plus that part of the domestic law of the United States "by which it gives effect to rules of international law" or "that otherwise involves matters of significant concern to its foreign relations." RESTATEMENT, FOREIGN RELATIONS § 2 (Proposed Official Draft 1962).

feres with the proper conduct of our foreign relations."[161] The district court in *Rich*, moreover, rejected the argument that the Department of State's suggestion conflicted with the Tate Letter, stating flatly "that no policy with respect to international relations is so fixed that it cannot be varied in the wisdom of the Executive."[162] Lower court decisions[163] and Department pronouncements[164] reflect a belief that political considerations should dominate the approach to immunity questions. It is but a short step to the position that comity, as determined by the executive, is the controlling factor.

The answer to this approach is that it overclarifies the present state of case law in the United States. Courts have followed the Department's suggestions because they deemed them persuasive or binding on the international law issue in dispute. For all intents and purposes, they simply have delegated the decision-making process on the immunity question. Certainly they have not articulated the belief that they were delegating "only the presence or absence of a factual situation that invokes the immunity."[165] Even if they had, it would be a distinction without a difference, save for the fact that

[161] See text at note 52 *supra*.

[162] See text at note 97 *supra*.

[163] See, *e.g.*, Weilamann v. Chase Manhattan Bank, 21 Misc. 2d 1086, 1087, 192 N.Y.S.2d 469, 471 (Sup. Ct. 1959): "The policies of the Department of State with respect to immunity of foreign nations and their property from local litigation are supreme. By virtue thereof, litigation on a local level may be required to be suspended in favor of negotiation on a diplomatic level."

[164] While the Tate Letter spoke of "a shift in policy," 26 DEP'T STATE BULL. 984, 985 (1952), it contained no intimation that the Department's adoption of the restrictive theory was qualified by the dictates of foreign relations. *Cf.* Cardozo 472-73. The memorandum of the United States filed with the Supreme Court in the *Rich* case, however, takes the position that the Department may deviate from its views expressed in the Tate Letter whenever it deems other considerations paramount.

> That letter does set forth the considerations which the Department will take into account in determining whether or not to recognize a claim of immunity by a foreign sovereign. But it is wholly and solely a guide to the State Department's own policy, not the declaration of a rule of law or even of an unalterable policy position; and, in addition, it sets forth only some of the governing considerations and does not purport to be all-inclusive or exclusive.

1 INT'L LEGAL MATERIALS 288-89 (1962). Thus the Department "may sometimes decide that for reasons of policy the Tate letter must be wholly disregarded, as it presumably did in the *Bahia de Nipe* [*Rich*] case." Cardozo 474.

[165] *Id.* at 472.

they would be less subject to the charge of judicial abdication. To the plaintiffs in *Rich,* it meant little whether comity qualified the international law rule or whether the rule was suspended for reasons of foreign policy.

The Cardozo thesis, in short, is no more than an attempt to provide a juridical justification for allowing the Department of State to decide sovereign immunity cases as it sees fit. Aside from the due process questions thus raised, the acceptance of this thesis would undermine, in the name of "flexibility,"[166] the restrictive theory of immunity which has evolved so slowly over the past forty years. "The word 'flexibility'," as Falk so aptly observes, "is a euphemism for the liberation of the executive from standards and rules, even those of his own fashioning."[167] The executive, as *Banco Nacional de Cuba v. Sabbatino* once again demonstrates, always wishes the maximum amount of flexibility on the ground that it can handle matters affecting international relations more effectively.[168] This desire for flexibility, however, must be balanced against other factors. The most important consideration is the need for the progressive development of a consistent body of law on the question of sovereign immunity which would make justiciable the maximum number of disputes involving foreign sovereigns.[169] This objective is more likely to be achieved if the courts, by according executive pronouncements great rather than conclusive weight, retain their freedom of decision in these cases. By so doing they will pass upon more cases, and their decisions will be given more respect. The second important factor militating against complete executive flexibility, mentioned but not fully developed by Cardozo, is the question of due process. As Mr. Justice Brandeis cautioned in another context, "the doctrine of the separation of powers was adopted by the Convention of 1787,

[166] See text at note 97 *supra.*

[167] FALK, *op. cit. supra* note 84, at 154.

[168] See Brief for the United States as Amicus Curiae, pp. 2-3, Banco Nacional de Cuba v. Sabbatino, 376 U.S. 398 (1964), 2 INT'L LEGAL MATERIALS 1009 (1963).

[169] The acceptance of the "comity" approach would permit inconsistent decisions in similar cases. See text at and accompanying note 156 *supra.* Indeed, the outcome of any case would be in doubt throughout the course of litigation, since the Department of State always could change its mind about what comity currently required. *Cf.* Stephen v. Zivnostenska Banka, note 83 *supra.* See also Timberg, *supra* note 72, at 115-18.

not to promote efficiency but to preclude the exercise of arbitrary power."[170]

THE DUE PROCESS PROBLEMS RAISED BY DEPARTMENT OF STATE SUGGESTIONS OF IMMUNITY

The due process problems, which have been suggested above,[171] became acute only when the Department of State endorsed the restrictive theory of sovereign immunity in the Tate Letter. Ex parte determinations by the executive, as Cardozo was quick to point out, constituted a threat to due process.[172] He recently reiterated that:

> whether the courts treat these interventions as conclusive or only of "great weight," a litigant has a just complaint if they occur before he has had a chance to argue for the kind of intervention he thinks proper in his case. When he is arguing about the policy, the facts or the law, he deserves a day in court.[173]

Nevertheless, until a recent change in practice "the Department has not considered that it ought to solicit the plaintiff's view."[174] Such was the case in *Rich*, where the district court was notified of the Department's suggestion of immunity by telephone and hastily drafted letter. Apparently the Department, in the normal case, now notifies the plaintiff when a request for immunity has been made by a foreign country and affords him the opportunity of presenting his views in the matter.[175]

---

[170] Myers, Adm'x v. United States, 272 U.S. 52, 293 (1926) (dissenting opinion).

[171] See text at notes 85-91 *supra*.

[172] See note 89 *supra*. See also Comment, *Procedural Aspects of a Claim of Sovereign Immunity by a Foreign State*, 20 U. PITT. L. REV. 126 (1958).

[173] Cardozo 463.

[174] Griffin, *Adjective Law and Practice in Suits Against Foreign Governments*, 36 TEMP. L.Q. 1, 4 (1962). See also Comment, *supra* note 64, at 291.

[175] An Associate Reporter for the Restatement has furnished this writer with a revised Reporters' Note describing the Department's unpublicized new procedure, the only significant feature of which appears to be notification. The Note points out that "although the attorney for the plaintiff now is advised that he may be heard on the issue of immunity, the burden is still on him to make his views heard by the State Department. There is no formal procedure on which he can rely determining the time and manner of presentation of his views and it is up to him to take advantage of the opportunity offered by the State Department."

A former Department of State attorney acknowledged several years ago that "the Department's decision ought not to be taken without giving the plaintiff an opportunity to be heard. However, the Department is not in a position to conduct a trial-type hearing on the question whether a suggestion of immunity should issue because the Department does not possess the requisite quasi-judicial power."[176] Jessup supports this conclusion, contending that "if the State Department were to set up a procedure for hearings, its exercise of a judicial function would merely be more apparent."[177] Cardozo, who justifies the Department's determination under the executive's foreign relations power, regards the above arguments as no bar to the establishment of a timely hearing process which would assure the private litigant of an opportunity "to be heard when the policy decision is being formulated."[178] It is difficult to reconcile his commendable zest for procedural due process with the fact that, under his comity thesis, the executive retains the right for overriding reasons of policy to bestow immunity regardless of the legal merits of a case.[179] A formal hearing, for instance, would have been meaningless in *Rich*, save perhaps to record how the aims of foreign policy can be furthered at the expense of the rights of individuals.

Assuming, however, that the Department's suggestions should be entitled only to "great weight," the necessity for a bona fide hearing with adequate procedural safeguards becomes apparent. Unfortunately, the Department has taken no steps to formalize its decision-making process.[180] Timberg describes the present situation:

[176] Griffin, *supra* note 174, at 4.

[177] JESSUP, *op. cit. supra* note 13, at 83-84. *Accord*, Dickinson, *The Law of Nations as National Law: "Political Questions,"* 104 U. PA. L. REV. 451, 478 (1956).

[178] Cardozo 464.

[179] One has the same difficulty with a similar analysis presented in Comment, *supra* note 76, at 1152. Consistency would seem to require the payment of compensation to the private litigant whose action is dismissed following receipt of an executive suggestion based upon overriding political factors. See text at notes 196-208 *infra*.

[180] "Firm administrative procedures, if ever thought of, were doubtless deemed inconsistent with the flexibility, informality and secrecy necessary to the conduct of international affairs." Timberg, *Wanted: Administrative Safeguards for the Protection of the Individual in International Economic Regulation,* 17 AD. L. REV. 159, 163 (1965). See text accompanying note 175 *supra*.

The State Department not only has no special competence for deciding questions of international law and making quasi-judicial factual determinations, but labors under heavy disadvantages as compared with the courts. In the first place, the State Department has no satisfactory procedure for ferreting out the truth about obscure or contested facts. Also, it is completely lacking in facilities for developing an open record, to which the foreign governmental defendant and the private plaintiff can both contribute the evidence in their possession, and their respective appraisals of the facts and of the legal inferences to be drawn from the facts. Because there is no opportunity to develop such a record, the private parties affected by the State Department's quasi-judicial determinations are deprived of elementary administrative safeguards usually available to litigants.[181]

Therefore he suggests "replacing, wherever possible, the Department's present informal procedures with formal administrative procedures incorporating the maximum feasible amount of public notice, statement of applicable standards, public hearing and explanation of grounds of agency decision."[182] Even then the courts should not consider the Department's suggestions binding, for, "inevitably, there is pressure on the State Department to determine legal issues on the basis of diplomatic relations and temporary political expediency."[183] In the *Rich* case, for instance, far from exercising a judicial check upon executive expediency, the courts unhesitatingly accepted a suggestion of immunity formulated with no hearing whatsoever. Furthermore, they completely ignored the argument that this procedure deprived the claimants of their property without due process of law.[184] Yet it seems irrefutable that the courts' bland acquiescence did deprive various claimants of the opportunity to assert two substantive rights: (1) title to certain property in question; and (2) satisfaction from certain "nonsovereign" sovereign property of claims reduced to judgments.

On the first point, the discussion above demonstrates that the courts should not automatically accept as true the allegations as to ownership of property made by a foreign sovereign and rubber-

---

[181] Timberg, *op. cit. supra* note 74, at 48-49.

[182] Timberg, *supra* note 180, at 168. Another former Department of State attorney agrees that greater procedural protections are necessary. Bilder, *The Office of the Legal Adviser*, 56 AM. J. INT'L L. 633, 667 (1962).

[183] Timberg, *op. cit. supra* note 74, at 65-66.

[184] See text at note 100 *supra*.

stamped by the Department of State,[185] for to do so "is to deprive the plaintiff of any forum in which a right to assert a claim exists, and this, it is submitted, is a deprivation of substantive due process."[186] While refusal to accept such allegations would force the foreign sovereign to appear in court, thereby causing a supposed "affront" to its dignity, even Cardozo admits that "it would not be a particular hardship or indignity to a friendly foreign sovereign to be required to prove its ownership of particular property in one of our courts."[187]

The New York courts in *Stephen v. Zivnostenska Banka* distinguished *Rich* and held that suggestion of immunity does not preclude judicial determination of questions of title, since "the adjudication of rights to property in the custody of the court and within its jurisdiction is a judicial function."[188] The decision, which is one of the few instances of late where the judiciary has asserted its independence, represents "an exemplary attempt to erect a judicial limitation on the State Department's control of litigation through the device of suggestions of immunity."[189] It takes into account the proper allocation of functions between the two branches of government, prevents the executive from overstepping its constitutional powers, and assures the private litigant that his property rights will not be taken without due process of law. Moreover, hopefully it may signal a willingness to re-evaluate the respective functions of the two branches with respect to other aspects of an immunity case. Thus, "if the boundaries erected by the court in the principal case are accepted, the way may then be open for a consideration of the question whether the State Department's inappropriateness as an adjudicatory

[185] See text at notes 111-22 *supra*. Although the courts have done so in many cases, including *Rich*, it has been suggested that "when the executive asserts the power to determine the outcome of a judicial proceeding the facts of which do not bring it clearly within the scope of traditionally exercised executive powers, . . . the propriety of conceding such power to the executive is at least questionable." Comment, *supra* note 132, at 1611.

[186] Comment, *supra* note 64, at 309.

[187] Cardozo 476. "[H]istory does not support the proposition that to withhold a suggestion of immunity until the foreign government establishes its title in court would be vexatious to foreign affairs." Comment, *supra* note 64, at 298.

[188] 12 N.Y.2d 871, 186 N.E.2d 676, 235 N.Y.S.2d 1 (1962), *affirming on opinion below* 15 App. Div. 2d 111, 120, 222 N.Y.S.2d 128, 137 (1st Dep't 1961).

[189] Note, 61 MICH. L. REV. 396, 401 (1962).

body should also preclude it from determinations of particular defendants' rights to the claim of sovereign immunity."[190]

On the second point, the decision in *Rich* accepted as binding an international law determination made by the Department of State which, if measured against its own previously proclaimed international standard, was clearly erroneous.[191] Carrying sugar on a tramp steamer, Cardozo agrees, warrants no immunity under the restrictive theory.[192] Yet the Department's suggestion of immunity and its unquestioning acceptance by the court combined to deprive "a private party—a plaintiff with a claim against the government or its property—of a right or remedy conferred on that party by Federal or state law."[193] Substantive due process is ignored once again in the interest of amicable foreign relations.

While the courts in *Rich* should have given the Department's suggestion "great weight," they also should have recognized that this very practice developed because the executive allegedly possesses special *expertise* on matters of international law. Where, as here, the suggestion is completely at odds with the Department's announced interpretation of international law, it should be rejected out of hand, with the courts looking to other evidences of the applicable legal standard.[194] Indeed, even if the suggestion had been reconcilable with the Tate Letter, it should not be deemed binding on the courts, according to Briggs.

> The "Tate" letter was nothing but a statement of policy of the United States, which was not conclusive in the courts. It was valuable because it indicated a trend in international law. It was a trend away from absolute immunity, which has been widely established, toward the exception in matters *jure gestionis*. The "Tate" letter was valuable, because it did state a trend for the guidance of the courts, and in itself, because it was an official finding, if I might say that, of the executive branch of the United States. It is one of the elements which

[190] *Id.* at 402.
[191] See text at note 162 and accompanying note 164 *supra*.
[192] Cardozo 474.
[193] Timberg, *supra* note 180, at 159.
[194] Even one supporter of executive paramountcy makes the reservation that "the State Department's certifications should be binding upon a court only where they effectuate an established international legal contention advanced by the United States with reasonable consistency." Franck, *supra* note 114, at 1118.

will be taken into consideration, along with comparable attitudes of other states, in the formulation of a modified customary rule of international law, avoiding the old doctrine of absolute immunity.[195]

Where the courts, as in *Rich,* abdicate their duty to decide this legal question of immunity, they in effect place their judicial seal of approval upon what may be an arbitrary executive determination. In this manner they may compound a denial of due process.

Assuming, *arguendo,* that the requirements of foreign relations in a rare case might dictate the suspension of the rule of law, such as occurred in *Rich,* can it not be argued that this intervention by the Department of State constitutes the taking of private property for a public purpose compensable under the Fifth Amendment? This argument has been presented persuasively in an excellent law review note, in which the notewriter contends:

> The government's certification should be treated as an exercise of the exclusive power of the President in the field of international relations that, like every other governmental power, must be exercised in subordination to the provisions of the Constitution. Even if the State Department has authority to prevent recovery of property by its owner in the interests of amicable international relations, it should not have the power to deprive the individual of his interest in the property without paying just compensation. In *Seery v. United States* [127 F. Supp. 601 (Ct. Cl. 1955), *cert. denied,* 359 U.S. 943 (1959)] the Court of Claims held that if an executive agreement interferes with private property rights, compensation must be paid. In *Rich,* since less than an agreement—an ex parte determination—may have taken property, a remedy should exist in the Court of Claims. . . . The court should hold that an incorrect certification is a "taking" by the United States, since in the absence of such a certification the courts would not give the property to the foreign sovereign.[196]

Under this argument, "and if the restrictive view of immunity, *i.e.,* no immunity for a sovereign acting in a commercial capacity, is accepted, as the Supreme Court has indicated that it should be, a certification by the Secretary of State that a commercial ship is free from attachment for a private debt could be considered a taking for which compensation must be paid."[197] This approach also would produce

195 PROCEEDINGS 135-36.
196 Note, 50 CALIF. L. REV. 559, 564 (1962).
197 *Id.* at 565.

other desirable results. "If the government must bear the expense of the certifications, the President may be more likely to require a hearing of the plaintiff's claim before a decision is reached. Except in the cases where the immediate release of the attached property is an absolute necessity, the Secretary of State will probably revert to the pre-1941 policy of transmitting the sovereign's pleas without comment."[198]

This argument, which has not been tested before the Court of Claims, would have to withstand at least three objections. In the first place, it might be argued "that the taking was done by the foreign sovereign and merely acknowledged by the State Department."[199] Analogies might be made to the lump sum settlement of international claims, where the United States waives the claims of its citizens against a foreign country in return for a sum which, when distributed, only partially pays their claims.[200] As Oliver has shown, the waiver of claims does not constitute a compensable taking, since "the United States through the executive agreement does not take away any material thing—the other country did that."[201] However, this situation is distinguishable in that without the executive's assistance the claimants would have possessed only unenforceable claims, whereas "in a case in which the court defers to an incorrect certification of immunity, the claimant loses what would otherwise have been an existing property right."[202]

[198] *Id.* at 566.

[199] *Id.* at 564.

[200] See generally LILLICH, INTERNATIONAL CLAIMS: THEIR ADJUDICATION BY NATIONAL COMMISSIONS 29-34 (1962).

[201] Oliver, *Executive Agreements and Emanations from the Fifth Amendment*, 49 AM. J. INT'L L. 362, 365 (1955).

[202] Note, 50 CALIF. L. REV. 559, 564 n.38 (1962). It also is distinguishable on the theoretical ground that individuals, who are not subjects of international law and hence have no standing to assert an international claim against a foreign country, must look to their governments for protection, and by espousing such a claim the United States is deemed to make the claim its own. See, *e.g.*, Z. & F. Assets Corp. v. Hull, 311 U.S. 470, 487 (1941). Thus, in theory, any waiver is not a compensable taking, since it is the government's and not the individual's right that is being compromised. *Quaere*: does an individual's private grievance become an international claim only when he seeks government assistance or may the government take the initiative and treat his grievance as a claim, thereby constitutionally foreclosing the individual's right to pursue domestic remedies? This problem will be considered in a more general context in Chapter VI.

A second objection which might be raised is the Cardozo thesis or a variant thereof. Should the Supreme Court ever decide that the application of the doctrine of sovereign immunity turns upon the executive's determination of the needs of comity, then of course the individual would have no right that could be taken, since by definition whatever right he has to have the restrictive doctrine applied depends upon the benevolent graces of the executive.

Finally, it might be argued that an unwarranted suggestion of immunity does not deprive the private litigant of any right, since even under the restrictive theory of sovereign immunity he would not be able "to satisfy a judgment ensuing from the suit because, in the Department's view, under international law the property of a foreign sovereign is immune from execution even in a case when the foreign sovereign is not immune from suit."[203] This distinction between "immunity from jurisdiction" and "immunity from execution," recognized in the *Rich* case,[204] has been followed in subsequent decisions.[205] However, doubt has been expressed about whether international law really requires absolute immunity from execution,[206] and American courts, if they were free to pass upon the question without executive intervention, might well hold that it does not.[207] Thus a suggestion of immunity when none was called for would prevent the private litigant from obtaining a possibly valuable judg-

[203] 54 AM. J. INT'L L. 643 (1960). See also RESTATEMENT, FOREIGN RELATIONS § 72 (Proposed Official Draft 1962).

[204] 197 F. Supp. 710, 722-23 (E. D. Va. 1961), *aff'd*, 295 F.2d 24 (4th Cir. 1961).

[205] Lower court cases consistently hold that "a claim of immunity may be asserted as to property sought to be levied upon, after a judgment has been entered." State v. Dekle, 137 So. 2d 581, 582 (Fla. 1962). See also National Institute of Agrarian Reform v. Kane, 153 So. 2d 40 (Fla. 1963); United States v. Harris & Co. Advertising, Inc., 149 So. 2d 384 (Fla. 1963).

[206] Timberg, *op. cit. supra* note 74, at 54-55. See also SWEENEY, *op. cit. supra* note 55, at 46-51 (1963). A leading publicist concluded a decade ago that "it is significant that states affected by measures of execution have not as a rule protested against it as being unlawful." H. Lauterpacht, *The Problem of Jurisdictional Immunities of Foreign States*, 28 BRIT. YB. INT'L L. 220, 242 (1951).

[207] *Cf.* Harris & Co. Advertising, Inc. v. Republic of Cuba, 127 So. 2d 687, 692 (Fla. 1961), 13 SYRACUSE L. REV. 169 (1961), where in the absence of Department of State intervention a Florida court intimated that execution against Cuban goods and chattels was permissible. *Cf.* Berlanti Construction Co. v. Republic of Cuba, 145 So. 2d 256 (Fla. 1962). See also McDOUGAL & BURKE, *op. cit. supra* note 32, at 152-53.

ment. Moreover, even if the private litigant who has reduced his claim to judgment cannot obtain satisfaction by way of execution, the judgment does have some moral value, such as the weight it lends to a possible international claim espoused by the United States.[208] One must conclude, therefore, that this objection to the notewriter's due process argument, along with the prior two, is without merit.

A Suggested Approach

The rationale behind the development of the international law rule of sovereign immunity—comity—is consistent with the doctrine of restrictive immunity set forth by the Department of State in the Tate Letter. Seen in proper perspective, the absolute immunity concept, which reached its high-water mark in the *Pesaro* decision, was a temporary aberration from a pragmatic rule which permits immunity from judicial scrutiny of truly "sovereign" functions. Moreover, further efforts to restrict this immunity to "hard core" sovereign functions should be encouraged, since "immunity is hostile to the policy of extending law to cover in an orderly and a just fashion as many controversies involving international law as possible."[209]

During the past twenty-five years, courts in the United States have raised doubts about their commitment to international law by gradually abdicating their functions in sovereign immunity cases to the point where, as in *Rich,* they have become virtual arms of the executive. While suggestions of immunity issued by the Department of State properly were considered binding during the days of absolute immunity, and while they should be treated with great respect even today, there is no good reason, constitutional or otherwise, why they should be accorded unquestioned deference in the future, especially when the Department goes beyond its proper function of deciding the status of foreign sovereigns and advising the courts on questions of international law.

Too often in recent years untested claims of foreign relations needs have been advanced by the Department to sugarcoat obvious

---

[208] Friedmann, *supra* note 32, at 479 n.11. See also PROCEEDINGS 23-24 (Yingling).

[209] FALK, *op. cit. supra* note 84, at 167. See McDOUGAL & BURKE, *op. cit. supra* note 32, at 139-40. "The obvious shortcoming of the restrictive principle in relation to recommended community policy is that it does not go far enough in denying immunity." *Id.* at 155.

extensions of executive power, power exercised unchecked by constitutional provisions requiring procedural and substantive due process. Lack of concern for the interests of private litigants is apparent from the Department's refusal to establish a formal administrative process which would guarantee all parties a day in court before the issuance of a so-called suggestion. Again, lack of concern is apparent from the Department's failure to propose legislation definitely assuring a remedy in the Court of Claims to those private litigants whose rights, enforceable in the absence of an unwarranted suggestion of immunity, are sacrificed in the interests of nebulous foreign objectives. Why, for example, should the United Fruit Sugar Company in *Rich* be deprived of its rights in order that Eastern Air Lines or others be made whole?[210]

A candid appraisal of the chances of remedial action by the Department of State or the courts along the lines suggested in this Chapter inevitably leads to the conclusion that the possibility of such action is remote. The Department obviously is content with its present position in the immunity process, which in Roger Fisher's phrase allows it to control a lawsuit's "outcome by putting the executive thumb on the scales. . . ."[211] The courts, including the Supreme Court, if *Rich* has been read correctly, are not anxious to rethink their views on the subject.[212] Thus congressional action appears to be the only remedial approach now available.[213]

---

[210] See Cardozo 466-67. A hijacked Electra airplane belonging to the airline was returned by Cuba about this time.

[211] PROCEEDINGS 104.

[212] But see text accompanying note 66 *supra*. The Court's opinion in Banco Nacional de Cuba v. Sabbatino, 376 U.S. 398 (1964), to the extent that it demonstrates a lack of enthusiasm for the so-called *Bernstein* exception to the act of state doctrine, may portend an "agonizing reappraisal" of the wisdom of its accepting executive control in sovereign immunity cases. Stephen v. Zivnostenska Banka, note 83 *supra*, also may be the proverbial straw in the wind.

[213] In view of article III, section 2 of the Constitution, which provides, *inter alia*, that the federal judicial power shall extend to controversies "between a State or the Citizens thereof, and foreign States, Citizens or Subjects," there is no reason why Congress could not enact legislation requiring the courts to take jurisdiction of sovereign immunity cases and decide them according to international law, assuming of course that the present deferential posture of the courts is not required by the Constitution. *Cf.* Stevenson, *The State Department and Sabbatino—"Ev'n Victors Are by Victories Undone,"* 58 AM. J. INT'L L. 707, 709-11 *passim* (1964).

Pleas to Congress for the enactment of a general statute abolishing or limiting the immunity of foreign sovereigns are not new. One issued on the heels of the Supreme Court's decision in *Pesaro*,[214] and similar suggestions have been made down through the years.[215] In 1948 a notewriter, anticipating the Tate Letter, recommended that the Department of State adopt a declaration or that Congress enact a statute limiting a sovereign's immunity.[216] Considering the Department's post-Tate vacillation, the writer was extremely perceptive when he added the caveat that

> since a mere declaration is easily modified, it may not be sufficient in itself to curtail expedient decisions significantly. If diplomatic pressures were allowed to force an *ad hoc* grant of immunity to one nation despite the declaration, it would then be difficult to deny that privilege to any friendly nation. By its relative inflexibility, legislation would obviate this difficulty.[217]

Days after the decision in *Rich*, Senator Ervin introduced such a bill in Congress designed "to provide means of redress for the unlawful seizure of American property by foreign governments."[218] S. 3795,[219] introduced again during this Congress as S. 1894,[220] amends 28 U.S.C. § 1332 (1958), which gives federal district courts original jurisdiction of all civil actions where the matter in controversy exceeds the sum or value of $10,000 and is between, *inter alia,* citizens of a State and foreign states or citizens or subjects thereof, by adding the following new subsection:

> (c) If the matter in controversy in any such action involves, or arises out of, an act of a foreign state in violation of general principles of international law, or of a treaty to which the United States and the foreign state are signatories, *it shall be no bar to the maintenance of the action that it is brought against a sovereign state, with-*

---

[214] Sanborn, *supra* note 38, at 28.
[215] See, *e.g.*, Hervey, *The Immunity of Foreign States When Engaged in Commercial Enterprises: A Proposed Solution*, 27 MICH. L. REV. 751, 774-75 (1929).
[216] Note, 58 YALE L.J. 176 (1948). *Cf.* Franck, *supra* note 114, at 1118.
[217] Note, *supra* note 216, at 182.
[218] 108 CONG. REC. 22460 (1962).
[219] S. 3795, 87th Cong., 2d Sess. (1962).
[220] S. 1894, 89th Cong., 1st Sess. (1965). Senator Ervin also introduced the same bill during the last Congress. See S. 576, 88th Cong., 1st Sess. (1963).

out its consent, or that it involves the validity of official acts of such state.[221]

Citing the *Rich* decision, the Senator explained that the bill sought to remedy "this intolerable jurisdictional impasse . . . thought to be required by the doctrines of sovereign immunity and the act of state."[222] He argued:

> If a seizure of property of a U.S. citizen has been made in violation of international law or of a treaty to which we are signatory, no reason of logic, fairness, or international law or morality ought to prevent U.S. courts, having the property within the U.S. jurisdiction, from having jurisdiction to restore the property to its rightful owner, or compensating him for its seizure.[223]

While the above bill may serve to generate debate about the course of congressional action in the field of sovereign immunity, in its present form it does not remedy all the defects in the present state of the law. In the first place, it negates a claim of immunity only where the action is grounded upon a foreign state's violation of general principles of international law or a treaty. Hence, while it would cover expropriation cases, it would not apply to an ordinary action arising from a breach of contract or from negligence. True, the bill does not require the granting of immunity in such cases, and probably courts would allow it only rarely, but it is just such rare cases as *Rich* that must be avoided if remedial legislation is to be

---

[221] Emphasis added. Since this deprivation of a foreign sovereign's immunity from jurisdiction does not reach its immunity from execution, see text at notes 203-208 *supra*, the bill provides for a new section, 28 U.S.C. § 1655A, which states:

> It shall be no objection to the issuance of mesne or final process with respect to property, as provided by rule 64 of the Rules of Civil Procedure promulgated under this title, that the property is owned by a foreign state, if it is used in or acquired from commercial activities by such foreign state, or has been acquired by it as a result of acts against an American citizen or corporation in violation of general principles of international law or of a treaty to which the United States and the foreign sovereign are signatories.

[222] 108 CONG. REC. 22461 (1962).

[223] *Ibid.* "Legislation pursuant to the bill I am introducing would offend no recognized principles of international law. . . . Surely, a state may provide means for restoring to its citizen-owners property within its own jurisdiction which has been illegally taken by another state, in violation of its express obligations and agreements." *Ibid.*

effective. The bill should be widened to eliminate the defense of sovereign immunity in all but "hard core" cases.

Secondly, while the intent of the bill is obviously to remove the Department of State from its dominant role in the process of determining immunity and substitute a judicial determination of the question, it is by no means clear that the Department, if it retained a voice on the key question of whether the actions of the foreign state contravened international law, could not control the outcome of cases as it does at present. A delicate as well as difficult drafting problem arises here, but perhaps it could be solved by specifying the sources to which the judiciary should refer in determining any international law questions, listing as a subsidiary source entitled to "great weight" the advice of the Department of State.

Finally, the bill applies only to federal courts and hence would not cover those cases where, for want of diversity or a $10,000 claim, the action is brought in a state court.[224] Since, as Jessup has observed, "any question of applying international law in our courts involves the foreign relations of the United States and can thus be brought within a federal power,"[225] the bill should be revised or recast to apply to state courts as well.[226]

Subject to the above reservations, S. 1894 is an adequate first draft which merits the consideration of foreign investors, international lawyers, and, ultimately, Congress. While to date it has not received the attention that it and the problem to which it is addressed deserve, current debate on the so-called Sabbatino Amendment, analyzed in Chapter II, may help to focus attention on this problem too. Hopefully, in the near future a single statute may wipe away the cobwebs of judicial deference that have gathered during the past quarter century, restore to the courts their abdicated role as expositors of the international law rule of sovereign immunity, and thereby afford a small measure of increased protection to Americans who have valid claims against foreign countries.

[224] See Stephen v. Zivnostenska Banka, note 83 *supra*.

[225] Jessup, *The Doctrine of Erie Railroad v. Tompkins Applied to International Law*, 33 Am. J. Int'l L. 740, 743 (1939).

[226] *Cf.* Banco Nacional de Cuba v. Sabbatino, 376 U.S. 398 (1964).

II.

Act of State

UNDER THE so-called "act of state doctrine," courts in the United States have refused to inquire into the validity of certain acts of foreign states,[1] whether alleged to violate the municipal law of the foreign state[2] or the public policy of the United States,[3] on the ground that by automatically applying the foreign state's law as "a rule for their decision"[4] the courts prevent the vexing of the peace of nations.[5] The Supreme Court first acknowledged the doctrine in a sovereign immunity case, *Underhill v. Hernandez,*[6] where Mr. Chief Justice Fuller prefaced his opinion with the following dictum:

[1] The legal literature contains little discussion of just what actions by foreign states constitute "acts of state." The Restatement, acknowledging that judgments of courts may be acts of state, concludes that typical actions treated as acts of state "are executive and legislative measures giving effect to governmental decisions on major issues of policy, such as public versus private ownership of property, taxation, regulation of business enterprise, distribution of goods in the economy and the classification, for purposes of different treatment, of various groups in the society, including aliens." RESTATEMENT, FOREIGN RELATIONS, Explanatory Notes § 41, comment *c* at 130-31 (Proposed Official Draft 1962). See also RESTATEMENT, FOREIGN RELATIONS § 28a (Tent. Draft No. 4, 1960). Since the taking of property by a foreign state is clearly an act of state, the definitional problem is avoided in this Chapter, which will consider the application of the "act of state doctrine" from the viewpoint of property protection.

[2] RESTATEMENT, FOREIGN RELATIONS § 42 (Proposed Official Draft 1962). See text at notes 25 & 111 *infra*.

[3] RESTATEMENT, FOREIGN RELATIONS § 43 (Proposed Official Draft 1962). See text at notes 26 & 112 *infra*.

[4] Ricaud v. American Metal Co., 246 U.S. 304, 309 (1918).

[5] "To permit the validity of the acts of one sovereign State to be reexamined and perhaps condemned by the courts of another would very certainly 'imperil the amicable relations between governments and vex the peace of nations.'" Oetjen v. Central Leather Co., 246 U.S. 297, 304 (1918). See generally RE, FOREIGN CONFISCATIONS chs. 3, 5, 11 (1951).

[6] 168 U.S. 250 (1897).

Every sovereign State is bound to respect the independence of every other sovereign State, and the courts of one country will not sit in judgment on the acts of the government of another done within its own territory. Redress of grievances by reason of such acts must be obtained through the means open to be availed of by sovereign powers as between themselves.[7]

While the doctrine has been applied by the courts of other major Western countries, such as France, Germany and Great Britain,[8] it is not a rule of public international law,[9] but "a principle of judicial self-restraint and deference to the rôle of the executive or political branch of government in the field of foreign affairs."[10]

Recently, nationalization laws and decrees of foreign states have given rise to many potential act of state cases. In the typical situation, a foreign state, such as Cuba, takes the property of an American citizen located within its territory and transfers it to a third party, who then brings the property into the United States. If American courts were to apply the act of state doctrine, an action by the former owner against the third party to recover the property would be dismissed without a consideration of the validity of Cuba's taking of the property. Some courts[11] and most writers,[12] however, have taken the position that the act of state doctrine does not preclude the examination of the validity of foreign nationalization

[7] *Id.* at 252.

[8] RESTATEMENT, FOREIGN RELATIONS, Explanatory Notes § 41, Reporters' Note 1, at 134-36 (Proposed Official Draft 1962).

[9] RESTATEMENT, FOREIGN RELATIONS, Explanatory Notes § 41, comment *g* at 134 (Proposed Official Draft 1962). See text at notes 60 & 156 *infra.* The International Law Association adopted this position in 1962 by about 324 votes to 24 with 2 abstentions. INTERNATIONAL LAW ASSOCIATION, REPORT OF THE FIFTIETH CONFERENCE xiv, 131, 618 (1963).

[10] *Id.* at 155 (Report of the Special Committee of the American Branch of the International Law Association on the "Act of State" Doctrine). "If, in an act of state case, the second State reviews the act of the first State on its merits and refuses to give it effect, the former has not committed a wrong under international law and the latter has no basis for a claim against it." *Ibid.* Both this sentence and the statement in the text were approved by an overwhelming vote of the International Law Association. See note 9 *supra.*

[11] A collection of cases may be found in the opinion of the court of appeals in Banco Nacional de Cuba v. Sabbatino, 307 F.2d 845, 855 n.6 (2d Cir. 1962).

[12] A list of authorities may be found in the district court's opinion in Banco Nacional de Cuba v. Sabbatino, 193 F. Supp. 375, 380 n.7 (S.D.N.Y. 1961).

laws and decrees *under international law*.[13] This view received substantial support in 1959 from a well-known report by the Committee on International Law of the Association of the Bar of the City of New York, which stated that "the available precedents do not require the conclusion that United States courts are barred from examining the validity of foreign acts of State in violation of international law."[14]

Relying heavily upon this report, the tentative draft of the American Law Institute's Restatement of the Foreign Relations Law of the United States adhered to this view the following year.[15] Finding that "no American case has raised the question of application of the doctrine"[16] when a foreign act of state is alleged to violate international law, the Restatement concluded:

> In this absence of controlling precedent, courts of the United States would appear to be free to consider on its merits the act of a foreign state charged to be in violation of, or in conflict with, international law. As international law is part of the law of the United States, and applicable directly in its courts, the question whether it has been violated should be considered as a legal question not subject to suspension in order to prevent embarrassment in the conduct of foreign affairs.[17]

The Restatement's position, which read precedent to permit an "international law exception" to the act of state doctrine, came under attack by several international lawyers at the 1960 meeting of the American Law Institute[18] and at the Third Summer Conference on

[13] Compare text at notes 2 & 3 *supra*.

[14] COMM. ON INT'L LAW, N.Y.C.B.A., A RECONSIDERATION OF THE ACT OF STATE DOCTRINE IN UNITED STATES COURTS 11 (1959). The report is commended in Hyde, *The Act of State Doctrine and the Rule of Law*, 53 AM. J. INT'L. L. 635 (1959) and criticized in Reeves, *Act of State Doctrine and the Rule of Law—A Reply*, 54 AM. J. INT'L L. 141 (1960).

[15] RESTATEMENT, FOREIGN RELATIONS § 28d(2) at 14 (Tent. Draft No. 4, 1960).

[16] RESTATEMENT, FOREIGN RELATIONS, Explanatory Notes § 28d, comment *e* at 19 (Tent. Draft No. 4, 1960). This statement has been called "flatly wrong and confusing" by METZGER, INTERNATIONAL LAW, TRADE AND FINANCE 69 (1962). A later draft of the Restatement modifies the phraseology somewhat. RESTATEMENT, FOREIGN RELATIONS § 43, Reporters' Note 3, at 142-43 (Proposed Official Draft 1962).

[17] RESTATEMENT, FOREIGN RELATIONS, Explanatory Notes § 28d, comment *e* at 20 (Tent. Draft No. 4, 1960).

[18] 37 ALI PROCEEDINGS 568-608 (1960).

International Law held at the Cornell Law School in June, 1960.[19] In an effort to quiet these critics, the Reporters for the Restatement subsequently retreated from their firm stand in support of the above exception to the more cautious line that "it is possible but not certain that courts in the United States will develop an exception to the act of state doctrine . . . where a violation of international law is charged."[20] By this time, moreover, the first case squarely presenting this possibility was working its way up through the federal courts.

Banco Nacional de Cuba v. Sabbatino, undoubtedly one of the most important international law cases to be decided by national courts during this century, was not the typical act of state case given above.[21] Farr, Whitlock and Company, a New York commodity broker, had entered into contracts for the purchase of sugar with a wholly-owned Cuban subsidiary of Compania Azucarera Vertientes-Camaguey de Cuba (C.A.V.), itself a Cuban corporation over 90 percent owned by residents of the United States. On the day that the sugar was being loaded aboard ship, C.A.V. was nationalized by the Cuban government. Thereafter, in order to obtain the required consent of the Cuban government to have the loaded ship depart, Farr, Whitlock & Co. entered into contracts with Banco Para el Commercio Exterior de Cuba, the government's representative, identical in terms with the earlier contracts it had made with C.A.V.'s subsidiary. The ship then sailed for Casablanca, Morocco.

The bills of lading for the shipment of sugar were assigned

---

[19] INTERNATIONAL LAW IN NATIONAL COURTS, PROCEEDINGS OF THE THIRD SUMMER CONFERENCE ON INTERNATIONAL LAW 61-124 (1960) [hereinafter cited as PROCEEDINGS].

[20] RESTATEMENT, FOREIGN RELATIONS, Explanatory Notes § 44, comment *b* at 145 (Proposed Official Draft 1962). The Reporters also inserted the following disclaimer:

> The Institute takes no position whether . . . [the act of state doctrine] permits examination in the United States of the validity of an act of a foreign state challenged as in conflict with international law but calls attention to the fact that in such situations there is no precedent expressly contrary to the possibility that an act so challenged could be examined.

RESTATEMENT, FOREIGN RELATIONS, Explanatory Notes § 43, Caveat at 141 (Proposed Official Draft 1962). While it may be going too far to say that this later draft "bears only remote resemblance to the [tentative] version," M. H. Cardozo, *Judicial Deference to State Department Suggestions: Recognition of Prerogative or Abdication to Usurper?,* 48 CORNELL L.Q. 461 (1963), it certainly does not constitute a strong endorsement of the international law exception.

[21] See text following note 10 *supra.*

by Banco Para el Commercio Exterior de Cuba to Banco Nacional de Cuba, also an instrumentality of the Cuban government, which in turn sent them to its agent in New York for presentation to Farr, Whitlock & Co. for payment. The latter accepted the documents, negotiated the bills of lading to its customer, and received payment of the purchase price. However, it did not pay the proceeds to Banco Nacional's agent but to one Peter L. F. Sabbatino, a receiver appointed at the behest of a stockholder of C.A.V. pursuant to Section 977-b of the New York Civil Practice Act.[22] Banco Nacional thereupon brought an action in the United States District Court for the Southern District of New York, alleging that Farr, Whitlock & Co. had illegally converted the bills of lading and the proceeds, and also praying that Sabbatino be enjoined from exercising jurisdiction over the sums paid to him. As a defense against Banco Nacional's motion for summary judgment, the defendants claimed that the Cuban decree nationalizing C.A.V.'s property was not enforceable in the United States.[23] It was the consideration and disposition of this claim by Judge Dimock in the district court that turned *Sabbatino* into a landmark case.[24]

DISTRICT COURT OPINION

The threshold problem faced by Judge Dimock in determining the enforceability of the Cuban nationalization decree was whether

[22] This section, now distributed among Sections 1202, 1203, 1207 and 1218 of the New York Business Corporation Law, authorizes the appointment of a receiver for the New York assets of a nationalized foreign corporation. See Comment, *Foreign Nationalization: A Statutory Remedy in New York*, 13 SYRACUSE L. REV. 555 (1962).

[23] If the decree was unenforceable, then courts in the United States would consider C.A.V. the owner of the sugar at the time when Banco Para el Commercio Exterior de Cuba purported to sell it to Farr, Whitlock & Co. Therefore Banco Nacional would have no right to enforce, as it attempted to do, the contract of sale.

[24] Banco Nacional de Cuba v. Sabbatino, 193 F. Supp. 375 (S.D.N.Y. 1961). An often perceptive but sometimes uneven analysis of the district court's opinion may be found in Falk, *Toward a Theory of the Participation of Domestic Courts in the International Legal Order: A Critique of* Banco Nacional de Cuba v. Sabbatino, 16 RUTGERS L. REV. 1 (1961), revised and reprinted as Chapter V of FALK, THE ROLE OF DOMESTIC COURTS IN THE INTERNATIONAL LEGAL ORDER (1964) [hereinafter cited as FALK]. Other law review comments, including numerous student notes, are collected in Dawson & Weston, *Banco Nacional de Cuba v. Sabbatino: New Wine in Old Bottles*, 31 U. CHI. L. REV. 63 n.2 (1963).

the act of state doctrine precluded judicial inquiry into its validity. With respect to the defendants' argument that the decree was invalid since it had not been published in the *Official Gazette* of Cuba, the court held that it could "not refuse to enforce the nationalization decree on the ground that it did not comply with the formal requisites imposed by Cuban law. . . ."[25] Nor did the court consider itself "free to refuse enforcement to the nationalization decree because it violates the public policy of the forum."[26]

Having thus applied the act of state doctrine, Judge Dimock proceeded to the heart of his opinion:

> The crucial question remains, however, whether this court can examine the validity of the Cuban act under international law and refuse recognition to the act if it is in violation of international law. Apparently, no court in this country has passed on the question.[27]

Noting that "foreign forums have evidenced some willingness to examine the validity of foreign acts under international law," the court acknowledged that "by far the strongest support for such examination has come from legal commentators and textwriters."[28] After balancing the reasons for refusal to examine the validity under international law of the Cuban decree against the reasons supporting such examination, Judge Dimock reached the "inescapable" con-

---

[25] 193 F. Supp. at 379, citing RESTATEMENT, FOREIGN RELATIONS § 28d(1) (Tent. Draft No. 4, 1960). See text at note 2 *supra*.

[26] 193 F. Supp. at 379-80. See text at note 3 *supra*. It has been argued that "the result [in *Sabbatino*] might have been better reached if the court had avoided . . . the act of state doctrine and in accordance with the basic conflict of laws principle, simply refused to give effect to foreign acts which produce results contrary to the public policy of the forum." Garretson, *International Law*, 1961 ANN. SURVEY AM. L. 1, 24. Falk, who urges "respect for foreign economic acts of state . . . to keep pure the role of domestic courts as agents of the horizontal international legal order," Falk, *Jurisdiction, Immunities, and Act of State: Suggestions for a Modified Approach*, in ESSAYS ON INTERNATIONAL JURISDICTION 14 (1961), adopts a "preferred position" attitude toward foreign governmental acts seriously abridging fundamental human rights, suggesting that in such cases the courts create "a limited public policy exception to the standard practice of deference." FALK 104. Compare COMM. ON INT'L LAW, *op. cit. supra* note 14, at 6-8, 11-12. The viability of Falk's distinction has been questioned. See Dawson, Book Review, 16 SYRACUSE L. REV. 192, 197 (1964).

[27] 193 F. Supp. at 380, citing RESTATEMENT, FOREIGN RELATIONS § 28d(2) and comment *e* (Tent. Draft No. 4, 1960). See text at and accompanying note 16 *supra*.

[28] 193 F. Supp. at 380.

clusion that "the decree in the present action is subject to examination in the light of the principles of international law."[29]

Whether one views Judge Dimock's opinion as constituting a "restriction of the act of state doctrine"[30] or a refusal "to extend the act of state doctrine"[31] depends upon one's view of the prior state of the law.[32] That moot debate will not be reopened here.[33] What is more important is ascertaining why Judge Dimock deemed himself free to examine the validity under international law of the Cuban decree. Was he adopting the Restatement position allowing the examination of foreign acts of state allegedly violating international law? Or was he conditioning his examination of the Cuban decree upon the tacit acquiescence of the Department of State— manifested in three diplomatic notes declaring the Cuban nationalization measures to be violative of international law?[34] Judge Dimock's approach to *Sabbatino* strongly suggests the first alternative,[35] although his opinion does not expressly adopt the Restate-

[29] *Id.* at 382.

[30] Comment, 75 HARV. L. REV. 1607, 1615 (1962).

[31] Coerper, *The Act of State Doctrine in the Light of the* Sabbatino *Case*, 56 AM. J. INT'L L. 143, 145 (1962).

[32] Metzger, for instance, took the position that the district court's opinion restricted the doctrine, since he believed it "applicable even if the validity of the act of the foreign state is sought to be re-examined because it is deemed to be in violation of international law." METZGER, *op. cit. supra* note 16, at 68. The Association of the Bar of the City of New York, on the other hand, viewed the opinion as a refusal to extend the doctrine. See text at note 14 *supra*.

[33] Whether prior case law required the application of the act of state doctrine when the act allegedly violated international law is a moot question after the Supreme Court's decision in the present case, at least insofar as acts involving the taking of property, the subject matter of this Chapter, are concerned. See text at note 163 *infra*. The question remains alive, however, with respect to other types of acts. As Falk rightly observes, the Supreme Court's decision "definitely does not formulate an absolute act of state doctrine. Courts are urged to pursue a flexible approach determining in each context whether the policies served by the act of state doctrine would, on balance, be served by its application to the facts of the particular controversy." Falk, *The Complexity of Sabbatino*, 58 AM. J. INT'L L. 935, 939 (1964) [hereinafter cited as Falk, *Complexity*].

[34] 193 F. Supp. at 381 n.11.

[35] From his opinion, which cites the Restatement five times, there is little doubt that Judge Dimock intended to fit the facts of the case into the Restatement's framework and supply a "controlling precedent" supporting its position. See text at note 17 *supra*. This surmise is reinforced by the fact that the issue on which Judge Dimock decided the case apparently was not briefed or argued by either of the defendants. Petition for Writ of Certiorari, p. 7 n.1.

ment's tentative position.[36] Indeed, by raising and then rejecting one possible reason for refusing to examine the validity under international law of the Cuban decree—the desire not to embarrass the executive in its conduct of foreign relations—the court resurrects the ghost of *Bernstein*.

Under what may be called the "green light" theory of the *Bernstein* cases,[37] a court will apply the act of state doctrine unless it is shown by "positive evidence" that it is the "positive intent" of the Department of State to relax the doctrine's application.[38] In the second *Bernstein* case, which has been called "the only case in which the State Department has suggested to a court that it could ignore or should ignore the Act of State Doctrine,"[39] a letter to plaintiff's counsel published in the form of a Department of State press release, expressing no objection to judicial consideration of the foreign act of state, was held to constitute sufficient evidence of such intent.[40] Having received the green light, the Second Circuit in *Bernstein* proceeded to dispose of the case on its merits.

Was Judge Dimock using the *Bernstein* precedent in *Sabbatino* when he cited the three Department of State notes? A close reading of his opinion points to a negative answer. As demonstrated above, Judge Dimock was operating within the Restatement frame of

---

Moreover, the Supreme Court subsequently interpreted the opinion in this fashion. Banco Nacional de Cuba v. Sabbatino, 376 U.S. 398, 406 (1964).

[36] Falk observes that Judge Dimock's opinion in "*Sabbatino* follows the Restatement approach, although it did assure itself that no executive embarrassment would follow from an inquiry into the status of the Cuban acts under international law." FALK 105. He concludes that "Judge Dimock's view of executive participation allows only for an initial veto of the normal judicial application of international law." *Id.* at 95 n.95. To the extent that Judge Dimock's opinion is interpreted as permitting "affirmative executive policy" to act as a "check" upon a court's ability to pass upon the validity under international law of foreign acts of state (*id.* at 91, 92 n.88), it cannot be squared with the tentative draft of the Restatement, which considered a court's jurisdiction in such situations "not subject to suspension in order to prevent embarrassment in the conduct of foreign affairs." See text at note 17 *supra*. For reasons given in the text at notes 41-52 *infra*, this writer does not accept Falk's analysis of the district court opinion on this point.

[37] Bernstein v. Van Heyghen Freres S.A., 163 F.2d 246 (2d Cir.), *cert. denied*, 332 U.S. 772 (1947); Bernstein v. Nederlandsche-Amerikaansche Stoomvaart-Maatschappij, 210 F.2d 375 (2d Cir. 1954). See Comment, 62 COLUM. L. REV. 1278, 1310 (1962).

[38] 163 F.2d at 251.

[39] PROCEEDINGS 105 (Metzger).

[40] 210 F.2d at 376.

reference, and the tentative draft of the Restatement clearly rejected the green light theory when the foreign act of state allegedly violated international law.[41] Even if the three diplomatic notes cited in *Sabbatino* constituted sufficient "positive intent" to permit the use of the *Bernstein* approach,[42] which of course was debatable,[43] there is nothing in the opinion indicating that the court used them for this purpose.[44] Having considered the "basic reason" for judicial refusal to examine the validity of foreign acts of state—"a wise recognition of and respect for the sovereignty of each state within its own territory"[45]—and dismissed it as inapplicable to the *Sabbatino* situation,[46] Judge Dimock proceeded to demonstrate why another reason for the rule also was without merit.

> Judicial refusal to inquire into the validity of an act of a foreign state has also been due to a desire not to embarrass the Executive in its conduct of foreign relations. See Bernstein v. Van Heyghen Freres

[41] See text at note 17 and accompanying notes 35 & 36 *supra*.

[42] "It is felt that a model for this decision could have been found in the *Bernstein* litigation." Note, 3 B.C. IND. & COM. L. REV. 282, 285 (1962).

[43] The government, which at this stage of the proceedings was the model of equivocation, later asserted that it was "perfectly plain that the [*Bernstein*] exception is not applicable in this case since the executive statement which it requires has not been made. . . ." Brief for the United States as Amicus Curiae, pp. 34-35, 2 INT'L LEGAL MATERIALS 1020 (1963) [hereinafter cited as Brief]. See text at note 144 *infra*.

[44] The district court decision has been construed as a liberalized version of *Bernstein*, with the requirement of "positive evidence" of "positive intent" being met by something less than express executive approval. Note, 30 FORDHAM L. REV. 523, 528-29 (1962). As Falk ably demonstrates, "an external intergovernmental note of protest sent to the Cuban government is not equivalent to an internal mandate specifically directed at American domestic courts." FALK 90. Therefore, if one assumes that Judge Dimock was following *Bernstein*, it is correct to conclude that he misused, or at least misread, those cases. *Id.* at 91-92. This Chapter rejects that assumption, and with it much of Falk's criticism of Judge Dimock's opinion. Falk's analysis is extremely incisive, however, when applied to Judge Waterman's Second Circuit opinion. See text at and accompanying notes 95-104 *infra*.

Quaere: If the district court was following *Bernstein*, why did it devote three pages of its opinion to the consideration of policy factors underlying a question it believed "no court in this country has passed on . . ."? 193 F. Supp. at 380. Surely a short paragraph citing *Bernstein* would have been adequate had the court been so disposed.

[45] *Id.* at 381.

[46] "The basis for such recognition and respect vanishes, however, when the act of a foreign state violates . . . the standards imposed by international law. There is an end to the right of national sovereignty when the sovereign's acts impinge on international law." *Ibid.*

S. A., 2 Cir., 163 F. 2d 246, certiorari denied 332 U.S. 772, 68 S. Ct. 88, 92 L. Ed. 357. The United States State Department has, however, delivered a note to the Cuban Government declaring the very nationalization law which plaintiff seeks to enforce to be in violation of international law. It can scarcely be believed therefore that judicial examination of the decree in the light of international law would embarrass the Executive.[47]

Bernstein is cited by the court as a judicial articulation of one reason often urged in support of the act of state doctrine, and the Department of State notes are used to demonstrate that this reason disappears when the act in question violates international law. While the passage indicates an awareness of executive sensitivity,[48] the extract, by itself and in the context of the entire opinion, does not support the conclusion that the court was following the green light approach.[49] Nor is there anything in it to warrant the statement that the case *"explicitly* allows the executive view of foreign affairs to act as a potential check upon the scope of normal review."[50] What rôle, if any, the executive should play in act of state cases was left unsaid. The conclusion seems inescapable, then, that the court "chose to break new ground by basing its holding on the proposition that the 'act of state' doctrine does not bar examination of foreign acts of state where such acts violate international law."[51] The Proposed Official Draft of the Restatement so interprets the district court opinion.[52]

[47] *Ibid.*

[48] "Since the Executive position was clearly [*sic*] stated, it can be concluded that the court did not totally discard the rationale designed to prevent embarrassment of the Executive Branch." Note, 47 IOWA L. REV. 765, 770 (1962). See also RESTATEMENT, FOREIGN RELATIONS, Explanatory Notes § 43, Reporters' Note 3, at 143 (Proposed Official Draft 1962).

[49] See text at and accompanying notes 41-44 *supra*.

[50] FALK 92 n.88. (Emphasis added.) See also Falk, *The Sabbatino Controversy*, in THE AFTERMATH OF SABBATINO 5, 10, 13 (1965) [hereinafter cited as Falk, *Controversy*]. While the opinion is somewhat less than precise at this point, it certainly does not "explicitly" uphold the assertion in the text. It may well be that Judge Dimock assumed the possibility of an executive veto in cases like *Sabbatino*, but he never explicitly stated his views on the question.

[51] Note, 60 MICH. L. REV. 231, 233 (1961). Banco Nacional de Cuba construed the district court's opinion in this fashion, Brief for Appellant, pp. 10-11, Banco Nacional de Cuba v. Sabbatino, 307 F.2d 845 (2d Cir. 1962), as did the Supreme Court. See text accompanying note 35 *supra*.

[52] See RESTATEMENT, FOREIGN RELATIONS, Explanatory Notes § 43, Re-

Having concluded that the Cuban nationalization decree was subject to examination under international legal standards, the court held that the decree was "a patent violation of international law" because: (1) it was not reasonably related to a public purpose; (2) it discriminated against United States nationals; and (3) it did not provide adequate compensation.[53] This Chapter will not explore the court's determination of the substantive international law issue, except to note that Judge Dimock considered it one for the court.[54] Observing that the Department of State had previously declared the decree to be in violation of international law,[55] he added that "the facts and law of the case, irrespective of that determination of the Executive, require the same conclusion by the Judicial [*sic*] with regard to the decree."[56] Thus, as Falk states, "it would be incorrect to attribute the result in *Sabbatino* to judicial abdication in the face of executive policy."[57]

In sum, the district court's decision in *Sabbatino* staked out a large area where, without the necessity of executive permission, the act of state doctrine was not to apply. The decision thus avoided making the courts mere "conduits for the fulfillment of executive policy,"[58] while at the same time raising hopes "that individuals injured by foreign acts of state in violation of international law might more often obtain a day in court."[59] The increased availability of municipal courts, in turn, would contribute to the clarification

porters' Note 3, at 143 (Proposed Official Draft 1962), stating that the opinion "tends to support an exception to the doctrine where the act of a foreign state is challenged under international law, but also involves executive indications related to § 44 [which restates *Bernstein* approach]." A comment to section 44 notes that "it is possible but not certain that courts in the United States will develop an exception to the act of state doctrine, independent of the rule stated in this Section, where a violation of international law is charged." RESTATEMENT, FOREIGN RELATIONS § 44, comment *b* at 145 (Proposed Official Draft 1962). See text accompanying note 35 *supra*.

[53] 193 F. Supp. at 384-86 *passim*.

[54] Dawson and Weston exhaustively consider this issue in their article cited in note 24 *supra*.

[55] 43 DEP'T STATE BULL. 171 (1960).

[56] 193 F. Supp. at 384.

[57] FALK 83. He cautions, however, that domestic courts "tend to invoke norms that correspond with the national preference. *Sabbatino* is itself an illustration of institutionalized bias." *Id.* at 75. But see text at and accompanying note 307 *infra*.

[58] *Id.* at 95 n.95.

[59] COMM. ON INT'L LAW, *op. cit. supra* note 14, at 15.

of international law on such questions as nationalization. The boldness of the district court's opinion automatically elevated the decision to leading case status, making *Sabbatino* the subject of much comment as the case went up on appeal. Unfortunately, the decision by the Second Circuit, while affirming the judgment of the district court, represented a retreat on all the above points.

Second Circuit Opinion

The court of appeals, when it turned its attention to the act of state doctrine, acknowledged that it was "one of the conflict of laws rules applied by American courts" and "not itself a rule of international law."[60] Citing numerous cases where courts of other countries have inquired into the legality of steps taken by foreign sovereigns,[61] the court traced the history of the doctrine in American jurisprudence and listed instances where it had been recognized and applied by the Second Circuit and other courts.[62] Then Judge Waterman, writing for a unanimous court, reached the heart of his opinion, the rationale behind the Second Circuit's exception to the act of state doctrine.

> However, when the executive branch of our Government announces that it does not oppose inquiry by American courts into the legality of foreign acts, an exception to the judicial abnegation required by the act of state doctrine has arisen and has been recognized both in this circuit and elsewhere. In *Bernstein v. N.V. Nederlandsche-Amerikaansche Stoomvaart-Maatschappij,* 210 F.2d 375 (2d Cir. 1954) (*per curiam*), when we received word from the State Department that it was State Department policy to permit American courts to pass on the validity of acts done by Nazi officials, our court rescinded its earlier mandate based upon the act of state doctrine, preventing the district court from questioning the validity of the acts of the German Nazi government. See 173 F.2d 71 (2d Cir. 1949). . . .
> *This exception is applicable to the case before us.* While the case has been pending we have been enlightened, as the court was in the *Bernstein* case, *supra,* as to the attitude of the Department of State.

---

[60] Banco Nacional de Cuba v. Sabbatino, 307 F.2d 845, 855 (2d Cir. 1962).

[61] *Id.* at 855 n.6.

[62] *Id.* at 855-57. Among the cases cited were the first *Bernstein* decision, note 37 *supra,* and Republic of Cuba v. Pons, 294 F.2d 925 (D.C. Cir. 1961), *cert. denied,* 368 U.S. 960 (1962), 13 Syracuse L. Rev. 327 (1961). See text accompanying note 105 *infra.*

... These statements are somewhat ambiguous, perhaps intentionally so. But at the least they express a belief on the part of those responsible for the conduct of our foreign affairs that the courts here should decide the status here of Cuban decrees.[63]

The import of the above passage is obvious. The Second Circuit forced *Sabbatino* into the *Bernstein* mold.[64] Rejecting by implication the promising exception introduced by Judge Dimock and commented upon by the Proposed Official Draft of the Restatement,[65] the court of appeals applied the act of state doctrine, and with it the *Bernstein* exception, to a case where the validity of the foreign act had been challenged under international law. The fact that the court perceived the Department of State's green light (albeit through a glass, darkly), not the fact that the Cuban decree was alleged to violate international law, operated to permit the consideration of the case on its merits. While the Second Circuit reached the same result as the district court, its reasoning is far less satisfactory.

In the first place, Judge Waterman's opinion "extends" rather than "restricts" the scope of the act of state doctrine.[66] The court implies that, absent Department of State consent, the doctrine would apply. Hence a broad exception based upon an alleged violation of international law is replaced by a narrow exception conditioned upon the wishes of the executive. As Metzger, a supporter of this approach, has observed, "it is unlikely that there would be many cases in which the State Department would convey directly to a court such a 'supervening expression of Executive policy'."[67] Thus, compared with the district court's opinion, the opinion of the court of appeals markedly decreases the availability of municipal courts to determine upon the merits cases involving acts of foreign states.

This injection of political considerations into the judicial process,

[63] 307 F.2d at 857-58. (Emphasis added.)
[64] The possibility of such an approach had been recognized. See text at and accompanying notes 41-44 *supra*.
[65] See text accompanying note 52 *supra*.
[66] See text at and accompanying notes 30-32 *supra*.
[67] METZGER, *op. cit. supra* note 16, at 74. Elsewhere he has stated that "except in the very odd situation, the Act of State Doctrine would be applied lock, stock, and barrel, as it has been. . . . As I visualize it, the upshot of the existing law is that [the] Act of State Doctrine will apply, except in a very odd case and very infrequently." PROCEEDINGS 105.

which allows the Department of State to change a lawsuit's "outcome by putting the executive thumb on the scales,"[68] is rationalized on the ground that the wholesale examination of foreign acts of state under international law upon occasion might embarrass the executive in its conduct of foreign affairs.[69] This argument, one of the most overrated in the annals of American legal history, is no more appealing in the context of the act of state doctrine than it is when the question of sovereign immunity is involved.[70] The question of whether a foreign act of state violates international law, like the issue of sovereign immunity, is a juridical question, and "the duty of the courts to render a decision on the merits should not be subordinated to political considerations on no more solid grounds than exaggerated apprehension of national prejudice to the conduct of United States foreign relations."[71] In addition, toleration of executive intervention, as Falk warns, "is itself a deprecation of the commitment to international law. The prestige of international law in domestic courts is undermined if its application depends upon a prior political authorization."[72]

A corollary to the embarrassment argument, suggested but not

[68] *Id*. at 104 (Fisher).

[69] "My own feeling on the matter is that the present posture of the law as reflected in the second *Bernstein* case, namely, that the Act of State Doctrine of judicial abstention will apply unless the State Department indicates to the court that foreign relations, in effect, will not be vexed and that, consequently, it is appropriate, in the Department's view, for the court to go to the merits, this present state of the law is just about where the law ought to be.

"This, it seems to me, derives from the basic rationale of the Doctrine, which is a foreign relations doctrine. The courts say, in effect, 'Since our judging of a foreign act affecting persons or property within a foreign country's jurisdiction could lead to foreign relations vexation, we, the court, do not feel confident that we will be able to make a judgment on that vexatious question; since the political arm of the government, which is supposed to be cognizant of the foreign relations implications, is best able to give a judgment on that, we will abstain, unless we get a statement from the foreign relations arm of the government that it is all right that we proceed, their having taken into account foreign relations considerations.' " *Id*. at 84 (Metzger).

[70] For a discussion of this argument in the sovereign immunity context, see Chapter I.

[71] COMM. ON INT'L LAW, *op. cit. supra* note 14, at 11.

[72] FALK 93. On a more theoretical level, he contends that executive intervention "relegates the role of domestic courts as agents of a nascent international legal order to the marginal circumstance where the political considerations bearing on the controversy are ambiguous or nonexistent." *Id*. at 88. See text at and accompanying note 67 *supra*.

developed in Judge Waterman's opinion,[73] is the contention that permitting courts to pass upon the validity under international law of foreign acts of state

> would be a most ineffective tool to achieve just compensation for all former owners, and would in all likelihood actually hinder the kind of government to government negotiation for a settlement which, if recent history is any indication, is the most effective way to secure the maximum compensation obtainable, and to distribute it equitably.[74]

There is a certain plausibility in this argument. In the absence of available international remedies, often the only avenue of redress open to a person who has been injured by the wrongful act of a foreign state is the diplomatic espousal of his claim by the Department of State.[75] When the wrong arises from the nationalization of property, it is most likely that his claim, along with those of many other claimants, will be handled by means of a lump sum settlement between the United States and the foreign country.[76] In the postwar period, lump sum settlements have been received from the Communist countries of Yugoslavia, Rumania, Poland and Bulgaria, and in all probability such a settlement will be negotiated someday with the Republic of Cuba.[77] While these settlements only partially compensate claimants for the loss of their property, they are a method of securing some redress and thus are generally favored by claimants. "This traditional method of settlement is impaired," it is argued, "when a foreign municipal court attempts to give relief by passing judgment on the contested official act of the government."[78]

Is it really impaired? No categorical answer can be given, the lower court decisions in *Sabbatino* being the first instance in America where the act of state doctrine has not been applied and the claimant

[73] 307 F.2d at 857. It later became one of the government's major arguments. See text at and accompanying note 142 *infra*.

[74] METZGER, *op. cit. supra* note 16, at 74. See FALK 101, 103; Comment, 75 HARV. L. REV. 1607, 1616 (1962).

[75] LILLICH & CHRISTENSON, INTERNATIONAL CLAIMS: THEIR PREPARATION AND PRESENTATION ch. VI (1962).

[76] LILLICH, INTERNATIONAL CLAIMS: THEIR ADJUDICATION BY NATIONAL COMMISSIONS 10, 102 (1962).

[77] See Chapter V for a discussion of lump sum claims agreements.

[78] FALK 97.

relegated to "the poverty and inadequacy of the international remedies. . . ."[79] If, as some assert, "negotiations through diplomatic channels are unlikely to result in prompt or adequate relief,"[80] it would seem that there is little to impair. In *Sabbatino*, for instance, Judge Waterman observes with respect to the Cuban nationalization decrees that "no aid appears to be available through diplomatic channels to the injured parties."[81] Even if the situation with respect to Cuba had not reached rock bottom, it is doubtful whether one or more judicial decisions passing upon the international legal validity of the Cuban decrees would have made much difference. Certainly the court's action in the *Rich* case[82] did not seem to improve the diplomatic climate to any great degree, and the application of the act of state doctrine in the *Pons* decision[83] also had little observable effect. Lump sum settlements, being politically negotiated compromises, involve many practical considerations,[84] but with one exception there is little evidence that the position of municipal courts has been an important factor during negotiations.[85]

[79] COMM. ON INT'L LAW, *op. cit. supra* note 14, at 2. Falk himself recognizes the weakness of international remedies. FALK 65 n.3.

[80] Comment, 75 HARV. L. REV. 1607, 1618 (1962).

[81] 307 F.2d 868-69. The Department of State, while it received claims for eventual action, never espoused them against Cuba nor negotiated for their settlement by a lump sum. *Hearings on the Claims of U.S. Nationals Against the Government of Cuba Before the Subcommittee on Inter-American Affairs of the Committee on Foreign Affairs*, 88th Cong., 2d Sess. 141-42 (1964) (remarks of Hon. Leonard C. Meeker). See also the last two Sections of Chapter V.

[82] See the extended discussion of this case in Chapter I.

[83] See note 62 *supra*. In *Pons* the Cuban government successfully invoked the doctrine as a defense to a counterclaim. The case is distinguishable on its facts from *Sabbatino*, however, since the act involved the taking of property belonging to a Cuban national and hence raised no violation of international law question.

[84] LILLICH, *op. cit. supra* note 76, at 106-09.

[85] In Stephen v. Zivnostenska Banka, 12 N.Y.2d 781, 186 N.E.2d 676, 235 N.Y.S.2d 1 (1962), affirming 15 App. Div. 2d 111, 222 N.Y.S.2d 128 (1st Dep't 1961), the Department of State, in a suggestion of sovereign immunity made to a court with respect to certain assets claimed by Czechoslovakia, indicated that the Czech Government, if its claim of immunity was not granted, intended to deduct the amount of these assets from the pending lump sum settlement of Czech nationalization claims. 15 App. Div. 2d at 118-19, 222 N.Y.S.2d at 136. Timberg notes that this deduction, even if it were agreed upon by United States negotiators, "probably amounts at most to 4 or 5 mills on each dollar of provable claims. . . ." Timberg, *Expropriation Measures and State Trading*, 55 A.S.I.L. PROCEEDINGS 113, 120 (1961). Nevertheless, the govern-

Even assuming that the possibilities of executive embarrassment and of hindrance to claims negotiations justify handling cases like *Sabbatino* under the *Bernstein* approach, the manner in which the Second Circuit went about searching for the necessary green light presented serious problems. The first *Bernstein* case, it will be recalled, indicated that the court would relax its application of the act of state doctrine upon the showing by "positive evidence" that it was the "positive intent" of the Department of State to permit such relaxation.[86] This "definitive expression of Executive Policy," as it was referred to in the second *Bernstein* case, was satisfied there by a letter to plaintiff's counsel expressing no objection to judicial examination of the foreign act of state.[87] If one views Judge Dimock's district court opinion as an application or misapplication of the *Bernstein* approach,[88] then the three diplomatic notes declaring the Cuban decrees violative of international law must constitute the green light. Falk, assuming for purposes of argument the wisdom of judicial deference, contends that these notes do not constitute the express mandate required by the *Bernstein* precedent. "Why," he asks, "should a domestic court pay any attention whatsoever to a note that passes between states on a diplomatic level?"[89]

---

ment later raised the unsubstantiated argument that allowing courts to adjudicate act of state cases "might even destroy contemporaneous negotiations in which the United States might be persuading the foreign state to make substantial or even full reparations to all United States nationals. . . ." Brief 29-30, 2 INT'L LEGAL MATERIALS 1019 (1963).

[86] 163 F.2d at 251.

[87] 210 F.2d at 375-76. "Freedom to review can develop from an express executive pronouncement for a particular case, a general statement for all cases emanating out of a particular government's course of action, or a fair implication from public declarations and positions of the executive branch." Cardozo, *supra* note 20, at 481. On the last alternative, see the text accompanying note 89 *infra*.

[88] See note 44 *supra*. This writer, once again, does not.

[89] FALK 81. The brief filed by the Solicitor General in the *Rich* case, decided after the district court's decision in *Sabbatino* but before the opinion by the court of appeals, demonstrates why general pronouncements are an untrustworthy guide for judicial conduct under the green light theory. For there the Solicitor General, advocating the application of the act of state doctrine, contended that "it would not be inconsistent for the State Department to challenge the validity of the Cuban expropriation under international law, and at the same time to accept the validity of the confiscation of American property located in Cuba, so far as our domestic courts are concerned." Quoted from Petition for Writ of Certiorari, p. 26. See also Brief for Petitioner, pp. 26-27, 2 INT'L

Judge Waterman's Second Circuit opinion openly followed the *Bernstein* cases but omitted reference to the three diplomatic notes. Instead, the court saw its green light in three off-the-record pieces of correspondence. The first of these was a letter from the Legal Adviser of the Department of State to counsel for the amici curiae in the case, two sugar companies. The court quoted this letter as follows:

> "The Department of State has not, in the *Bahia de Nipe* case or elsewhere, done anything inconsistent with the position taken on the Cuban nationalization by Secretary Herter. *Whether or not these nationalizations will in the future be given effect in the United States is, of course, for the courts to determine.* Since the *Sabbatino* case and other similar cases are at present before the courts, any comments on this question by the Department of State would be out of place at this time. As you yourself point out, statements by the executive branch are highly susceptible of misconstruction."[90]

The second communication relied upon by the court, from the Under Secretary of State for Economic Affairs to counsel for the amici curiae, stated only that the letter writer, the Legal Adviser and the Secretary of State all agreed that " 'the Department should not comment on matters pending before the courts.' "[91] Lastly, the court quoted a telegram sent by the Department to litigants in a Florida state court action involving the Cuban nationalization decrees: " 'Effect in U.S. of Decrees, etc. of Castro regime is question for court in which case heard'."[92] Judge Waterman acknowl-

---

LEGAL MATERIALS 1147 (1963). This extract shows quite clearly that the executive branch did not intend the three diplomatic notes to serve as the "definitive expression of Executive Policy" in Cuban act of state cases, if indeed they were ever intended to serve the purpose for which Falk suggests Judge Dimock used them.

[90] 307 F.2d at 858. (Emphasis added.) The italicized sentence of the Legal Adviser came as a surprise after the Department of State's intervention in the *Rich* case. Unfortunately, as eventually demonstrated in *Sabbatino*, the Department never has deemed comments upon pending cases "out of place."

[91] *Ibid.* This statement must come as a surprise to counsel in many sovereign immunity cases, especially in Stephen v. Zivnostenska Banka, note 85 *supra*.

[92] 307 F.2d at 858. The case, Kane v. National Institute of Agrarian Reform, 18 Fla. Supp. 116 (Cir. Ct. 1961), is discussed in Bayitch, *International Law, Fifth Survey of Florida Law 1959-1961*, 16 U. MIAMI L. REV. 240, 271-72 (1961). It is ironic to note that, despite the existence of this telegram, the court in *Kane* presumably based its refusal to apply the act of state doctrine upon

edged that the above three statements "are somewhat ambiguous, perhaps intentionally so," but he concluded that "at the least they express a belief on the part of those responsible for the conduct of our foreign affairs that the courts here should decide the status here of Cuban decrees."[93] Since the Department of State "has expressed a lack of concern as to the outcome of the litigation,"[94] the court decided that it was free to determine the case on its merits.

The Second Circuit, in using the green light theory, introduced two modifications to the *Bernstein* approach. First, it found the required executive approval in informal, off-the-record correspondence—two letters to counsel for the amici curiae and a telegram directed to litigants in a pending Florida action. In the second *Bernstein* case executive policy was evidenced by a formal Department of State press release as well as by a letter to counsel.[95] There is good reason to require such a formal pronouncement. Letters to amicus curiae, even if unambiguous, are a haphazard method of communicating executive approval to a court. They are not part of the record. They need not be shown to counsel for the parties. They may be used or withheld to suit the purposes of the recipient. In short, their use in this fashion rubs against the grain of due process.[96]

Telegrams and other communications in unrelated litigation are an even more untrustworthy guide for judicial action under *Bern-*

---

the alleged violation of international law, following the district court opinion in *Sabbatino*, and not upon the green light theory. Rather prophetically, in view of Judge Waterman's Second Circuit opinion in *Sabbatino*, Bayitch observed that "with this telegram in hand, the court [in *Kane*] could have completely ignored the act of state doctrine and followed the two *Bernstein* cases." *Id.* at 272.

The case was reversed on appeal, however, the appellate court applying the act of state doctrine across-the-board and rejecting both the international law and *Bernstein* exceptions. Unlike Judge Waterman, it saw no green light in the Department of State's telegram. "We are unable to agree with the effect appellees give to the telegram. The extent to which the telegram can be given effect is simply that the Executive Department of the United States Government will not interpose itself one way or the other in this litigation." National Institute of Agrarian Reform v. Kane, 153 So. 2d 40, 44 (Dist. Ct. App. Fla. 1963). See Note, 13 KAN. L. REV. 159 (1964).

[93] 307 F.2d at 858.
[94] *Id.* at 858-59.
[95] 210 F.2d at 376.
[96] See Brief for Petitioner, pp. 51-53, 2 INT'L LEGAL MATERIALS 1153-54 (1963).

stein. Assuming, as Judge Waterman does, that executive approval is required before a court may disregard the act of state doctrine, why should approval in one of a class of cases, even when expressed in general terms, be regarded as approval in all similar cases? The possibility exists that the executive branch may have decided that our foreign affairs permitted an exception in one particular case, while requiring the doctrine's application in all others. And if the executive branch actually takes different positions in different cases, should the court then be free to select the executive communication that is called to its attention or fits its purpose?

Here, for instance, Judge Waterman took notice of a "somewhat ambiguous" telegram to a lower state court, while presumably ignoring a flatly contrary statement made by the Department of Justice on behalf of the Secretary of State in a proceeding before the Supreme Court of the United States in the *Rich* case.[97] There, with 5,000 tons of expropriated sugar involved, the Solicitor General strongly argued for the application of the act of state doctrine:

> This act-of-state doctrine prevents any inquiry by our courts into the acts of the Cuban Government in Cuba which, in this case, may have resulted in the expropriation or confiscation of sugar or other property owned by petitioner in Cuba.
>
> .   .   .   .   .
>
> This doctrine applies with full force to preclude judicial review, in domestic courts, even where the act of the foreign state is asserted, as here, to be in conflict with or in violation of international law.[98]

That Judge Waterman, if informed of this statement, should have taken it into consideration seems too obvious to belabor. What weight he should have given it is another matter. Did it outweigh the telegram in the *Kane* case,[99] that telegram having come directly from the Department of State? If so, what about the two letters to counsel for the amici curiae?[100] Did they not tip the scales against judicial abstention? These questions highlight the difficulty in trying to divine executive policy in a particular case from conflicting pro-

---

[97] See text accompanying notes 89 & 92 *supra.*
[98] Quoted from Petition for Writ of Certiorari, pp. 26-27.
[99] See text at and accompanying note 92 *supra.*
[100] See text at notes 90-91 *supra.*

nouncements made in other proceedings.[101] Certainly this departure from *Bernstein* would be an unwise one bound to inject yet another aspect of uncertainty into act of state cases.

The second modification of *Bernstein* introduced by the court of appeals concerned the substance rather than the manner of the executive communication. In *Bernstein*, "positive evidence" of the Department of State's "positive intent" to give the green light was made the *sine qua non* of judicial disregard of the act of state doctrine. The court saw this green light in a formal Department of State communication which stated that its policy was " 'to relieve American courts from any restraint upon the exercise of their jurisdiction to pass upon the validity of the acts of Nazi officials'."[102] The "somewhat ambiguous" statements in *Sabbatino* cast a far weaker light. The Department, specifically stating that any comments by it would be out of place, said only that the effect of the Cuban nationalization decrees was a question for the court. Judge Waterman interpreted these statements as allowing the court to ignore the act of state doctrine and decide the case on its merits. An alternative (and, as we now know, more accurate) reading would have been that the Department intended the court to apply usual case law, including the act of state doctrine and the *Bernstein* exception, and in the absence of affirmative executive approval refuse to go into the case's merits.[103] In any event, one may apply Falk's analysis of Judge Dimock's opinion to the opinion of Judge Waterman and conclude that it states "a confusing approach to the relation between executive and judiciary in matters of foreign relations, an approach that neither agrees with precedents nor enunciates an acceptable new direction of policy."[104]

The position of the courts after the Second Circuit's *Sabbatino*

[101] Falk agrees that Judge Waterman's decision "aggravates *Bernstein* by resting executive authorization upon dubious collateral communications rather than by making the suspension of the act of state doctrine depend upon a formal and direct instruction from the executive to the judiciary." FALK 123.

[102] 210 F.2d at 376.

[103] "Whatever the proper limits of the *Bernstein* exeption to the act-of-state doctrine, we think it plain that the court of appeals in this case erred in holding that the State Department here had issued a '*Bernstein* letter.' " Brief 39, 2 INT'L LEGAL MATERIALS 1021 (1963).

[104] FALK 95.

decision, therefore, seemed to be as follows. If the executive branch remained silent, the act of state doctrine would be applied.[105] If the executive expressly indicated that the court might consider a case on its merits, under the *Bernstein* approach the court might do so.[106] What had been added was a liberal construction of *Bernstein* which saw a green light in a seemingly neutral statement by the executive branch, thus making it much easier for litigants to avail themselves of the *Bernstein* exception. Rejecting the presumption that the doctrine applies unless the Department of State specifically advises to the contrary,[107] Judge Waterman seemed to be establishing a presumption of the green light when the Department spoke.[108] This attitude, coupled with the court's acceptance of informal, off-the-record manifestations of the green light, would afford many more litigants a remedy in American courts. While any modification of *Bernstein* was welcome, certainly the Second Circuit's was less gratifying than the district court's. For an alleged violation of international law was no longer sufficient to create an exception to the act of state doctrine: some degree of executive intervention, even if in another case, was required. The courts' rôle as conduits of

[105] See Republic of Cuba v. Pons, note 62 *supra*, where the Court of Appeals for the District of Columbia applied the act of state doctrine to a counterclaim by a Cuban national. Since no violation of international law was alleged, the decision is distinguishable from the district court's opinion in *Sabbatino*. In addition, the Department of State had not responded to the court's invitation to file a brief, so the decision may be distinguished from the court of appeals opinion in *Sabbatino* on the ground of no executive approval. In a dissent, Judge Burger interpreted the Department's silence to mean that the court was free to adjudicate the case. 294 F.2d at 927. See Comment, 75 HARV. L. REV. 1607, 1619 (1962). See also text at note 107 *infra*. *Quaere*: could not the court have cited the *Kane* telegram, as did Judge Waterman, and on this basis have refused to apply the doctrine? See text accompanying note 92 *supra*.

[106] Since under the Second Circuit's *Sabbatino* a court might find its green light in correspondence made in connection with an entirely different case, other courts then might be able to consider similar cases on their merits. See *quaere* note 105 *supra*.

[107] Among others, Metzger (PROCEEDINGS 86-87) and Reeves (*id*. at 81) have advocated the continuance of this presumption and Fisher (*id*. at 86) and Stevenson (*id*. at 89) have opted for its reversal.

[108] "[I]f the executive says anything, no matter to whom and no matter how coyly and obliquely, then a court is permitted to construe these communications as indicative of an executive's will not to be embarrassed if the courts inquire into the validity of the foreign acts." FALK 119.

executive policy was thus further solidified, incompatible as this may be with the concept of the rule of law.[109]

Having decided that it was able to pass upon the merits of the case by taking advantage of the *Bernstein* exception to the act of state doctrine, the court then faced the question of the validity of the Cuban decree. Like the district court,[110] the court of appeals took the position that it could not hold the decree invalid because it violated Cuban law[111] or because it was contrary to American public policy.[112] However, once again like the district court,[113] it held that it could inquire into the Cuban "decree's consistency with international rules of law."[114] The court thus reached the same three-pronged argument of invalidity raised by Farr, Whitlock below—that the decree violated international law because: (1) adequate compensation was not provided; (2) the purpose of the seizure was retaliation against the United States; and (3) the expropriation was discriminatory in operation.[115]

The court's determination of this substantive international law issue need not be fully explored in this Chapter.[116] Prefacing his dis-

[109] Falk, who deems the Second Circuit's decision to be "a distinct improvement over Judge Dimock's opinion with regard to the external or foreign relations aspects of the case," nevertheless finds that "in the matter of the proper character of executive-judicial relations in an international law case—the internal aspects—Judge Waterman accentuates, rather than corrects, the failings of Judge Dimock. The ideal of judicial independence is shamelessly sacrificed without any development of defensive or limiting principles." *Id.* at 116, 116-17.

[110] See text at and accompanying notes 25-26 *supra*.

[111] 307 F.2d at 859.

[112] *Ibid.* Taking note of "the admonition that public policy is an 'unruly horse . . . ,' " the court concluded that the "decision of this case based upon the public policy of this forum is undesirable because reliance upon such a basis for decision results in a nationalistic, or municipal, solution of a problem that is clearly international." *Ibid.* Thus the court avoids the charge of "institutionalized bias" that might arise from a decision based upon public policy. See text accompanying notes 26 & 57 *supra*.

[113] See text at note 29 *supra*.

[114] 307 F.2d at 859. The court aptly observed that "although it can be argued that nationalistic prejudice could affect the decision in cases of this sort, it is also often claimed that other biases in various obnoxious forms are present in the minds of judges in other types of cases." *Id.* at 860. Compare text accompanying note 112 *supra*.

[115] See text at note 53 *supra*.

[116] For a thoughtful analysis of this issue, see Dawson & Weston, note 24

cussion with the needless dicta that "the law of nations is a hazy concept"[117] and that "anyone who undertakes a search for the principles of international law cannot help but be aware of the nebulous nature of the substance we call international law,"[118] Judge Waterman sought to find and apply international law free from "institutionalized bias" or executive pressure.[119] Stating the traditional international law rule requiring the payment of just compensation,[120] he also took note that:

> Tremendous social and cultural changes are occurring in many parts of the world today. Many countries have acted upon the principle that, in order to carry out desired economic and social reforms of vast magnitude, they must have the right to seize private property without providing compensation for the taking. They argue that because of the paucity of funds in their governmental coffers, it would be impossible to carry out large-scale measures in the name of social welfare if they had to provide compensation immediately, or even if required of them later. . . . It is commonplace in many parts of the world for a country not to pay for what it takes.[121]

Then, leaning over backward to avoid a "partisan posture,"[122] he refused to decide the "difficult question" of "whether a government's failure, in and of itself, to pay adequate compensation for the property it takes is a breach of international responsibility. . . ."[123]

---

supra. See also Stevenson, *The Sabbatino Case—Three Steps Forward and Two Steps Back*, 57 AM. J. INT'L L. 97, 99 (1963).

[117] 307 F.2d at 859.

[118] *Id.* at 860.

[119] Compare the approach of the district court at notes 55-57 *supra.* See also text at and accompanying note 121 *infra.*

[120] 307 F.2d at 863.

[121] *Id.* at 864. Elsewhere the court speculated that perhaps "international law is not violated when equal treatment is accorded aliens and natives, regardless of the quality of the treatment or the motives behind that treatment." *Id.* at 867. Such statements, coming from an eminent jurist on one of the most respected courts in the United States, are bound to undercut the Department of State's argument for prompt, effective, and adequate compensation in nationalization cases. Indeed, before the Supreme Court the government acknowledged that "the statement in the Court of Appeals opinion expressing doubt as to the law of compensation has already hurt the Department of State in negotiation." Summary of Oral Argument, 2 INT'L LEGAL MATERIALS 1128, 1134 (1963). No further demonstration that the court was free of "institutionalized bias" is necessary.

[122] FALK 114.

[123] 307 F.2d at 864. Compare Judge Dimock's position which viewed the

Instead, he conditioned his holding upon a finding that the Cuban decree was an act of reprisal against the United States which discriminated against United States nationals and therefore violated international law.[124] The holding, more narrow and limited than that of the district court,[125] is spelled out quite clearly:

> Since the Cuban decree of expropriation not only failed to provide adequate compensation but also involved a retaliatory purpose and a discrimination against United States nationals, we hold that the decree was in violation of international law.[126]

The decree having violated international law, Judge Waterman reasoned that Banco Nacional de Cuba's title was invalid and therefore affirmed the district court's dismissal of the complaint.[127] Both courts thus reached the same destination, although the route taken by the Second Circuit was far less satisfactory.

SUPREME COURT OPINION

Banco Nacional, in its petition for a writ of certiorari to review the judgment of the court of appeals, relied on two main points: (1) that the decisions conflicted with prior cases like *Ricaud*,[128] which it contended had applied the act of state doctrine "even where the property confiscated by the foreign government was that of an American citizen";[129] and (2) that the decision's use of *Bernstein* was inappropriate, since "that case is clearly distinguishable. We

---

failure to provide adequate compensation as an independent ground for holding the Cuban decrees violative of international law. 193 F. Supp. at 385.

[124] 307 F.2d at 868. Judge Dimock had held that the Cuban decrees violated international law on both of these independent grounds. 193 F. Supp. at 384-85.

[125] See text at notes 53-54 *supra*.

[126] 307 F.2d at 868. Any possible idea that Judge Waterman intended to hold the decrees invalid on three independent grounds is dispelled by his phrasing of the question for decision. *Id.* at 864. The Supreme Court later agreed with this construction of the court of appeals' opinion. Banco Nacional de Cuba v. Sabbatino, 376 U.S. 398, 407 (1964).

[127] The court rejected the argument that the nationalization decree vested good title to the sugar in Cuba, subject only to a duty to pay compensation for the taking. *Id.* at 869. Compare Domke, *Indonesian Nationalization Measures Before Foreign Courts*, 54 AM. J. INT'L L. 305 (1960) and Wortley, *Indonesian Nationalization Measures—An Intervention*, 55 AM. J. INT'L L. 680 (1961) with Baade, *Indonesian Nationalization Measures Before Foreign Courts—A Reply*, 54 AM. J. INT'L L. 801 (1960).

[128] See note 4 *supra*.

[129] Petition for Writ of Certiorari, p. 9.

have here no 'positive evidence' of an intent by the executive to relax the Act of State Doctrine."[130] The Solicitor General, requested by the Supreme Court to express the views of the United States, submitted a memorandum suggesting that the case be reviewed.[131] Although the memorandum purported not to be "an expression of the views of the executive branch upon the substantive merits of the questions presented,"[132] it nevertheless impliedly supported the petitioner's first point and openly advocated its second. Taking no position on whether the *Bernstein* exception was "a permissible or desirable limitation on the Act of State doctrine,"[133] the Solicitor General went on to state flatly that the court of appeals had erred in assuming that it had a *Bernstein* letter before it.[134] The Supreme Court thereupon granted the petition for certiorari.[135]

If, as Domke had observed, the Solicitor General's memorandum was not "a favorable omen for the protection of property rights of Americans,"[136] the brief upon the merits filed by the United States as amicus curiae was yet another sign of impending disaster.[137] Wholeheartedly embracing the act of state doctrine, the government denied the existence of an "international law" exception and argued that "the balance of considerations strongly favors retention of the traditional act of state doctrine in such cases."[138] The brief relied upon four policy arguments: (1) "American judicial decisions applying international law would have, at best, only occasional application to foreign acts of state."[139] (2) "Decisions invalidating foreign

[130] *Id*. at 10. See text at notes 86-94 *supra*.

[131] Memorandum for the United States, 2 INT'L LEGAL MATERIALS 212 (1963).

[132] *Id*. at 10, 2 INT'L LEGAL MATERIALS at 221.

[133] *Id*. at 6, 2 INT'L LEGAL MATERIALS at 217.

[134] *Id*. at 7, 2 INT'L LEGAL MATERIALS at 218. The memorandum is discussed in FALK 131-32.

[135] 372 U.S. 905 (1963).

[136] Domke, *The Present American Attitude Towards Nationalization of Foreign-Owned Property*, 1963 DUKE L.J. 281, 289.

[137] Indeed, as far back as 1961 the handwriting was on the wall. In denying the application for a stay made by the United Fruit Sugar Company in the *Rich* case, discussed in Chapter I, the Chief Justice, after citing the standard sovereign immunity cases, "added reference to the classic Act of State decisions: 'Also *Underhill* v. *Hernandez*, 168 U.S. 250, 252, and *Ricaud* v. *American Metal Co.*, 246 U.S. 304, 309.'" Petition for Writ of Certiorari, p. 19.

[138] Brief 25, 2 INT'L LEGAL MATERIALS 1018 (1963). See text at notes 11-20 *supra*.

[139] *Id*. at 26, 2 INT'L LEGAL MATERIALS at 1018. "At best, American applica-

acts of state would have disruptive effects upon international transactions."[140] (3) "American judicial decisions in act of state cases would not be likely to advance the development of principles of international law."[141] (4) "The primary and most satisfactory way to deal with foreign acts of state which violate international law is the exercise of diplomacy."[142]

The brief, while taking no position on the *Bernstein* exception,[143] also made it crystal clear that this exception, even if it should receive Supreme Court approval, was not applicable here.

> Whatever the proper limits of the *Bernstein* exception to the act-of-state doctrine, we think it plain that the court of appeals in this case erred in holding that the State Department here had issued a

tion of international law to the foreign sovereign's act will be sporadic and hap-hazard, depending upon wholly fortuitous circumstances, such as the foreign property, or the assignee of the foreign government, coming into the United States. . . . Nor could such decisions hope to achieve any general redress of the wrong committed by the foreign government as it affects American nationals; they could only give relief to parties who, by chance, are able to bring suit in an American court." *Ibid.*

[140] *Ibid.* "Unquestionably, decisions like those below, while they will be unable to afford any general remedy against infractions of international law or to exert any comprehensive effect upon the foreign conduct involved, will, by threatening to cloud the title to nationalized property, serve to disrupt international commercial transactions. There is no reason to believe that such decisions would, on the other hand, exert economic pressure which might ultimately deter countries from undertaking to nationalize privately owned assets. Nationalizations are significantly, if not primarily, influenced by political rather than commercial considerations." *Id.* at 26-27, 2 INT'L LEGAL MATERIALS at 1018.

[141] *Id.* at 27, 2 INT'L LEGAL MATERIALS at 1018. "Decisions by American courts striking down foreign official acts of state which impair American property interests will probably not be viewed abroad as dispassionate applications of neutral international principles. More likely, they will frequently be seen in many other nations as reflecting merely parochial American views partisan to American national interests." *Id.* at 27-28, 2 INT'L LEGAL MATERIALS at 1018.

[142] *Id.* at 28, 2 INT'L LEGAL MATERIALS at 1018. This argument, which received twice as much space in the government's brief as the other three combined, reflects the brief's underlying rationale: a belief in "the primacy of foreign affairs and the superior pragmatics of executive settlement." FALK 136. This rationale is considered extensively in the text at notes 213-40 *infra*.

[143] Brief 34-38, 2 INT'L LEGAL MATERIALS 1020-21 (1963). Upon oral argument before the Supreme Court, "Mr. Katzenbach stated that the Government was not then urging that the Bernstein exception be either approved or abandoned. The Government was not taking any position on this. And it was not relevant to this case. In this case there had been no Bernstein letter purporting to remove the act of state bar to judicial consideration of the foreign act." Summary of Oral Argument, 2 INT'L LEGAL MATERIALS 1133 (1963).

"*Bernstein* letter." A full account of the correspondence relied upon
by the court of appeals . . . makes it plain that the court of appeals'
holding was erroneous.[144]

Since even the liberal construction of *Bernstein* adopted by the
court of appeals required some degree of executive assent before a
court might consider an act of state case on its merits,[145] this stand
by the government forced the respondent[146] and amici curiae supporting it[147] to forsake the Second Circuit's approach and concen-
trate upon the "international law exception" advanced in the district
court's opinion. Such was the posture of the case when it came before
the Supreme Court.

   In an historic opinion Mr. Justice Harlan, writing for a majority
of eight, first rejected the respondent's contention that the petitioner,
an instrumentality of a government with which the United States
does not maintain diplomatic relations, be denied access to American
courts.[148] Holding that any relationship, short of war, with a recognized sovereign power embraces the privilege of resorting to such
courts,[149] the Court then turned to the question whether the act of
state doctrine served to sustain petitioner's claims. Quoting "the
classic American statement of the act of state doctrine"[150] found in
Underhill v. Hernandez,[151] Mr. Justice Harlan surveyed later

[144] Brief 39, 2 INT'L LEGAL MATERIALS 1021 (1963).

[145] See text at note 105 *supra*. In the abundance of precaution, the government's brief devoted four pages to refuting the proposal of the Association of
the Bar of the City of New York that executive silence be treated as the
equivalent of a *Bernstein* letter. *Id.* at 43-46, 2 INT'L LEGAL MATERIALS at 1022-
23. See note 14 *supra* and text at notes 259-64 *infra*.

[146] The briefs for the respondent Farr, Whitlock & Co., together with the
briefs for the petitioner, are reprinted in 2 INT'L LEGAL MATERIALS 1142-91
(1963). Also included is the brief of C.A.V., which the Supreme Court allowed
to appear as amicus curiae but not as a party.

[147] Amici curiae briefs supporting the respondent's position were filed by the
North American Sugar Industries, Inc. (formerly the Cuban-American Sugar
Company) and the Cuban American Sugar Mills Company; the Committee on
International Law of the Association of the Bar of the City of New York; the
Executive Committee of the American Branch of the International Law As-
sociation; and the American Bar Association. The A.B.A. brief was limited to
the question of whether Cuba's acts violated international law. The Pan-Ameri-
can Insurance Company filed an amicus curiae brief supporting the petitioner.

[148] 376 U.S. at 408-10. See Falk, *Complexity* 949-51.

[149] 376 U.S. at 410.

[150] *Id.* at 416.

[151] See text at note 7 *supra*.

decisions, including *Oetjen* and *Ricaud*, and concluded that "none of this Court's subsequent cases in which the act of state doctrine was directly or peripherally involved manifest any retreat from *Underhill*."[152] Noting that the decision by the court of appeals relied upon the *Bernstein* exception, the Court made it clear that any such exception did not apply to *Sabbatino*.

> This Court has never had occasion to pass upon the so-called *Bernstein* exception, nor need it do so now. For whatever ambiguity may be thought to exist in the two letters from State Department officials on which the Court of Appeals relied, . . . is now removed by the position which the Executive has taken in this Court on the act of state claim. . . .[153]

The case turned, therefore, upon whether the Court accepted either of the two main contentions urged by the respondent against the doctrine's application: (1) that the doctrine did not apply to acts of state which violated international law; or (2) that the doctrine was inapplicable unless the executive specifically interposed it in a particular case.[154]

Mr. Justice Harlan first examined the foundations on which the act of state doctrine rests.[155] The doctrine, according to the Court, is not compelled "either by the inherent nature of sovereign authority . . . or by some principle of international law."[156] Moreover, "the text of the Constitution does not require the act of state doctrine;

[152] 376 U.S. at 416.

[153] *Id.* at 420. See also *id.* at 436.

[154] *Id.* at 420. The Court also considered and rejected the argument that the doctrine could not be invoked by a foreign government suing in American courts. *Id.* at 437-39. Compare the typical act of state case in the text following note 10 *supra*.

[155] For a superb analysis of possible foundations, see Henkin, *The Foreign Affairs Power of the Federal Courts:* Sabbatino, 64 COLUM. L. REV. 805 (1964).

[156] 376 U.S. at 421. "That international law does not require application of the doctrine is evidenced by the practice of nations. Most of the countries rendering decisions on the subject fail to follow the rule rigidly. No international arbitral or judicial decision discovered suggests that international law prescribes recognition of sovereign acts of foreign governments, . . . and apparently no claim has ever been raised before an international tribunal that failure to apply the act of state doctrine constitutes a breach of international obligation." *Id.* at 421-22. See text at and accompanying note 9 *supra*. The Court added that "if international law does not prescribe use of the doctrine, neither does it forbid application of the rule even if it is claimed that the act of state in question violated international law." *Id.* at 422.

it does not irrevocably remove from the judiciary the capacity to review the validity of foreign acts of state."[157] Nevertheless, the doctrine has " 'constitutional' underpinings,"[158] a phrase which apparently means that it reflects "the proper distribution of functions between the judicial and political branches of the Government on matters bearing upon foreign affairs."[159] Furthermore, since the problems surrounding the act of state doctrine are "intrinsically federal," its scope "must be determined according to federal law."[160]

> [I]t is plain that the problems involved are uniquely federal in nature. If federal authority, in this instance this Court, orders the field of judicial competence in this area for the federal courts, and the state courts are left free to formulate their own rules, the purposes behind the doctrine could be as effectively undermined as if there had been no federal pronouncement on the subject.[161]

Thus the Court concluded that the act of state doctrine is a rule of "federal-judge-made law," "federal-court-built law," or "federal judicial law" binding upon state as well as federal courts.[162]

---

[157] *Id.* at 423. Stevenson quickly noted that this determination "that the act of state doctrine is judicial rather than Constitutional, suggests that an Act of Congress requiring the courts to apply international law (or a statutory declaration of the applicable principles thereof) as the rule of decision in 'act of state' cases would be upheld." Stevenson, *The State Department and Sabbatino— "Ev'n Victors Are by Victories Undone,"* 58 AM. J. INT'L L. 707, 711 (1964). See text at notes 328-38 *infra.*

[158] 376 U.S. at 423. "It arises out of the basic relationships between branches of government in a system of separation of powers. It concerns the competency of dissimilar institutions to make and implement particular kinds of decisions in the area of international relations. The doctrine as formulated in past decisions expresses the strong sense of the Judicial Branch that its engagement in the task of passing on the validity of foreign acts of state may hinder rather than further this country's pursuit of goals both for itself and for the community of nations as a whole in the international sphere." *Ibid.*

[159] *Id.* at 428. See Falk, *Complexity* 940.

[160] 376 U.S. at 427. The Court felt "constrained to make it clear that an issue concerned with a basic choice regarding the competence and function of the Judiciary and the National Executive in ordering our relationships with other members of the international community must be treated exclusively as an aspect of federal law." *Id.* at 425.

[161] *Id.* at 424.

[162] *Id.* at 426. See Henkin, *supra* note 155, at 811-13. Compare Maw, Comments, 5 HARV. INT'L L. CLUB J. 221, 223-24 (1964). The question whether New York law applied and whether New York had an act of state doctrine had been raised after oral argument before the Supreme Court in a supplemental

With these important preliminary matters out of the way, Mr. Justice Harlan turned to a consideration of the scope of the doctrine and its applicability to the facts of *Sabbatino*. Commendably, the decision, although noting that "the plain implication of all these opinions . . . is that the act of state doctrine is applicable even if international law has been violated," does not apply "the wisdom of the precedents" mechanically.[163] Indeed, it acknowledges that the doctrine's continuing vitality depends upon its capacity to meet present needs. Balancing the "relevant considerations," the Court rejects claims of an absolute act of state doctrine and reaches a more narrow holding, a holding covering only those acts which involve the taking of property.[164]

> Therefore, rather than laying down or reaffirming an inflexible and all-encompassing rule in this case, we decide only that the Judicial Branch will not examine the validity of a taking of property within its own territory by a foreign sovereign government, extant and recognized by this country at the time of suit, in the absence of a treaty or other unambiguous agreement regarding controlling legal principles, even if the complaint alleges that the taking violates customary international law.[165]

Before evaluating the reasons advanced by Mr. Justice Harlan in support of the above holding, three potential limitations to the doctrine's application contained therein warrant mention.[166] In the first place, its scope is restricted to those acts of a foreign sovereign government occurring "within its own territory. . . ." Thus courts in the United States need not give effect to acts affecting interests

---

brief prepared by the Association of the Bar of the City of New York. COMM. ON INT'L LAW, N.Y.C.B.A., THE EFFECT TO BE GIVEN IN THE UNITED STATES TO FOREIGN NATIONALIZATION DECREES 30-34 (1964).

[163] 376 U.S. at 430, 431. See text at and accompanying notes 30-36 *supra*.

[164] Writers with such opposite viewpoints as Stevenson, *supra* note 157, at 707, and Falk, *Complexity* 935, agree on this point.

[165] 376 U.S. at 428.

[166] "These grounds for refusing deference to a foreign governmental act are not made to appear exclusive or determinative in the *Sabbatino* opinion. They are enumerated as considerations that a domestic court should properly take into account when the application of the act of state doctrine is challenged by a litigant. It is important to realize this. . . . Other matters could presumably also enter the balance. Therefore, there are no rigid guidelines laid down as to when a court should refrain from applying the act of state doctrine." Falk, *Complexity* 943.

outside the territory of the "taking" country.[167] Secondly, the doctrine is limited to acts of governments "extant and recognized by this country at the time of suit. . . ." Hence the courts need not give effect to the acts of nonexistent or unrecognized governments.[168] Finally, and most important, the doctrine is inapplicable if "a treaty or other unambiguous agreement regarding controlling legal principles" exists. This last exception, not without ambiguity itself, reflects the Court's adoption and apparent reformulation of Falk's "consensus" approach to the act of state doctrine.[169] Clarification of the opinion on this point requires a brief explanation of Falk's thesis.

Joining issue with international lawyers who have urged the courts to reject the act of state doctrine and assume a more active role in the application and creation of international law rules, Falk contends that "rules of deference applied by domestic courts advance the development of international law faster than does an indiscriminate insistence upon applying challenged substantive norms in order to determine the validity of the official acts of foreign states."[170] "Rather than risk the bias of decentralized review," he argues, "it is preferable to insist upon deference, relying upon diplomatic pressure and supranational review for the application of substantive standards of international law."[171] However, Falk appends a major qualification to his arguments for judicial deference, deeming it "inappropriate if the subject matter of dispute is governed by substantive norms of international law that are adhered to by an overwhelming majority of international actors."[172]

[167] See RESTATEMENT, FOREIGN RELATIONS § 46 (Proposed Official Draft 1962). For a critique of this "principal qualification," see Henkin, *supra* note 155, at 828. Of course, an international agreement might require the courts to give effect to such acts. See, *e.g.*, United States v. Pink, 315 U.S. 203 (1942).

[168] "The balance of relevant considerations may also be shifted if the government which perpetrated the challenged act of state is no longer in existence, as in the *Bernstein* case. . . ." 376 U.S. at 428. See RESTATEMENT, FOREIGN RELATIONS § 45 (Proposed Official Draft 1962). See also Metzger, *Act-of-State Doctrine Refined: The Sabbatino Case*, [1964] SUP. CT. REV. 223, 234 n.31 (questions use of term "extant") [hereinafter cited as Metzger]. For a critique of this qualification generally, see Henkin, *supra* note 155, at 829.

[169] See text accompanying note 26 *supra*.

[170] FALK 6-7.

[171] *Id.* at 106.

[172] *Id.* at 9.

Only in matters of "legitimate diversity," situations where "there is no global consensus in favor of making universal a single substantive standard," should courts apply the act of state doctrine.[173]

Mr. Justice Harlan obviously accepted Falk's consensus argument, which had not been briefed or argued by the parties or by amici, for shortly before the holding quoted above appears the following sentence.

> It should be apparent that the greater the degree of codification or consensus concerning a particular area of international law, the more appropriate it is for the judiciary to render decisions regarding it, since the courts can then focus on the application of an agreed principle to circumstances of fact rather than on the sensitive task of establishing a principle not inconsistent with the national interest or with international justice.[174]

By making the presence or absence of consensus the key to the application of the act of state doctrine, the Court departs sharply from the unqualified teachings of *Underhill v. Hernandez*.[175] As Metzger ably demonstrates, the holding in *Sabbatino* constitutes both a "reformulation and modification of *Underhill*'s statement of the doctrine," albeit one which offers little relief to private parties in cases involving the taking of property.[176]

While adopting Falk's thesis lock, stock and barrel, Mr. Justice Harlan's formulation of the *Sabbatino* holding, barring the application of the act of state doctrine in those cases where there exists "a treaty or other unambiguous agreement regarding controlling legal principles" but invoking it when "the complaint alleges that the taking violates customary international law," serves only to prompt confusion.[177] By stating the holding in conclusory fashion before discussing the lack of consensus on the question of property takings,

[173] *Id.* at 127 n.29.

[174] 376 U.S. at 428. The Court's adoption of the Falk thesis also is apparent from its subsequent misapplication of the consensus test to the facts of *Sabbatino*. See text at notes 195-212 *infra*.

[175] See text at note 7 *supra*.

[176] Metzger 229 and following.

[177] Henkin, for example, states that "the Court concluded that the fact that an act of state violates customary international law does not detract from the rationale of Act of State and will not warrant an American court to deny it effect." Henkin, *supra* note 155, at 828. This statement appears to be an overgeneralization. See text at and accompanying note 182 *infra*.

the Court leaves the impression that its modification of the *Under-hill* rationale is limited to situations where the relevant international law standard is contained in an international agreement.[178] With respect to cases involving the taking of property, to which the decision is limited, this impression is correct, but only because the Court examines the customary international law governing foreign expropriations and finds a consensus wanting.[179] In other words, the Court concludes that in expropriation cases today consensus may be found only in international agreements.[180] This conclusion, how-ever, does not mean that the Court, in a case involving a different kind of foreign act, may not invoke the *Sabbatino* rationale, find a consensus regarding the relevant customary international law rule, and pass upon the act's validity thereunder. The Court, in fact, devotes a footnote to just this possibility.

> There are, of course, areas of international law in which consensus
> is greater and which do not represent a battleground for conflicting
> ideologies. This decision in no way intimates that the courts of this
> country are broadly foreclosed from considering questions of inter-
> national law.[181]

Customary international law, then, still may play a rôle in certain act of state cases.[182]

Mr. Justice Harlan's unfortunate phrasing of the *Sabbatino* holding, which has caused some commentators to question the Court's commitment to Falk's approach,[183] may spawn further con-

[178] See Metzger 233-34.

[179] See text at notes 195-212 *infra.*

[180] See text at notes 182-84 *infra. Quaere:* "May we not expect that the Court's diffidence to pass on questions of international law would not extend to cases where the states concerned have—without a joint declaration or agree-ment—nevertheless independently accepted certain governing principles? Should the doubts cast by newly emergent states cloud the law recognized by, say, the United States and Canada?" Laylin, *Holding Invalid Acts Contrary to Interna-tional Law—A Force Toward Compliance,* 58 A.S.I.L. PROCEEDINGS 33, 35 (1964). See Falk, *Complexity* 945, stating that *Sabbatino* requires only "a consensus at least wide enough to embrace the parties to the dispute." Compare text at note 172 *supra.*

[181] 376 U.S. at 430 n.34.

[182] "*Sabbatino* makes it very clear that a domestic court that confronts a set of facts for which the rules are supported by a consensus is not bound to apply the act of state doctrine. . . ." *Id.* at 941. See also *id.* at 941-42.

[183] *Cf.* Henkin, *supra* note 155, at 829: "It is not clear whether the Court is distinguishing between treaty and customary law, reflecting the view that all

fusion. For instance, to what international agreements relating to property protection may one look to find the required consensus? Metzger raises just this question.

> Does "treaty or other unambiguous agreement regarding controlling legal principles" refer solely to nation-to-nation agreements, whether in the form of treaties, conventions, exchanges of notes, or similar writings expressing commitments of sovereign governments as between one another, whether bilateral or multilateral? Or does it also include contracts between a government on one side and a private foreign corporation on the other? It seems clear that the Court was referring solely to government-to-government commitments, because the binding character of government commitments to private corporations is itself one of the "issues in international law today on which opinion seems to be so divided," with very substantial opinion considering that such a breach is not in itself an international law violation.[184]

Stevenson, on the other hand, interprets the ambiguously phrased "unambiguous agreement" in contrary fashion. "In addition to international treaties," he suggests, "there may, of course, be other agreements by foreign states, including agreements with foreign private investors, which recognize the controlling legal principles."[185] On balance, Metzger's gloss on this aspect of the Court's opinion appears more convincing.

The confusion caused by the "treaty" limitation stems in part from the fact that nowhere does Mr. Justice Harlan articulate the reasons for its inclusion or consider its possible effects. Conceivably the clause was missing from the draft of the majority opinion and was inserted later in response to Mr. Justice White's vigorous dissent.[186] This possibility at least would explain the Court's failure

---

nations recognize treaty obligations, and therefore acts of state which violate treaties may perhaps be disregarded without damage to international relations. This assumes that in relations between nations all treaties and all violations are of equal weight; it gives equal lack of weight to all customary international law, although even the Soviet Union and the new nations accept and assert the paramountcy of some customary international law. Perhaps the Court would really distinguish between treaty and universally agreed customary law, on the one hand, and, on the other, alleged customary principles that are challenged by some nations." See also text accompanying note 180 *supra*.

[184] Metzger 234-35.
[185] Stevenson, *supra* note 157, at 710.
[186] The dissent appears aimed at a majority opinion containing no treaty

to develop the point elsewhere in its opinion. In any event, the Court's limitation, now applicable to the acts of state of only nineteen countries,[187] "promises small effect, so small as to make one wonder whether, had it been fully aware of the likely results, it might have decided to restate *Underhill* unmodified for the purposes of the expropriating acts of foreign states."[188] Moreover, as Metzger convincingly shows, many of the reasons advanced by Mr. Justice Harlan to support the doctrine's application in expropriation cases apply with equal strength to acts whether in violation of treaty provisions or customary international law.[189]

To support its reformulation of Falk's consensus approach, the Court seeks to establish that there exists a diversity of opinion concerning the relevant international law standards applicable to the Cuban decree. "There are few if any issues in international law today," the majority opinion states, "on which opinion seems to be so divided as the limitations on a State's power to expropriate the property of aliens."[190] Reviewing the traditional rule that "a taking is improper under international law if it is not for a public purpose,

---

limitation. Thus, in his first paragraph Mr. Justice White states that "the Court expressly extends its ruling to *all acts of state* expropriating property," 376 U.S. at 439 (emphasis added), and twice thereafter he construes the majority opinion to apply to *"any"* act of a foreign state expropriating property. *Id.* at 459 (emphasis added). "The act of state doctrine formulated by the Court," he concludes, "bars review in this case and will do so in *all others involving expropriation of alien property. . . ." Id.* at 464 (emphasis added). Since it seems unlikely that Mr. Justice White completely misconstrued the scope of the majority's holding, one may speculate whether the treaty limitation was not missing from Mr. Justice Harlan's draft opinion. Part VI of the majority opinion, it may be recalled, concludes with the observation that the Court's holding maintains "intact the act of state doctrine in this realm of its application." *Id.* at 437.

[187] "The nineteen treaties that were negotiated and have entered into force since 1945 were with Belgium, China, Denmark, Ethiopia, France, Federal Republic of Germany, Greece, Iran, Ireland, Israel, Italy, Japan, Korea, Luxembourg, Muscat and Oman, the Netherlands, Nicaragua, Pakistan, and Vietnam." Metzger 235 n.34.

[188] *Id.* at 236-37.

[189] *Id.* at 237-40. Steiner, citing the Court's reliance upon the government's argument that the executive is able to obtain compensation for all claimants, notes that its holding could vitiate this same argument. "Even had the action of Cuba violated a bilateral treaty with the United States, the arguments in favor of marshaling assets for an eventual settlement and of noninterference with Executive initiatives might have the same validity. The bare fact of an alleged treaty violation, rather than an alleged violation of customary international law, might not brighten prospects for effective remedies." Steiner, Introduction, 5 HARV. INT'L L. CLUB J. 209, 211 (1964).

[190] 376 U.S. at 428.

is discriminatory, or is without provision for prompt, adequate, and effective compensation,"[191] the Court notes that Communist and newly independent and underdeveloped countries have questioned its continued validity.[192] Moreover, Mr. Justice Harlan finds it "difficult to imagine the courts of this country embarking on adjudication in an area which touches more sensitively the practical and ideological goals of the various members of the community of nations."[193] Therefore, while stopping short of saying that "there is no international law standard in this area," the Court finds such a lack of consensus that it seems the matter "not meet for adjudication by domestic tribunals."[194]

The majority opinion's approach to ascertaining consensus may be faulted on three grounds. In the first place, although the Court "is rather vague about just what are the customary rules that lack a supporting consensus,"[195] Mr. Justice Harlan focuses mainly upon the highly controversial question of compensation.[196] By selecting this rule to test for consensus to the exclusion of others, the Court pretty much determines the outcome of the case. As Falk observes:

> It makes a great deal of difference whether one is denying a consensus for the rule that "prompt, adequate, and effective compensation" must accompany a valid expropriation rather than for the rules that prohibit discrimination against the nationals of one country or forbid a confiscatory expropriation in which no compensation at all is offered.[197]

[191] *Id.* at 429.

[192] *Id.* at 429-30.

[193] *Id.* at 430.

[194] *Id.* at 428 n.26.

[195] Falk, *Complexity* 944.

[196] Later in its opinion, the Court considers the respondent's contention "that, even if there is not agreement regarding general standards for determining the validity of expropriations, the alleged combination of retaliation, discrimination, and inadequate compensation makes it patently clear that this expropriation was in violation of international law." 376 U.S. at 433. Strangely enough, the Court implies that even the existence of a consensus on this minimum standard would not preclude the application of the act of state doctrine. "If this view is accurate, it would still be unwise for the courts so to determine. Such a decision now would require the drawing of more difficult lines in subsequent cases. . . ." *Ibid.* Hence, not only a lack of consensus, but the possibility of such a lack in a future case, necessitates the application of the doctrine. Compare Falk, *Complexity* 944: "Of course, the most controversial aspect of *Sabbatino* involves the determination that no consensus exists to support those rules of international law that condemn a confiscatory and discriminatory taking."

[197] *Ibid.*

In any case, it is hard to understand why the supposed lack of consensus as to compensation precludes the Court from considering whether the needed consensus underlies other rules in the area of expropriation.[198] Even the author of the consensus approach acknowledges that the Supreme Court "over-generalizes the customary norms at stake to be apparently conterminous with the entire law of foreign investment and, thereby, forfeits the opportunity to suspend the operation of the act of state doctrine by narrowing the norms at issue to those prohibiting discriminatory and confiscatory taking."[199]

Secondly, assuming *in arguendo* that the Court correctly restricted its inquiry to the compensation question alone, Mr. Justice Harlan effectively controls the outcome of the consensus test by phrasing the rule in terms of "prompt, adequate, and effective compensation." To paraphrase Falk, it makes a great deal of difference whether one is denying a consensus for the rule so stated rather than for a rule requiring the payment of some lesser standard of compensation. Ample evidence from the district court's opinion,[200] C.A.V.'s brief[201] and the amicus curiae brief of the American Bar Association[202] was before the Court to establish that international law requires the payment of *some* compensation.[203] Moreover, the

---

[198] As Mr. Justice White stresses in his dissenting opinion, lack of consensus on "the clearly discrete issue of adequate and effective compensation" does not mean a lack of consensus on all rules governing foreign expropriations. 376 U.S. at 465 n.22.

[199] Falk, *Complexity* 947. "The *Sabbatino* majority does not seem sensitive to the importance of identifying rather specifically the customary norms that are in issue. Judge Waterman, in the Circuit Court of Appeals, was very careful to state his holding in terms far narrower than those used by Judge Dimock to void Castro's expropriation in the District Court. It might be argued that *Sabbatino* should have affirmed the decision of the Circuit Court, substituting its rationale for exceptions to act of state deference for Judge Waterman's strained and misguided conclusion that the Executive had written, in effect, a *Bernstein* letter." *Id.* at 944. See also Falk, *Controversy* 40.

[200] See text at notes 53-57 *supra*.

[201] See Brief of C.A.V., pp. 35-53, 2 INT'L LEGAL MATERIALS 1165-69 (1963).

[202] See Brief of the American Bar Association as Amicus Curiae, reprinted in 8 A.B.A. INT'L & COMP. L. BULL. No. 1, at 45 (1964).

[203] Dawson, one writer cited by the Court to show a lack of consensus in the area of expropriation, 376 U.S. at 428 n.26, actually takes the position that, "while nations and lawyers indeed dispute the compensatory standard applicable to nationalized property, they all recognize that *some* compensation should be accorded deprived aliens. Whether this recognition is codified in the governing

amicus curiae brief of the Committee on International Law of the Association of the Bar of the City of New York called the Court's attention to resolution 1803 (XVII) adopted by the General Assembly of the United Nations on December 14, 1962, by a vote of 87 to 2 with 12 abstentions, stating that persons whose property is taken "shall be paid appropriate compensation . . . in accordance with international law. . . ."[204] This resolution, not mentioned by the Court, constitutes the strongest possible evidence of a consensus supporting the requirement of compensation. By ignoring all this data and concentrating instead on the relatively easy task of showing dissensus on the "prompt, adequate, and effective" standard, "the Supreme Court may have misapplied the very theory it invoked to overturn the lower courts."[205]

Finally, by concluding that no consensus existed after what, at best, can be called a cursory look at relevant authorities, Mr. Justice Harlan's opinion illustrates how the consensus approach can produce even worse effects than those which allegedly would follow from the Court's adoption of the international law exception to the act of state doctrine. The government's brief, pointing out that this exception "would, of necessity, by [*sic*] applicable whenever such a violation is merely *alleged* by a party whose interests have been affected by the foreign act,"[206] argued that "executive diplomatic action may be seriously impeded or embarrassed by American judicial decisions which undertake, in domestic lawsuits, to pass

---

law of the various legal systems or whether it is merely given tacit support through treaties or negotiated compensation agreements would seem of little relevance. The Cuban compensatory plan, however, based upon a totally illusory funding system and payable in bonds that were never printed, did not recognize this basic universal norm of international behavior." Dawson, *Current Decisions*, 8 A.B.A. INT'L & COMP. L. BULL. No. 2, at 28, 33 (1964). See also Dawson & Weston, *supra* note 24, at 101: "The Cuban legislation pursuant to which C.A.V. was nationalized failed to meet the most minimal compensatory requirements of the Law of State Responsibility."

[204] U.N. GEN. ASS. OFF. REC. 17th Sess., Supp. No. 17, at 15 (A/5217) (1962), reprinted in 57 AM. J. INT'L L. 710, 712 (1963). See Schwebel, *The Story of the U.N.'s Declaration on Permanent Sovereignty over Natural Resources*, 49 A.B.A.J. 463 (1963). See also Gess, *Permanent Sovereignty Over Natural Resources*, 13 INT'L & COMP. L.Q. 398, 420-29 (1964).

[205] Dawson, *supra* note 203, at 32.

[206] Brief 29, 2 INT'L LEGAL MATERIALS 1019 (1963). Lowenfeld suggests that this "argument which seeks to graft an exception onto the act of state doctrine in effect destroys it." Lowenfeld, Comments, 5 HARV. INT'L L. CLUB J. 215, 218 (1964).

upon the validity of foreign acts."[207] As an example, the brief suggests that a decision by an American court holding that the foreign government's acts did not violate international law might seriously undercut contemporaneous diplomatic negotiations.[208] In oral argument before the Supreme Court, the now Attorney General buttressed this suggestion by contending that "the statement in the Court of Appeals opinion expressing doubt as to the law of compensation has already hurt the Department of State in negotiations."[209]

Whether or not the executive was hurt by the language of Judge Waterman, certainly it was dealt a mortal blow by Mr. Justice Harlan's superficial survey of the compensation question. If the casualness shown by the Court in handling this key preliminary point is indicative of how the consensus approach is to be applied, surely the possibilities of executive embarrassment are even greater than under the international law exception. For, despite the fact that consensus is merely a threshold question, a finding that it is lacking is bound to have an impact upon the attitude of other countries toward the customary international law rules governing expropriation.[210] The Court, evidently impressed by the executive's arguments concerning possible embarrassment, seemingly overlooked the potential for just such embarrassment inherent in the consensus approach. Mr. Justice White highlighted this inconsistency in trenchant fashion.

> I fail to see how greater embarrassment flows from saying that the foreign act does not violate clear and widely accepted principles of international law than from saying, as the Court does, that nonexamination and validation is required because there are no widely accepted principles to which to subject the foreign act.[211]

In short, whether or not the embarrassment argument is a valid one,

---

[207] Brief 29, 2 INT'L LEGAL MATERIALS 1019 (1963).

[208] *Ibid.*

[209] Summary of Oral Argument, 2 INT'L LEGAL MATERIALS 1134 (1963).

[210] "The problem of upholding in diplomatic and international arbitral proceedings the principle of just compensation will not be eased by the necessity of explaining away these references as having no relevance to the determination of international law standards but only to the Supreme Court's own standard for application of the self-imposed act of state doctrine." Stevenson, *supra* note 157, at 709.

[211] 376 U.S. at 465-66.

using it in one instance and ignoring it in another seems questionable.[212]

While the Court relies heavily upon the consensus approach to
justify its holding, great weight also is placed upon what Falk
correctly identifies as the "principal rationale" of the government's
brief: "the primacy of foreign affairs and the superior pragmatics of
executive settlement."[213] In view of "the State Department's unqualified allegations of the success of our diplomacy in obtaining
compensation for takings violating international law,"[214] allegations
accepted without question by Mr. Justice Harlan as evidence of
the Department of State's "ample powers to effect compensation,"[215]
it is not surprising that the Court should relegate American claimants
to diplomatic channels.[216]

> Following an expropriation of any significance, the Executive en-
> gages in diplomacy aimed to assure that United States citizens who
> are harmed are compensated fairly. Representing all claimants of
> this country, it will often be able, either by bilateral or multilateral
> talks, by submission to the United Nations, or by the employment
> of economic and political sanctions, to achieve some general redress.
> Judicial determinations of invalidity of title can, on the other hand,
> have only an occasional impact, since they depend on the fortuitous
> circumstance of the property in question being brought into this

[212] On the untenability of the embarrassment argument in general, see Brief
of the Committee on International Law of the Association of the Bar of the
City of New York as Amicus Curiae, pp. 19-22 [hereinafter cited as City Bar
Brief]. With respect to *Sabbatino* in specific, "not only has the Executive
branch neglected to present this Court with a single reason to support its
contention that an adverse judicial decision would 'embarrass' its position, but
it has itself previously pronounced its agreement with the adverse decision that
it fears, *i.e.*, that the confiscation was a violation of international law. See 43
DEP'T STATE BULL. 171 (1960)." Brief of the Executive Committee of the
American Branch of the International Law Association as Amicus Curiae, p. 18
[hereinafter cited as ILA Brief]. See also text at notes 68-72 *supra*.

[213] FALK 132, 136. See text at and accompanying note 142 *supra*.

[214] Stevenson, *supra* note 157, at 708.

[215] 376 U.S. at 436.

[216] Nevertheless, its across-the-board reliance on this argument is unusual in
view of its adoption of the consensus approach. Falk, for instance, finds the
argument persuasive "if confined to subject matter for which there is no consensus supporting a universal norm, but not otherwise. . . . Deference should be
primarily a consequence of diversity and understood as such, and should only
secondarily justify itself by foreign policy considerations or by the efficacy of
diplomatic settlement techniques." FALK 135.

country. . . . Piecemeal dispositions of this sort involving the probability of affront to another State could seriously interfere with negotiations being carried on by the Executive Branch and might prevent or render less favorable the terms of an agreement that could otherwise be reached.[217]

This hearty endorsement of the efficacy of diplomatic settlement techniques warrants brief examination.

When the act of state doctrine was elaborated in *Underhill v. Hernandez*,[218] diplomatic channels undoubtedly gave powerful states like the United States an effective means of protecting the interests of their citizens abroad. As Falk acknowledges, "intervention and the procedures of diplomatic settlement were available to resist serious infringements of property rights; broad settlements could be coerced or negotiated on a diplomatic level."[219] The range of sanctions which a state could invoke knew few limits in 1897. For example, the opinion by the court of appeals in the above case, quoted approvingly by the government in its *Sabbatino* brief,[220] states that it is "unnecessary" to subject the acts of states to examination in the courts of other states, since "foreign citizens can rely upon the intervention of their respective governments to redress their wrongs, *even by a resort, if necessary, to the arbitrament of war*."[221] While one may laud the abolition of "the threat or use of force" in such situations,[222] nevertheless it must be recognized that its prohibition deprives the diplomatic process of its most effective sanction.[223]

What, then, are the "ample powers" which the executive may use today to achieve a satisfactory settlement? The Court mentions multilateral talks, citing no instance where such a procedure has been followed, much less has been used successfully. The same

[217] 376 U.S. at 431, 432.
[218] See text at note 7 *supra*.
[219] FALK 103.
[220] Brief 15-16, 2 INT'L LEGAL MATERIALS 1015 (1963).
[221] Underhill v. Hernandez, 65 Fed. 577, 579 (2d Cir. 1895). (Emphasis added.)
[222] U.N. Charter art. 2, para. 4.
[223] "Whatever may have been an acceptable sanction for a violation of international law in the period prior to the Spanish-American War, it does appear unusual in 1963 for the Government to attempt to rationalize compulsory judicial abstention from a consideration of a violation of international law by a foreign state on the ground that war may provide an alternative." ILA Brief 43.

criticism applies to its reference to submitting claims to the United Nations. Economic sanctions? Chapter III describes the mixed results achieved by the Hickenlooper Amendment's use of foreign aid as a lever. Economic embargoes and the freezing of foreign assets also have left much to be desired, Cuba being a case precisely in point. Political sanctions? While they may be effective sometimes, in most cases, witness Cuba once again, they are not. Mr. Justice White, therefore, reflects the realities of the situation more accurately than the majority opinion when he concludes that "the availability and effectiveness of these modes of accommodation may more often be illusory than real."[224]

Perhaps the most common as well as satisfactory method by which the executive secures some redress for American claimants is the lump sum settlement device.[225] However, despite the claims made in the government's brief about the Department of State's impressive record of concluding such agreements,[226] claims so inflated that an impartial observer might think they had been advanced with tongue in cheek, lump sum settlements occur only sporadically and then insure only partial compensation.[227] Actually, while the Court acknowledges the importance of this diplomatic device for securing compensation, it places less stress on its efficacy than on the fact that claims agreements permit the executive branch to secure some degree of general redress for all American claimants.[228]

This "equitable" argument, advanced by commentators[229] and mentioned repeatedly in the government's brief,[230] constitutes an extension of the rationale of the *Pink* case to situations where no international agreement exists.[231] Of course, where diplomacy has functioned, as in *Pink*, the courts may be closed to individual litigants in the interest of all claimants, although this result has occasioned strong debate.[232] But to extend this principle to situations

---

[224] 376 U.S. at 460.

[225] See text at and accompanying notes 73-85 *supra*.

[226] Brief 30-32, 2 INT'L LEGAL MATERIALS 1019 (1963). The brief ignores "the grossly inadequate recovery" obtained from some countries. Stevenson, *supra* note 157, at 708 n.4. See also text at and accompanying note 305 *infra*.

[227] See generally Chapter V.

[228] 376 U.S. at 431-32.

[229] See text at note 74 *supra*.

[230] Brief 28-34 *passim*, 2 INT'L LEGAL MATERIALS 1018-20 (1963).

[231] See note 167 *supra*.

[232] Compare Borchard, *Extraterritorial Confiscations*, 36 AM. J. INT'L L. 275

where diplomacy has failed and no agreement exists, where the Court has only the government's assurances that "effective negotiations with Cuba to achieve some compensation for all American property which has been nationalized may well prove possible in the course of time,"[233] seems unwarranted. Moreover, as an amicus curiae brief contends, the approach taken to accomplish the result seems somewhat disingenuous.

> If now the United States wishes to marshal the proceeds of the property of C.A.V. and other particular interest for "all American interests," it should then ask that proceedings be stayed until enactment of legislation authorizing the Government to expropriate the property of these particular business interests for the public purpose of dividing it amongst "all American interests."
>
> . . . . .
>
> In the absence of legislation of this sort, or of a treaty, entitling the Department of State to take up the rights of certain American nationals for the benefit of a larger group, the courts are duty-bound, it is submitted, to keep themselves "free to apply public international principles in act of state cases" (Gov't Brief, p. 25).[234]

The Court sub silentio rejects this argument, in effect equating the possibility of an eventual settlement agreement with the existence of one. This optimistic belief in the efficacy of diplomatic remedies naturally lends some support to the Court's holding. However, Mr. Justice White's observation that "the possibility of alternative remedies, without more, is frail support for a rule of automatic deference to the foreign act in all cases"[235] contains a more realistic estimate of the value of resort to diplomatic channels today.

Furthermore, it may be asked why the possible existence of diplomatic remedies, traditionally the last resort of claimants, should compel claimants to forego judicial remedies in favor of a prolonged and uncertain method of settling international disputes. Diplomatic remedies should be in supplement to, not in derogation of, normal

---

(1942), with M. H. Cardozo, *The Authority in Internal Law of International Treaties: The Pink Case*, 13 SYRACUSE L. REV. 544 (1962).

[233] Brief 33, 2 INT'L LEGAL MATERIALS 1020 (1963).

[234] Brief of the North American Sugar Industries, Inc. as Amicus Curiae, pp. 25-26.

[235] 376 U.S. at 460. "To request the courts to abstain indefinitely from exercising jurisdiction upon such a highly speculative consideration does not appear to be reasonable." Brief of C.A.V., p. 29, 2 INT'L LEGAL MATERIALS 1163 (1963).

judicial remedies. "After a violation of international law has occurred," argues the above amicus curiae brief, "diplomacy is certainly *a* way to secure redress which *at times* is satisfactory, but it does not follow, nor is there anything to support the assumption in the Government Brief, that diplomacy is the *only* way."[236] The reasons why resort to municipal courts should at least coequal with diplomatic remedies are several. In the first place, "municipal courts may on occasions provide the only means for securing respect for International Law. . . ."[237] Secondly, permitting a judicial decision on what is fundamentally a legal question[238] certainly is preferable to turning the dispute into a political question.[239] Finally, the existence of a judicial remedy, even if it does not serve as a deterrent to foreign acts of state violating international law, may facilitate the conclusion of a more satisfactory diplomatic settlement with the expropriating country.[240]

The Court, having adopted Falk's consensus approach and supported it with arguments about the efficacy of diplomatic remedies borrowed from the government's brief, next devoted the equivalent of two full pages to refuting various "unpersuasive" arguments in favor of the international law exception to the act of state doctrine. Rejecting the contention that American courts could contribute significantly to the growth of international law,[241] Mr. Justice Harlan

[236] Brief of the North American Sugar Industries, Inc., *supra* note 234, at 23-24.

[237] 1 OPPENHEIM, INTERNATIONAL LAW 270 (8th ed., Lauterpacht 1955).

[238] "[R]estricting persons injured by a foreign state taking solely to diplomatic channels, and imposing upon their state the burden of making complaint in the first instance, is not only unjust but may well have the additional undesirable effect of bypassing any possibility of a judicial decision on what is fundamentally a legal question—whether or not the taking violates international law." City Bar Brief 20.

[239] Domke warns that "the courts should not abdicate their function to determine the private rights of American citizens, irrespective of the attitude the government has to take, the latter being guided by expediency which may be justified under existing political circumstances." Domke, *supra* note 136, at 289-90.

[240] This point is developed further in the text at notes 252-58 *infra*.

[241] "Mr. Seymour [counsel for C.A.V.] assailed the government's policy argument on the ground that it exaggerates the importance of the executive as an upholder of international law and minimizes the role of the courts as definers, upholders, and enforcers of international law. . . .

"The courts can make a valuable contribution to the development of international law, he stated. 'A brick placed in the wall of international law by an

concludes that "given the fluidity of present world conditions, the effectiveness of such a patchwork approach towards the formulation of an acceptable body of law concerning state responsibility for expropriations is, to say the least, highly conjectural."[242] Moreover, the contention "rests upon the sanguine presupposition that the decisions of the courts of the world's major capital exporting country and principal exponent of the free enterprise system would be accepted as disinterested expressions of sound legal principle by those adhering to widely different ideologies."[243] The Court's reasoning here closely parallels the arguments contained in the government's brief.[244]

The majority opinion, to quote Mr. Justice White, completely "ignores the historic role which this Court and other American courts have played in applying and maintaining principles of international law."[245] Of course, decisions by municipal courts in expropriation cases are a patchwork process, but it cannot be denied that they contribute in some measure to the development of "a comprehensive body of international law on the subject of the taking of alien-owned property."[246] Of course, decisions by municipal courts in different countries often conflict, but from such stuff is customary international law made and modified.[247] Indeed, by refusing to

authoritative court is better than a hole in the wall.' A court's deliberate declaration that international law has been violated will have an impact on the country involved and the lawyers of the world." Summary of Oral Argument, 32 U.S.L. WEEK 3159 (1963).

[242] 376 U.S. at 434.

[243] *Id.* at 434-35.

[244] See text at and accompanying notes 139 & 141 *supra.*

[245] *Id.* at 458. In McDougal's more sprightly phraseology, "it forsook the historic, creative role of the Supreme Court for the expression of timid and suicidal conceptions." McDougal, Comments, 58 A.S.I.L. PROCEEDINGS 49 (1964).

[246] City Bar Brief 22. "As is true with any rule of law, a few sound precedents establish guidelines by which persons seeking to avoid recourse to the courts tailor their conduct." *Id.* at 23.

[247] "Although foreign courts, in passing on expropriation decrees, have not yet arrived at a demonstrable consensus, the majority's argument overlooks the fact that the only likely alternative is a collection of still more divergent and conflicting statements by various foreign offices. Indeed, it seems likely that the availability of opinions from municipal courts would aid the International Court of Justice if it were ever called upon to review an expropriation case." *The Supreme Court, 1963 Term,* 78 HARV. L. REV. 143, 303-04 (1964). See also Jennings, *The Sabbatino Controversy,* 20 RECORD OF N.Y.C.B.A. 81, 82-83 (1965).

participate in the process of clarifying and applying the relevant international law standards and by adopting instead "a rule which restricts courts to a completely amoral attitude regarding foreign acts of state,"[248] the Court actually perpetuates the supposed lack of consensus so damaging to customary international law. Its decision creates expectations throughout the world, expectations which unfortunately will work in many areas to undercut the international standard protecting foreign investment.[249]

Moreover, the fact that decisions by American courts applying international law in expropriation cases might not be accepted everywhere as "disinterested expressions of sound legal principle" seems an odd reason for the Supreme Court of the United States to rely upon to deny relief in a case properly before it. Surely this problem arises whenever a municipal court is faced with any international law problem. Some countries may automatically regard decisions by American courts "as reflecting merely parochial American views partisan to American national interests."[250] Other countries, taking the possibilities of national bias into account, may accept them for their juridical worth. The reasoning in the majority opinion on this score, carried to its logical extreme, would deprive American courts of any effective role in the international legal order. To discount their decisions completely on the grounds of real or imagined bias demonstrates both a lack of understanding of the nature of international law and the process by which it is created and clarified.[251]

The second argument in support of the international law exception considered by Mr. Justice Harlan is the contention that the

[248] Comment, 57 YALE L.J. 108, 111 (1947).

[249] "If the courts of the leading power of the free world support by their silence or by their jurisprudential verbiage the notion that there is no international law, they certainly lend no support to the Department of State when it seeks to protect American interests abroad." JESSUP, THE USE OF INTERNATIONAL LAW 85 (1959).

[250] Brief 27-28, 2 INT'L LEGAL MATERIALS 1018 (1963).

[251] See generally McDougal, *supra* note 245, at 48-52 *passim*. Unlike the present Court, the Court ten years ago refused to award weight to an argument based upon possible "parochial bias." National City Bank v. Republic of China, 348 U.S. 356, 363 (1955). The bias argument is vitiated by a further fact: any decision of an American court not in conformity with international law may be protested by a foreign country through diplomatic channels and, ultimately, may be taken to the International Court of Justice. Stevenson, *supra* note 157, at 708. *Cf.* Jessup, *Has the Supreme Court Abdicated One of Its Functions?*, 40 AM. J. INT'L L. 168, 169 (1946).

resulting economic pressure would add materially to the protection of American investors. The expropriating country would be denied access to essential markets for the expropriating property, thus encouraging the settlement of claims, and other countries would be deterred from taking such action in the future. Argued an amicus curiae brief:

> Increased enforcement of and respect for the rule of law, which at the present time may most effectively be achieved if international law is applid by municipal courts, is the best guarantor of meaningful certainty in international trading and investment relationships generally. Automatic recognition by municipal courts of foreign takings violative of international law would have a crippling effect upon foreign investment, especially in the less developed areas, which it is the policy of the United States to encourage. . . . Private and governmental investors will take fewer risks if they may not look to an international investment climate in which the rule of law is supreme and may not be heard in any judicial tribunal to seek redress for unlawful takings.[252]

The Court was "not convinced, *even assuming the relevance of this contention.* Expropriations take place for a variety of reasons, political and ideological as well as economic."[253] When "the variety of means possessed by this country to make secure foreign investment" were considered, "the persuasive or coercive effect of judicial invalidation of acts of expropriation dwindles in comparison."[254] Citing as examples of executive leverage the Hickenlooper Amendment, economic embargoes and the freezing of assets in the United States, Mr. Justice Harlan concludes that "any country willing to brave any or all of these consequences is unlikely to be deterred by sporadic judicial decisions directly affecting only property brought to our shores."[255] On this point too the Court's reasoning closely follows the arguments of the government's brief.[256]

Admittedly, municipal courts may provide only occasional redress in expropriation cases. It may even be granted that their remedial

[252] City Bar Brief 24-25.

[253] 376 U.S. at 435. (Emphasis added.) Why the Court thought it necessary to assume the relevance of this contention is a mystery. Certainly the protection of American investment abroad is one of the most relevant policy factors in the case.

[254] *Ibid.*

[255] *Id.* at 436.

[256] See text at and accompanying note 139 *supra*.

benefits, on the whole, are less than those achieved by diplomatic remedies, although when one considers their possible deterrent effect, which Mr. Justice Harlan does not, it is hard to agree that their importance "dwindles in comparison." Nevertheless, leading international lawyers have testified how the availability of municipal courts has produced acceptable settlements in the past.[257] Surely this evidence should place judicial remedies outside the Court's self-imposed *de minimus* rule. However, the majority opinion ignores the possible effectiveness of the judicial sanction and, in a completely irrelevant final sentence, reaffirms the law priority that it puts upon the protection of United States investors: "If the political branches are unwilling to exercise their ample powers to effect compensation, this reflects a judgment of the national interest which the judiciary would be ill advised to undermine indirectly."[258]

Having disposed to its satisfaction of all arguments for an international law exception to the act of state doctrine, the Court turns to the respondent's second main contention, namely, that the doctrine should be applied only "when the Executive Branch expressly stipulates that it does not wish the courts to pass on the question of validity."[259] This "reverse-twist *Bernstein* exception,"[260] first recommended as the Court notes by the Association of the Bar of the City of New York,[261] had been attacked in the government brief.[262] Mr. Justice Harlan endorses the government's position in summary fashion:

> We should be slow to reject the representations of the Government that such a reversal of the Bernstein principle would work serious inroads on the maximum effectiveness of United States diplomacy.

[257] See, *e.g.*, Laylin, *supra* note 180, at 36-37. Argument of counsel before the British Foreign Compensation Commission in Application of Anisminic Ltd. revealed how a British mining company was able to achieve a speedy settlement with Egypt after threatening to sue continental purchasers of its manganese ore.

[258] 376 U.S. at 436.

[259] *Ibid.* See text at note 154 *supra*.

[260] Metzger, *op. cit. supra* note 168, at 241. For discussion of the *Bernstein* exception, which the Court found inapplicable here, see text at and accompanying notes 37-52, 86-109 and 153 *supra*. While the Court did not pass upon the exception, "the manner in which it stated the *Underhill* modification seems to have at once limited *Bernstein* to its facts and encapsulated it, and . . . the tone of its opinion probably serves notice upon the State Department to avoid invoking it." *Ibid.* Accord, Falk, *Complexity* 937-39.

[261] See note 14 *supra*.

[262] Brief 43-46, 2 INT'L LEGAL MATERIALS 1022-23 (1963).

Often the State Department will wish to refrain from taking an official position, particularly at a moment that would be dictated by the development of private litigation but might be inopportune diplomatically. Adverse domestic consequences might flow from an official stand which could be assuaged, if at all, only by revealing matters best kept secret. Of course, a relevant consideration for the State Department would be the position contemplated in the court to hear the case. It is highly questionable whether the examination of validity by the judiciary should depend on an educated guess by the Executive as to probable result and, at any rate, should a prediction be wrong, the Executive might be embarrassed in its dealings with other countries. We do not now pass on the Bernstein exception, but even if it were deemed valid, its suggested extension is unwarranted.[263]

These arguments against changing the *Bernstein* presumption of nonreview in the absence of an executive "green light" will be considered in the final section of this Chapter. Suffice to say now that Mr. Justice White advanced a strong case in favor of such a change.[264]

If, from the standpoint of Americans with investments abroad, the Second Circuit's opinion constituted a pyrrhic victory, certainly the Supreme Court's decision represents a complete rout.[265] The respondent and the amici curiae in *Sabbatino*, in Henkin's words, had squarely "rejected the notion that courts should abdicate judicial functions, and sacrifice rights of litigants, out of deference to the uncertain and unreliable aspirations of the Department of State for

[263] 376 U.S. at 436.

[264] "If my view had prevailed I would have stayed further resolution of the issues in this Court to afford the Department of State reasonable time to clarify its views in light of the opinion. In the absence of a specific objection to an examination of the validity of Cuba's law under international law, I would have proceeded to determine the issue and resolve this litigation on the merits." *Id.* at 472. Cardozo once suggested that the President "declare" that American courts were free to review foreign acts of state under international law, subject to a reverse-twist *Bernstein* exception. Cardozo, *supra* note 20, at 481.

[265] According to Snyder, the decision is a "body-blow to investors and potential investors of the United States who either have investments in or are contemplating investments in, newly developing nations." Snyder, Banco Nacional de Cuba v. Sabbatino: *The Supreme Court Speaks*, 16 SYRACUSE L. REV. 15, 37 (1964). Compare Goldie, The Sabbatino Case: *International Law versus the Act of State*, 12 U.C.L.A.L. REV. 107 (1964), with Reeves, *The* Sabbatino *Case: The Supreme Court of the United States Rejects a Proposed New Theory of Sovereign Relations and Restores the Act of State Doctrine*, 32 FORDHAM L. REV. 631 (1964).

diplomatic flexibility and the larger needs of American foreign policy."[266] The Court, on the other hand, found that the conduct of foreign affairs, especially the need of the executive to have a free hand negotiating future lump sum compensation agreements, required the application of an almost absolute act of state doctrine in expropriation cases. There is no doubt that these factors favor judicial deference in cases like *Sabbatino*. "But to adduce sound reasons for a policy of nonreview," Mr. Justice White reminds us, "is not to resolve the problem at hand, but to delineate some of the considerations that are pertinent to its resolution."[267] Unfortunately, despite its verbiage about balancing "relevant considerations," the Court accepts too readily the executive's claims to exclusive competence in this area.

The effect of *Sabbatino*, being limited to cases involving the taking of property, is to deprive American investors abroad of a possible judicial remedy and to remand them exclusively to diplomatic remedies for redress. The holding obviously lessens the protection accorded American investment overseas, a fact dimly perceived by the Court but held to be outbalanced by other factors. "Any legal principle," one counsel on the government's brief subsequently admitted in a moment of candor, "may hurt some one some of the time."[268] Surely this remark is hardly encouraging to the foreign investor. And surely all commentators who advocate that American courts apply international law to cases before them should not be charged, by some process of guilt-by-association, with the nefarious offense of harboring a desire "to enlist domestic courts in the struggle to make national views on the protection of foreign investment prevail in contemporary international law."[269]

Supporters of *Sabbatino*, who themselves have cautioned that its "permanent significance has . . . rather little to do with the legal protection of foreign investment,"[270] would do well to credit at least some of its critics with sharing a similar wide perspective. *Sabbatino*,

[266] Henkin, *supra* note 155, at 808.

[267] 376 U.S. at 447.

[268] Lowenfeld, *supra* note 206, at 220. He added: "We do not think the act of state doctrine will hurt any one class most of the time, and we believe that in the long run it will promote the overall interest of the nation, including that of the investing community." *Ibid.* No data is advanced to support this point.

[269] Falk, *Complexity* 936.

[270] *Ibid.*

in the view of many international lawyers, delimits too narrow an area for American courts in international law cases. The executive's pre-eminence in actual diplomatic negotiations, they believe, has obscured the fact that all three coordinate branches of government have important parts to play in the clarification and application of international law.[271] "Application by our courts of international law," it is maintained, "will assist the further judicial exposition of that law—which the political departments cannot do."[272] Indeed, there is strong evidence that on the very question of expropriation the executive is the branch taking the retrogressive position.[273]

In short, critics of *Sabbatino* are just as concerned with building and maintaining an international legal order encompassing the needs and aspirations of all states as are its most fervent supporters. With respect to takings of property, the extent of the *Sabbatino* holding, they contend that "the maintenance of both an international economy and stable community expectations about international law requires that courts apply international law when necessary for the protection of private rights."[274] Just as strongly they oppose the Court's "unhistoric and dangerous" rationale, applicable to other varieties of acts of state, under which the Court abdicates its function in this area, leaving American claimants "completely subject to any momentary determination of political expedience by the Executive."[275]

---

[271] "The plain fact is that the fixing of the fundamental objectives of our foreign policy is not, and cannot safely be made, a task for any single branch of our government. The executive is not the sole creator and judge of our objectives or even of the instrumentalities for the achievement of our objectives: the task is one for all the coordinate branches of our government. Surely no one could seriously propose that the fact that legislative action may impair what the executive branch considers our most desirable foreign policy could be justification for the Congress' automatic, compulsory abstention from its designated legislative function. It is no less unhistoric and dangerous to demand that the judiciary automatically and compulsorily abdicate and leave the assessment of the legality of the acts of a foreign government to the Executive, except where the Executive affirmatively seeks the assistance of the judiciary. The appropriate constitutional task for the Executive is not to seek to substitute itself for the other branches of the government but rather, within the broad outlines of the fundamental objectives established by all branches of government, to bring its unique competence for negotiation to bear in support of the decisions of the other branches of the government." ILA Brief 14-15.

[275] *Id.* at 54.

[273] See text at notes 307-08 *infra*.

[274] ILA Brief 52.

[272] City Bar Brief 6.

Neither the rights of individuals nor the cause of international law is served by a decision which arbitrarily politicizes a vast assortment of international disputes.

THE SABBATINO AMENDMENT

"Let us hope that it will not be nearly 100 years before *Sabbatino* meets its *Erie*."[276] This plea, uttered within a week of the Supreme Court's decision, heralded the commencement of a campaign to have Congress overturn the *Sabbatino* holding. Citing the Court's determination that the Constitution does not require the doctrine's application,[277] numerous international lawyers urged the adoption of a statute embodying an international law exception to the doctrine.[278] Even supporters of the decision recognized "the authority of Congress to deal with Act of State under its foreign affairs power."[279] The short of it is that six months after the Supreme Court had spoken a statute was pushed through Congress adopting, in substance, the international law exception approach originally urged in 1959 by the Association of the Bar of the City of New York.[280] The wheel had come full circle.

The vehicle used to accomplish this speedy reversal of *Sabbatino* was the Foreign Assistance Act of 1964, and once again, as with the Hickenlooper Amendment discussed in Chapter III, the congressional agent for "some oil companies and others"[281] was Senator Hickenlooper. The Senator introduced a bill which added a new subparagraph to section 620(e) of the Foreign Assistance Act of

[276] Maw, *supra* note 162, at 227.

[277] See text at and accompanying note 157 *supra*.

[278] *Id.* at 226; Laylin, *supra* note 180, at 36-39; Stevenson, *supra* note 157, at 709-11 *passim*.

[279] Henkin, *supra* note 155, at 821. "There can be little doubt that the Court would have to follow modifications in Act of State by act of Congress . . . ." *Id.* at 823.

[280] In addition to the authorities cited in the notes that follow, see Levie, *Sequel to Sabbatino*, 59 AM. J. INT'L L. 366 (1965), and Paul, *The Act of State Doctrine: Revived But Suspended*, 113 U. PA. L. REV. 691 (1965). See also Comment, 65 COLUM. L. REV. 530 (1965); Comment, 63 MICH. L. REV. 528 (1965); and Comment, 10 VILL. L. REV. 509 (1965).

[281] Metzger 242. This characterization of the amendment's backers seems somewhat slanted. Among the "others" supporting it were such impartial scholars as Baxter, Bishop, McDougal and "other distinguished law students who have attacked the Sabbatino decision as properly a critizable decision of the Supreme Court. . . ."110 CONG. REC. 18937 (daily ed., Aug. 14, 1964) (Senator Hickenlooper).

1961 providing that no court in the United States should decline, on the ground of the federal act of state doctrine, to determine on its merits any case in which an act of a foreign state occurring after January 1, 1959, was alleged to be in violation of international law, subject only to "the reverse-twist *Bernstein* exception that was specifically rejected by the Court."[282] According to the Senate Foreign Relations Committee, which adopted the amendment on July 10, 1964, without benefit of hearings:[283]

> The amendment is intended to reverse in part the recent decision of the Supreme Court in *Banco Nacional de Cuba v. Sabbatino.* . . .
>
> The effect of the amendment is to achieve a reversal of presumptions. Under the *Sabbatino* decision, the courts would presume that any adjudication as to the lawfulness under international law of the act of a foreign state would embarrass the conduct of foreign policy unless the President says it would not. Under the amendment, the Court would presume that it may proceed with an adjudication on the merits unless the President states officially that such an adjudication in the particular case would embarrass the conduct of foreign policy.[284]

To the foreign investor whose property has been taken this reversal of "presumptions" makes all the difference in the world. Instead of having to wait in vain for an executive green light, he is assured his day in court unless the executive, for overriding reasons of national policy, flashes a red light in his particular case.[285]

---

[282] Metzger 242. See H.R. 11380, § 301(b)(2), 88th Cong., 2d Sess. (1964).

[283] Metzger states that it was adopted "without an opportunity for the executive to present its views." Metzger 242. But see the "Statement by the Executive Branch" dated June 25, 1964, in *Hearings on S. 2659, S. 2662 & H.R. 11380 Before the Senate Committee on Foreign Relations*, 88th Cong., 2d Sess. 618 (1964), reprinted in 3 INT'L LEGAL MATERIALS 1077 (1964). Nevertheless, the undue haste displayed in pushing this bill through Congress permits one to question "the propriety of the 'procedures' used to secure the adoption of a piece of legislation reversing a fully reasoned Supreme Court decision, without meaningful hearings or an opportunity for the Executive Branch, charged as it is with the delicate task of guiding the United States through dangerous crises, to be heard on a matter that all acknowledge to involve the foreign relations of the United States in important ways." Metzger 245-46.

[284] S. REP. No. 1188, 88th Cong., 2d Sess. 24 (1964).

[285] "We are perfectly prepared to leave to the discretion of the President the decision as to whether the foreign policy interests of the United States require that a private litigant be denied his day in court and that the court

The amendment, as part of the Foreign Assistance Act of 1964, received the approval of the Senate on September 24, 1964, and went immediately to a conference committee. Although the House bill did not contain a comparable provision, the House managers, after expressing regret "that there had not been an opportunity for thorough study and full hearings on the subject,"[286] agreed to the amendment with several modifications.[287] As passed by both Houses, the Sabbatino Amendment provides as follows:

> Notwithstanding any other provision of law, no court in the United States shall decline on the ground of the federal act of state doctrine to make a determination on the merits giving effect to the principles of international law in a case in which a claim of title or other right is asserted by any party including a foreign state (or a party claiming through such state) based upon (or traced through) a confiscation or other taking after January 1, 1959, by an act of that state in violation of the principles of international law, including the principles of compensation and the other standards set out in this subsection: *Provided,* That this subparagraph shall not be applicable (1) in any case in which an act of a foreign state is not contrary to international law or with respect to a claim of title or other right acquired pursuant to an irrevocable letter of credit or not more than 180 days duration issued in good faith prior to the time of the confiscation or other taking, or (2) in any case with respect

---

be denied the ability to apply principles of international law in such a case. What we are not willing to do is to leave it as an inflexible presumption that the courts are absolutely precluded from making an inquiry into the validity of an uncompensated foreign taking when no one in the Government has even taken the trouble to determine whether the litigation would impinge upon the foreign policy interests of the Government." 110 CONG. REC. 18937 (daily ed., Aug. 14, 1964) (Senator Hickenlooper).

[286] H.R. REP. No. 1925, 88th Cong., 2d Sess. 16 (1964).

[287] "The committee of conference amended the Senate language to pinpoint its precise effect, making it clear that it does not apply if no violation of international law principles is found, or if the case involves a short term irrevocable letter of credit issued in good faith prior to the taking of property by a foreign state. The exception in those individual cases in which the President determines that judicial review of the foreign government's action is not in the U. S. foreign policy interest is preserved. An additional change was added to limit the application of the amendment to cases in which the proceedings are commenced before January 1, 1966. This limitation was approved with the understanding that the congressional committees concerned will make a full review and study of the matter during the next Congress and make a determination on the need for permanent legislation." *Ibid.*

to which the President determines that application of the act of state doctrine is required in that particular case by the foreign policy interests of the United States and a suggestion to this effect is filed on his behalf in that case with the court, or (3) in any case in which the proceedings are commenced after January 1, 1966.[288]

Before analyzing the policy arguments relevant to the amendment and considering its constitutionality, a brief description of the statute would be useful.

While, at first glance, the amendment appears to reinstate the broad international law exception laid down by the district court, actually it only modifies the Supreme Court's decision in the matter of presumptions, with the courts now being able to consider the international validity of foreign acts of state in the absence of an executive veto.[289] Thus the amendment, unlike Judge Dimock's opinion, does not read out the possibility of executive intervention.[290] On the other hand, the amendment is much preferable on this score to the decision of the Second Circuit, under which executive approval rather than an alleged violation of international law became the touchstone of justiciability.

The international law exception to the act of state doctrine spelled out in the amendment, it must be emphasized, applies only to acts which involve a "confiscation or other taking" of property. Here the amendment fits the Supreme Court's holding, which was limited to acts constituting a "taking of property," like a glove. "In substantive areas other than expropriation," Falk contends, "the *Sabbatino* approach to the act of state doctrine remains intact, being unaffected by the terms of the statute."[291] Thus, when the questioned act of state is not expropriatory in nature, the private party cannot rely on the amendment but must demonstrate the existence of a consensus on the applicable international legal standard.[292]

---

[288] Subsection 301(d)(4) of the Foreign Assistance Act of 1964, 78 Stat. 1013, 22 U.S.C.A. § 2370(e)(2) (Supp. 1964).

[289] 110 CONG. REC. 18936 (daily ed. Aug. 14, 1964) (Senator Hickenlooper). See text at and accompanying note 285 *supra*. To the extent that the *Sabbatino* decision eliminates the possibility of an excutive veto when consensus exists, the amendment modifies the decision on this score too.

[290] Falk interprets the amendment as a restatement of Judge Dimock's opinion. Falk, *Controversy* 42. See text at and accompanying note 50 *supra*.

[292] The original bill was not limited to expropriatory actions alone. See note 282 *supra*.

[291] *Ibid*.

The amendment defines the international law principles which the courts are to apply in act of state cases to include "the principles of compensation and other standards set out in this subsection," thereby incorporating the standards which the Hickenlooper Amendment enjoins the President to follow when determining whether to suspend foreign aid.[293] As Chapter III will demonstrate, these standards, especially insofar as they require the payment of full compensation in convertible foreign exchange, clearly exceed the standards demanded by customary international law.[294] Undoubtedly this provision, which requires American courts to follow the congressional view of customary international law in applying what purports to be an international law exception, is the weakest and least desirable in the Sabbatino Amendment. Should it be applied,

> we would be witnessing the spectacle of American courts deciding cases upon the basis of "international law" principles known not to be accepted as such by the international community. This would indeed be a curious way of showing that the rule of law as practiced in the United States deserves respect.[295]

Three exceptions to the international law exception are contained in the amendment. First, "in order to alleviate the opposition of at least one bank to the amendment,"[296] it is made inapplicable to cases involving "a claim of title or other right acquired pursuant to an irrevocable letter of credit of not more than 180 days duration issued in good faith prior to the time of the confiscation or other tak-

[293] "These principles as applied by our courts are to include the requirement for prompt, adequate, and effective compensation in cases of expropriation spelled out in the first part of section 620(e)." 110 CONG. REC. 22849 (daily ed., Oct. 2, 1964) (Mr. Adair). See also *id.* App. at A5157 (daily ed., Oct. 7, 1964) (Senator Hickenlooper). According to Senator Hickenlooper "a distinction must be drawn between the principles of compensation and other standards of international law presently set out in section 620(e) and technical provisions inserted by Congress to guide the executive branch in applying the [Hickenlooper] amendment to the aid program. The 6-month rule and the not less than 50 percent beneficially owned test are such technical provisions. They are not part of international law and are not included in the standards of international law referred to." *Id.* at 18946 (daily ed., Aug. 14, 1964).

[294] "These standards seem, if anything, to be in excess of the traditional rules of customary international law. As such, they repudiate the conclusion reached by the *Sabbatino* Court that international law is too indefinite in the expropriation area to permit its constructive application by domestic courts." Falk, *Controversy* 43. See also Metzger 246.

[295] *Ibid.*

[296] *Ibid.*

ing. . . ."[297] Secondly, as has been mentioned above, the amendment permits the executive branch to flash a red light and bring court proceedings to a halt.[298] Here it is important to note only that the President, in order to invoke this exception, must make a determination in "that particular case"[299] and then file "a suggestion to this effect . . . with the court. . . ."[300] Finally, the amendment does not apply if the taking occurred before January 2, 1959,[301] or if proceedings are commenced after January 1, 1966.[302] According to

[297] See text accompanying note 287 *supra*. "The exception does not give protection to innocent purchasers who do not finance through a letter of credit. It has been pointed out that 'the greater part of all United States imports are not financed by letters of credit.' Moreover, the exception does not apply if the transaction arises from a revocable letter of credit or if the letter is issued after the date the expropriation takes effect." Falk, *Controversy* 43.

With respect to innocent purchasers, Senator Hickenlooper has denied that the amendment would work an injustice to them, since it "does not dictate any result other than that a court would reach by 'a determination on the merits.' In such a determination the rights of the innocent third party would be protected. The existence of the amendment would, however, discourage purchases of expropriated property since the purchasers would be unable to rely automatically on the act of state doctrine and would have to establish their lack of notice of the violation of international law that took place in the seizure." 110 CONG. REC. 18946 (daily ed., Aug. 14, 1964).

[298] See text at notes 282-84 *supra*.

[299] See text accompanying note 287 *supra*. Hence a general determination that the foreign policy interests of the United States necessitate the application of the act of state doctrine as a matter of course will not suffice. *Cf.* Metzger 247: "The State Department should lose no time in recommending to the President that he cause to be filed in each pending case in American courts a suggestion that application of the act-of-state doctrine is required by the foreign policy interests of the United States pending 'thorough study and full hearings on the subject' by the House of Representatives and the Senate of the United States."

[300] This requirement of a direct communication from the executive to the court avoids the problems caused by the Second Circuit's liberal construction of *Bernstein*. See text at notes 86-101 *supra*.

[301] This date was picked because it marks "the coming to power of the Castro regime in Cuba and the beginning of the greatest series of illegal takings of American property in recent history. Some cutoff date is desirable and it is clear that prior to the Supreme Court's reversal of the lower courts in the Sabbatino case parties were not relying on any such drastic application of the act of state doctrine." 110 CONG. REC. 18946 (daily ed., Aug. 14, 1964) (Senator Hickenlooper).

[302] This time span might suggest that the amendment "relates to Cuban takings alone. This is not at all the case. Ceylonese, Algerian, United Arab Republic, Indonesian, Brazilian, Argentine, and perhaps other takings are also subjected to the judgment of American courts by the amendment." Metzger 247.

Senator Hickenlooper, this cutoff was inserted in the Sabbatino Amendment to give

> the Senate Foreign Relations Committee an opportunity to have hearings next year on how the amendment works in practice and whether it should be made permanent. I want to serve notice now that the burden will be on the State Department, which opposed the amendment, to give the amendment a chance to operate in practice and then to show us how the power of the President to suspend enforcement of the amendment in special cases for foreign policy reasons does not amply meet any problems that may arise in the actual conduct of foreign affairs.[303]

As the above extract indicates, the executive branch strongly opposed the inclusion of the amendment in the Foreign Assistance Act of 1964. While not questioning its constitutionality, the executive advanced its usual policy arguments against the amendment.[304] In a memorandum dated July 28, 1964, it contended that the amendment would not aid American claimants very much since little American-owned property taken abroad ever comes within the jurisdiction of American courts. Therefore, only a small percentage of the value of American property that had been expropriated would be recovered in judicial proceedings. Harking back to its shopworn argument about the efficacy of diplomatic remedies, the memorandum maintained that

> the amendment would have an unintended effect adverse to the interest of American claimants. Over the years, the State Department has pressed in claims settlements for adherence to a standard of prompt, adequate, and effective compensation. We have had a fair measure of success in obtaining satisfactory settlements.[305] If United

[303] 110 Cong. Rec. App. A5157 (daily ed., Oct. 7, 1964).

[304] Falk, discussing the executive memorandum quoted in the text that follows, states that it "did not attempt to defend the rationale of the Court, but confined its opposition to the argument that the statute would be a setback for the recovery prospects of American claimants in the expropriation context." Falk, *Controversy* 50. However, since an earlier executive memorandum not cited by Falk employs the Court's consensus argument, see note 309 *infra*, it is not quite accurate to say that "Congress acted without any presentation in defense of the Court." *Ibid.* Of course, the majority opinion had no *effective* advocate in Congress or, for that matter, in the executive branch.

[305] The modesty of the executive branch about its record in negotiating claims settlements would be admirable were it not a bit late in coming. Before the Supreme Court, it will be recalled, the government spoke of its unqualified "success" in compiling an "impressive" record of amicable settlements. Brief 30-31, 2 Int'l Legal Materials 1019 (1963).

States courts were to pass on the legality under the international law of foreign expropriations, and were to pass on the standards of compensation adhered to by a foreign government, we believe the negotiating position of the Executive would be undermined rather than strengthened. A review of U.S. court decisions, including the opinions of the District Court, the Court of Appeals, and the Supreme Court in the *Sabbatino* case, discloses that American judicial standards in regard to compensation are considerably lower than those pressed for by the Department of State in international claims negotiations. The end result, if the "Sabbatino" amendment were to become law, would probably be to decrease the over-all recovery by expropriated American property owners. Their loss would far outbalance such recoveries as might be made by the very small number of American claimants who could trace their property or locate foreign-government property to the United States.[306]

The above extract essentially restates the arguments made in the government's brief in *Sabbatino*, but it also contains one new and surprising contention: that the executive's negotiating position would be undermined were American courts permitted to pass on the validity of foreign expropriations because "American judicial standards in regard to compensation are considerably lower than those pressed for by the Department of State in international claims negotiations." If this argument infers that American courts have become so sophisticated on the measure of compensation required by international law that their determinations thereon would undercut the prompt, adequate, and effective demands of the Department of State, it comes like an ill wind out of the mouths of persons so recently citing the alleged "parochialism" of municipal courts as a reason for applying the act of state doctrine.[307] If, on the other hand, the argument means that the Department of State's position on the compensation question is untenable, and thus decisions by American courts must be forbidden lest they reveal this embarrassing fact, surely the time has come to put aside the act of state doctrine and face the facts. "Accurate descriptions of the emperor's state of dress are rarely unhealthy," Metzger suggests, "since the occasions when a myth is to be preferred to reality seldom occur, and the myth in

---

[306] Reprinted as Appendix C in Falk, *Controversy* 77.

[307] Especially Falk, *Controversy* 48-49, who cites the argument to support his conclusion that the Sabbatino Amendment actually would reduce the net recovery by Americans in the expropriation area. See text following this note.

this case had long since outlived its usefulness."[308] In any event, the argument is completely without merit at present, since in its final form the amendment incorporates the compensation standard of the Hickenlooper Amendment, which far exceeds the Department of State's demands.

An earlier memorandum dated June 25, 1964, while relying upon the efficacy of diplomatic remedies, also raised the consensus argument in support of the Supreme Court's decision.[309] In addition, it specifically attacked the amendment's reversal of presumptions.

(a) The President's choice of whether or not to object is not as a practical matter a real one. If the President were to decide to object in one case and not to object in another, he would only invite charges of discrimination by the country involved in the latter case and would run an unacceptable risk of an adverse effect on U.S. relations with that country. Moreover, failure to object would raise a question of U.S. adherence to its nondiscrimination pledges under international agreements, both bilateral and multilateral.

(b) The President is forced to decide whether a court ruling on the act of a foreign state was prejudicial to U.S. foreign policy at a time and in a manner chosen by private parties to a court case and not at the time and in the manner chosen by the President. This would be unwise. The Executive may be involved in sensitive negotiations on another subject with the Government whose act is being questioned. This means that the President would be forced to decide whether it is better for the court to pass on the validity of the act of the foreign state and risk a breakdown of the negotiations, or to foreclose a court decision on the merits of the case.[310]

Both these arguments, of course, had been made in the government's brief in *Sabbatino* and were accepted by the Supreme Court, which

[308] Metzger 232.

[309] "There is a wide divergence of views in the world today regarding the limitations on a state's power to expropriate the property of aliens and the sensitivity of this issue in international relations today. As the Supreme Court stated: 'It is difficult to imagine the courts of this country embarking on adjudication in an area which touches more sensitively the practical and ideological goals of the various members of the community of nations.' It would be most unwise for the Congress to reverse this rule of judicial restraint and force the courts of the United States to pass on issues which are politically sensitive and on which there is little consensus and few guiding precedents." *Hearings, supra* note 283, at 619, 3 INT'L LEGAL MATERIALS at 1078. See text at and accompanying notes 293-94 *supra*.

[310] *Ibid.*

noted that "a reversal of the *Bernstein* principle would work serious inroads on the maximum effectiveness of United States diplomacy."[311] Assuming the paramountcy of foreign affairs, they have some merit. As Falk has noted, "the resolution of this issue depends very much on how one weights flexibility in the pursuit of foreign policy as opposed to the judicial independence of domestic courts in international law cases."[312] However, most of the problems supposedly caused by the presence of the executive veto in the amendment can be remedied simply by eliminating it. Since the President's choice "is not as a practical matter a real one" anyway,[313] a strong argument can be made for deleting the provision permitting executive intervention.[314]

Rebutting the arguments of the executive branch contained in the above two memoranda,[315] Senator Hickenlooper himself placed a memorandum in the *Congressional Record* answering the government's main objections to the amendment.[316] Since the executive memoranda had not raised any constitutional objections to the amendment, this statement did not spell out the constitutonal basis for Congressional action. Elsewhere in the record, however, he stated that the amendment was "an exercise of Congress [*sic*] broad powers with respect to foreign commerce and investment. . . ."[317] Furthermore, taking up the assertion that the amendment

[311] 376 U.S. at 436. See Brief 43-46, 2 INT'L LEGAL MATERIALS 1022-23 (1963).

[312] Falk, *Controversy* 58.

[313] Metzger predicts that "the State Department would be likely to maintain silence in all cases except those which would be deemed to be fraught with the most severe consequences diplomatically. In consequence, the adoption of this reverse *Bernstein* exception would effectively eliminate the act-of-state doctrine in all but the few cases that absolutely required a State Department request that it be invoked in order to avoid diplomatic disaster. All of this was well known to the sophisticated lawyers urging the scheme, obviously desiring precisely that result." Metzger 243. But see *The Supreme Court, 1963 Term*, 78 HARV. L. REV. 143, 303 (1964) (predicting executive intervention as a matter of course). See also text accompanying note 299 *supra*.

[314] See text at notes 348-49 *infra*.

[315] In addition to the two memoranda just discussed, the executive branch filed comments with the conference committee which are reprinted as Appendix C. While all three memoranda purport to reflect the views of the "executive branch," it is understood that one major department originally had no objections to the Sabbatino Amendment.

[316] 110 CONG. REC. 18948 (daily ed., Aug. 14, 1964).

[317] *Id.* at 18946. "The amendment, which becomes part of a provision in the Aid Act designed to discourage foreign expropriations, is essential to make

would infringe on the constitutional responsibilities of the executive with respect to foreign relations, he replied:

> There can be no question that the amendment is a constitutional exercise of Congress [*sic*] powers with respect to the aid program, foreign commerce, and offenses against international law. There is nothing expressed or implied in the separation of powers that prohibits such an exercise of these powers.[318]

Within two months of the Sabbatino Amendment's enactment, its constitutionality was put to the test when the defendants and the third-party defendants in the continuing *Sabbatino* litigation, now entitled *Banco Nacional de Cuba v. Farr, Whitlock & Co.*,[319] moved in the district court to dismiss the action on the ground that the amendment bars recovery in the case. After raising the specious argument that the amendment was not intended to apply to actions pending at the time of its passage,[320] the plaintiff advanced two constitutional arguments: (1) that the amendment, assuming it does applying to pending litigation, is unconstitutional because it deprives a litigant of his property without due process of law;[321]

---

sure that the United States does not become a 'thieves market' for the product of foreign expropriations and to prevent an undermining of the concept that acts of state are subject to international law. Since the United States is in many cases the principal market for oil, minerals, or other products that might be expropriated, the Hickenlooper-Sparkman [Sabbatino] amendment has a very direct relation to the security of foreign investment." *Ibid.* On the relevancy of the amendment to the Foreign Assistance Act of 1964, compare the remarks of Congressman Morgan (amendment "nongermane") with those of Congressman Adair ("one of the most significant aspects of the bill"). 110 CONG. REC. 22848, 22849 (daily ed., Oct. 2, 1964). See also Falk, *Controversy* 56.

[318] 110 CONG. REC. 18946 (daily ed., Aug. 14, 1964).

[319] Civil Action File No. 60-3929 (S.D.N.Y. 1965).

[320] "There is no mandate in the Hickenlooper Amendment to justify retrospective operation; quite the contrary. The language of the statute, the purpose for which it was enacted, and the effect intended by its sponsors all point to a Congressional intent that the legislation should have prospective effect only." Memorandum of the Plaintiff, p. 3. Actually, the language of the amendment points to the opposite conclusion. Moreover, "even if subordinate sources of legislative history are to be consulted, no intent of Congress to exclude this or other pending cases from the ambit of the statute appears." Memorandum of C.A.V., p. 10. See also the convincing argument on this score in the Memorandum of the North American Sugar Industries, Inc. as Amicus Curiae, pp. 14-32.

[321] Memorandum of the Plaintiff, pp. 23-24.

and (2) that the amendment is unconstitutional because it constitutes a legislative interference with the functions of the judicial and executive branches.[322] The government, in an amicus curiae memorandum filed at the request of the district court, took the position that the amendment did not apply to a pending case,[323] but that if it did the amendment "could constitutionally be applied retroactively so as to affect this and similar cases."[324] The government's memorandum assumes sub silentio that the amendment is not an unconstitutional interference with judicial or executive functions.[325]

On the first point, the constitutionality of the amendment's retroactive application, there appears to be no legally recognizable property which could be taken by the amendment's application, since the plaintiff never has secured a final judgment in the case.[326] As the government's memorandum points out, "the mere fact that a lawsuit has been instituted, or that a legal proposition has been decided in a certain way by an appellate court (though no judgment has as yet been entered), does not in and of itself create a vested right."[327] Thus the amendment, if applied to the case, would not run afoul of the Fifth Amendment.

On the second point, the plaintiff argued that "Congress has no power . . . to compel a court to decide a case which it, in the sound exercise of its judicial discretion, has determined not to decide."[328] Conceding that it had not found any cases in point, it contended that

[322] *Id.* at 24-31.

[323] Memorandum of the United States as Amicus Curiae, pp. 9-21. "The position taken by the Government in its memorandum has the aspect of a post-hoc rationalization for an attempt to salvage all that can be salvaged of a legislative defeat. The Executive Branch opposed adoption of the Rule of Law Amendment. In doing so, it was quite clear [to the executive branch] that 'the amendment is intended to reverse the recent decision of the Supreme Court' in this case. Moreover, its spokesmen did not tell the Congress that the amendment would not be applicable to pending cases, although this would have been a compelling reason for urging that the amendment should not be adopted because it would not have one of its desired effects." Memorandum of the North American Sugar Industries, Inc. as Amicus Curiae, p. 30.

[324] Memorandum of the United States as Amicus Curiae, p. 22.

[325] *Id.* at 21-23.

[326] Memorandum of the North American Sugar Industries, Inc. as Amicus Curiae, pp. 32-33.

[327] Memorandum of the United States as Amicus Curiae, p. 22.

[328] Memorandum of the Plaintiff, p. 24. Falk states that it is "an open question" whether Congress has such power. Falk, *Controversy* 45.

Congress went beyond its power by seeking "to direct the courts to decide this political question."[329]

> Congress has no power to direct the Court to decide issues which, however they are presented to the Court, involve questions which are by their very nature not subject to judicial action. Whether this is true as to any particular case must of necessity be left to the courts; it is an essential part of the judicial power.[330]

In summary fashion, the plaintiff also challenged the constitutionality of the amendment on the ground that it interferes with the President's power over foreign relations.[331]

A constitutional basis for the amendment, in the opinion of this writer and other authorities, can be found in several powers of Congress.[332]

> In its purpose to protect United States investment in foreign countries and promote the movement of United States capital abroad, the amendment is a valid exercise of Congress' power to regulate *foreign commerce*. In its purpose to promote United States private investment in underdeveloped countries as part of the Foreign Assistance Program, the amendment is based upon Congress' power over *foreign relations*. In addition, the Constitution authorizes the Congress to define and punish . . . "Offences against the Law of Nations." U.S. Const., Art. I, § 8, cl. 10. In the amendment Congress has defined as *an offense against the law of nations* expropriations of property that violate principles of international law, including the principle of prompt, adequate and effective compensation.[333]

These sources of congressional power, moreover, are supplemented by

> a further aspect of Congressional power in this area: the well-settled power of Congress to regulate the exercise of the judicial function of the courts, to define their jurisdiction and to prescribe the law which they are to apply. . . . The plenary power of Congress over the courts is drawn from various sections of the Constitution, such

[329] Memorandum of the Plaintiff, p. 29.
[330] *Id.* at 30. Compare Falk, *Controversy* 46-47.
[331] Memorandum of the Plaintiff, pp. 30-31.
[332] See note 278 & 279 *supra*.
[333] Memorandum of the North American Sugar Industries, Inc. as Amicus Curiae, pp. 34-35. (Emphasis added.)

as Art. I, § 8, cl. 9 and Art. III, § 1; Art. III § 2, para. 2; and Art. VI, para 2.[334]

Thus, at least four bases can be advanced to support the enactment by Congress of the Sabbatino Amendment.

By exerting its legislative power in this manner, Congress has not encroached improperly upon either judicial or executive functions. The amendment, "far from being an assumption of judicial powers, is in form and substance a declaration of federal policy by the principal lawmaking body of the Government—the exercise of a function which is not merely within its power but is one of the central purposes for which it was created."[335] Congress, in short, has stepped in to change judicially created federal law.[336] Nor has Congress impinged unconstitutionally upon the powers of the executive branch. While the President is the sole agent of the United States in its conduct of foreign relations,[337]

> Congress has the power to establish the policies that the Executive is to carry out. In conducting the foreign relations of the United States the Executive Branch is under a duty to implement these policies and the Executive Branch has traditionally enforced and applied the statutory law of the United States validly enacted by Congress.[338]

The fact that the executive did not question the amendment's constitutionality when it was before Congress, coupled with its position in the pending litigation, indicates that it considers the statute a proper, albeit unwise, exercise of congressional power. Obviously the amendment will have some impact upon the manner in which the President conducts foreign relations in the future, but not every such impact renders a statute unconstitutional. If the Sabbatino Amendment is retained after January 1, 1966, presumably the executive

[334] Memorandum of C.A.V., pp. 17-18. Of course, this basis of power is not available to justify the amendment's applicability in state court proceedings. The amendment is not limited to cases arising in the federal courts. See text at note 288 *supra*.

[335] *Id.* at 19.

[336] *Id.* at 19-20.

[337] See, *e.g.*, United States v. Curtiss-Wright Export Corp., 299 U.S. 304, 319 (1936).

[338] Memorandum of the North American Sugar Industries, Inc. as Amicus Curiae, p. 39.

branch, as it did in the case of the Hickenlooper Amendment, will learn to live with it.

FUTURE DEVELOPMENTS

To a great degree, as Falk notes, one's attitude toward *Sabbatino* is shaped, not "by an appeal to logic or to legal authority," but by how one weighs a long list of variable factors.[339] Thus, to some international lawyers the decision was "heart-warming,"[340] while to others it represented "a body-blow to investors. . . ."[341] The full-scale hearings on whether to continue the Sabbatino Amendment, which took place during this session of Congress, offered a splendid opportunity for the legislative and the executive branches, together with international lawyers and foreign investors, to participate in the formulation of an act of state doctrine which would contribute both to the protection of American investment abroad and to the development of the international economic system. Although the hearings unfortunately were limited to the retention of the existing amendment and did not consider the relation of judicial remedies to other governmental programs for the protection of foreign investment,[342] they still are "likely to have a major impact upon the role of domestic courts in the international law field during the decade ahead."[343]

Enough has been said in this Chapter to indicate this writer's disenchantment with an act of state doctrine that precludes the application of international law to the conduct of foreign states. The Sabbatino Amendment, to the extent that it removes the bar of a near-absolute act of state doctrine and permits the examination under international law of the validity of foreign acts relating to the taking of property, is a desirable piece of legislation that warrants retention by Congress. Since even critics of the amendment apparently assume that it will be retained,[344] it is up to them and also to inter-

---

[339] Falk, *Controversy* 60.

[340] Metzger 242.

[341] See note 265 *supra*.

[342] On the need for Congress to widen the scope of its inquiry, see Falk, *Controversy* 53-54. See generally Chapter VI.

[343] Falk, *Controversy* 69.

[344] *Id.* at 56-58. After lengthy hearings on the amendment, *Hearings on H.R. 7750 Before the House Committee on Foreign Affairs,* 89th Cong., 1st Sess. 576-620, 991-1079, 1234-71 (1965), the House Committee recommended its extension for one year. H.R. REP. No. 321, 89th Cong., 1st Sess. 31-32 (1965). A provision to this effect is contained in the Foreign Assistance bill passed by

national lawyers interested in the protection of foreign investment to suggest helpful modifications of the amendment. For, as Falk has remarked, "even supporters of the Sabbatino Amendment think it could be improved in drafting and effectiveness."[345]

The most important needed modifications are three in number. In the first place, the Sabbatino Amendment should be extrapolated from the Foreign Assistance Act and placed in the Judicial Code where it belongs. While there is a causal connection between the Hickenlooper Amendment and the Foreign Assistance Act, Falk rightly points out that

> there is no reason, other than perhaps the tactical one of discouraging a veto, for locating the successor to the temporary Sabbatino Amendment in a subdivision of legislation dealing with foreign aid, thereby fostering the undesirable impression that the United States is coming increasingly to rely upon the foreign aid program to provide leverage for the protection of business interests abroad. To encourage such a view is to increase the plausibility of Communist and other anti-American propaganda around the world.[346]

Secondly, the reference to the Hickenlooper Amendment standard of compensation should be deleted from the amendment, permitting the courts to apply principles of compensation found in customary international law. If the opinions of courts in the United States on the validity of foreign acts of state are to carry any weight abroad, they must be based upon international law and not some parochial notions laid down by Congress.[347] Finally, the provision allowing the executive branch to intervene should be excised, since it "tends to politicize the courts and to reinforce their image as nationalized

---

the House. 111 CONG. REC. 11155 (daily ed., May 25, 1965). On the other hand, the Senate Committee on Foreign Relations, which held no hearings on the amendment this year, voted to make it permanent, S. REP. No. 157, 89th Cong., 1st Sess. 19 (1965), and the Foreign Assistance bill passed by the Senate reflects this recommendation. 111 CONG. REC. 13067 (daily ed., June 14, 1965). Thus the Sabbatino Amendment seems to be here to stay. Neither bill modifies it in any substantial fashion.

[345] Falk, *Controversy* 52.

[346] *Id.* at 56.

[347] *Id.* at 56-57. Chayes and Stevenson, former Legal Adviser of the Department of State and Chairman of the Committee on International Law of the Association of the Bar of the City of New York respectively, both agree on this point. Remarks of Abram Chayes and John R. Stevenson in New York City, Jan. 11, 1965. See also text at notes 293-95 *supra*.

decision-making tribunals."[348] While this provision was included to lessen executive objections to the amendment, it is unworkable in practice and constitutes an unnecessary limitation on the international law exception approach.[349]

Whether American courts can make a significant contribution to the development of international law in the field of expropriation if the Sabbatino Amendment stays on the books remains to be seen. Certainly the foreign policy needs of the executive branch, however, are not so pressing that Congress should forsake its opportunity to insure American investors whose property is taken abroad of an occasional remedy in American courts. The rights of private litigants should not be rendered subject, as they are today in sovereign immunity cases, to possible eradication by executive action based upon the real or imagined needs of foreign policy. To quote Falk once again, "we must not lose sight of the cause of individual justice according to law. Certainly an increase in the use of domestic courts to settle the controversies that arise in international life is, other considerations aside, a vital and progressive step toward an orderly and just world."[350] The Sabbatino Amendment is just such a step.

[348] Falk, *Controversy* 57.

[349] See text at notes 298-300 and 310-14 *supra*. Chayes has stated that the executive branch should have nothing at all to say about the application of the act of state doctrine. Remarks of Abram Chayes in New York City, Jan. 11, 1965.

[350] Falk, *Controversy* 69.

Part Two

PROTECTION BY THE GOVERNMENT

Even if the sovereign immunity rule and the act of state doctrine presented no problems, Americans whose foreign properties have been nationalized would obtain only sporadic relief through municipal courts. Congress, recognizing this fact and anxious to protect American foreign investment, has enacted two measures designed to afford investors a greater degree of general protection. The Hickenlooper Amendment, added to the Foreign Assistance Act in 1962, threatens countries which take American property without compensation with the termination of United States aid. The Investment Guaranty Program, instituted in 1948 and continually strengthened through the years, now permits American investors in less developed countries to insure their new investments against expropriation and other nonbusiness risks. The two Chapters in this Part argue that, while formal government participation definitely is needed to protect the property of Americans abroad, a self-help program which is not linked to foreign aid represents a sounder and in the long run a more effective approach.

III.

The Hickenlooper Amendment

BACKGROUND AND LEGISLATIVE HISTORY

AMERICANS WITH investments abroad have had a great deal of property taken since World War II.[1] While in some instances they have received partial compensation from lump sum settlements with and vested assets of the taking countries,[2] these investors also have learned the harsh fact that the "remedies available under existing law are far from satisfactory."[3] Economic measures and diplomatic pressures, of course, constitute possible sanctions.[4] Bilateral treaties providing for the protection of private foreign investment (the so-called FCN treaties) purport to provide protection to persons investing in certain countries.[5] The Investment Guaranty Program, discussed in Chapter IV, is an interesting self-help device of great potential. But these remedial measures are not available in all instances, and even when available they offer incomplete protection for American investors.

Such was the situation on February 16, 1962, when Governor Leonel Brizola of the Brazilian state of Rio Grande do Sul canceled the operating title of the Companhia Telefonica Nacional, a subsidiary of the International Telephone and Telegraph Company of

[1] S. REP. No. 1535, 87th Cong., 2d Sess., App. No. 8, at 91-95 (1962) (Letter from the Department of State to Senator J. W. Fulbright Concerning Expropriation of U.S. Private Investments, With Attachment—Major Instances of Expropriation of Property Belonging to U.S. Nationals Since World War II).

[2] See Chapter V.

[3] Young, *Remedies of Private Claimants Against Foreign States*, in 3 INSTITUTE ON PRIVATE INVESTMENT ABROAD 45, 99-100 (1961). See also COMM. ON INT'L LAW, N.Y.C.B.A., A RECONSIDERATION OF THE ACT OF STATE DOCTRINE IN UNITED STATES COURTS 1 (1959).

[4] See FATOUROS, GOVERNMENT GUARANTEES TO FOREIGN INVESTORS 355-57 (1962). For a powerful account of how nonlegal sanctions were brought to bear upon Iran after its 1951 nationalization of the oil industry, see Walden, *The International Petroleum Cartel in Iran—Private Power and the Public Interest*, 11 J. PUB. L. 64 (1962).

[5] FATOUROS, *op. cit. supra* note 4, at 92-101.

New York, and ordered the seizure of the company's properties for expropriation by the state.[6] Although I. T. & T. valued the telephone system at between $6,000,000 and $8,000,000, the governor had deposited only 149,758,000 cruzeiros (about $400,000 at the existing free rate of exchange) as an indemnity for the company's assets.[7] In a statement issued the following day, the Department of State, while recognizing Brazil's right "to expropriate property belonging to nationals of other countries for public purposes if provision is made for the payment of prompt, adequate and effective compensation," criticized the compensation offered by the governor as "so far below book value that the valuation appears to have been made unilaterally."[8] The Department also observed that the expropriation "appears to be a step backward in the mobilization of available resources for the success of the Alliance for Progress."[9]

Coming as it did just six weeks before former President Goulart's scheduled trip to Washington to obtain additional United States financial assistance, the expropriation of the I. T. & T. subsidiary, carried out by the state of Rio Grande do Sul, proved to be a source of embarrassment to the Brazilian federal government.[10] Upon the request of United States Ambassador Lincoln Gordon, the federal government agreed to use its good offices to obtain "fair payment" for the company's properties.[11] Talks soon broke down, however, just as rumblings from Congress became audible. In the House, Representative Alger suggested cutting off aid to Brazil if it refused to accept responsibility for Governor Brizola's action,[12] and in the upper chamber Senator Long argued that "we should not continue generous U. S. foreign aid at the same time that the aid's recipients are seizing, virtually without compensation, valuable property of those U. S. taxpayers who are paying for that very aid."[13] Sensing that in foreign aid it had, for the first time, an effective lever to safeguard the foreign investments of United States citizens against the threat of expropriation without just compensation, Con-

[6] N.Y. Times, Feb. 17, 1962, p. 1, col. 8.
[7] *Ibid.*
[8] N.Y. Times, Feb. 18, 1962, p. 33, col. 2.
[9] *Ibid.*
[10] *Id.* at cols. 5-6.
[11] *Id.* at cols. 3-4.
[12] 108 CONG. REC. 2699 (1962).
[13] 108 CONG. REC. 3134 (1962).

gress began a lengthy debate on the merits and mechanics of legislation linking aid and expropriation.

By March 1962, several bills on the subject had been introduced in Congress. Both the late President Kennedy[14] and Secretary of State Rusk[15] immediately opposed these bills as unwise and unnecessary. The Department of State, in a memorandum submitted to Congress, took the position that

> There are well-established diplomatic and legal procedures for securing fair compensation for U.S. citizens and corporations whose property abroad has been taken by the power of eminent domain. Most countries have laws governing the exercise of this power with provisions for compensation.
>
> In the recent case of expropriation by Brazil of an American-owned utility, any final judgment is now premature, pending possible settlement or judicial decision in a Brazilian court concerning the

[14] N.Y. Times, March 8, 1962, p. 14, col. 8. At his news conference on March 7, the President stated the Administration's position:

Nobody has ever questioned the right of any government to seize property, providing the compensation is fair.

The United States is involved with the Brazilian Government in attempting to adjust this matter. I can think of nothing more unwise than to attempt to pass a resolution at this time which puts us in a position not of disagreement with a governor of a state who is not particularly our friend, but instead, really, with the whole Brazilian nation, which is vital and which is a key and with which we must have the closest relations.

. . . . . .

And I must say that if you look at the map and realize the vitality of Brazil—I think that we ought to keep a sense of proportion.

We don't want to make those who dislike us work easy by reacting to things which happen in a way which strengthens them and weakens the influence of the United States.

[15] See, e.g., Hearings on S. 2996 Before the Senate Committee on Foreign Relations, 87th Cong., 2d Sess. (1962). Asked to explain Department of State policy toward countries which expropriate property of United States citizens, Secretary of State Rusk, testifying before the Senate Committee on Foreign Relations, explained that "our influence is used wherever it can be and persistently, through our embassies on a day-to-day basis, in our aid discussions and in direct aid negotiations, to underline the importance of private investment." Id. at 27. When former Senator Capehart objected to this policy, claiming that it offered no protection to an American investor and that the latter at least should be assured that aid would be discontinued to a country taking his property, Rusk replied that the United States could not "afford to stake its interests in other countries on a particular private investment in a particular situation. . . . [S]uch a provision would create very severe complications in our relations with other governments." Id. at 31.

fairness of the compensation. Any evaluation based on the sum deposited as compensation neglects the fact that in Brazil, as in the United States, the amount of that sum is subject to judicial review. If the evaluation is critical, it can only be based on an assumption that justice will not be done, an assumption the United States cannot and does not make.

Furthermore, diplomatic channels have been used in the past to help American citizens secure adequate compensation. The Department of State believes that as a result of discussions now taking place with the Brazilian Government, a fair settlement of this recent instance of expropriation will be achieved, acceptable to both the company and to Brazil.

We believe that the injection of the U.S. foreign assistance program into condemnation proceedings would at best advance the interests of the American citizen whose property is expropriated only marginally, and, on the other hand, it can seriously injure the vital U.S. national interests which the foreign assistance program is designed to further.[16]

Despite these pleas, Congress continued to debate the bills during the spring. Finally, on May 8, 1962, Senator Hickenlooper proposed his amendment to the Foreign Assistance Act, which required the President to cut off foreign aid to any country taking American property "without providing immediate and effective compensation . . . as required by international law, justice, and equity. . . ."[17]

After a long debate and several modifications,[18] the "Hicken-

---

[16] *Id.* at 557-58.

[17] 108 CONG. REC. 7893 (1962).

[18] See generally Lillich, *The Protection of Foreign Investment and the Foreign Assistance Act of 1962*, 17 RUTGERS L. REV. 405, 409-14 (1963). In the House, Representative Gallagher contended that the President should have some discretion in applying the subsection, since an automatic termination of aid would tie the President's hands and make the foreign assistance program inoperable. Supporting this view, former Representative Judd argued that

> this program is primarily to help the United States, and I do not think it is wise for us to take action which may make us feel better by getting rid of some of our adrenalin in proper indignation over the behavior of some people or some local authorities in another country, if in doing so we injure the United States of America.

Representative Zablocki pointed out that the amendment would make it impossible for the President to deal with a new government, even though friendly to the United States, if the previous government had seized American property. Representative Frelinghuysen declared that under the proposal the action of a

looper Amendment" was added to the Foreign Assistance Act of 1962, which the President signed into law on August 1, 1962.[19] The amendment, section 620(e) of the Act, presently reads as follows:

> (e) The President shall suspend assistance to the government of any country to which assistance is provided under this *or any other* Act when the government of such country or any gov-

political subdivision or governmental agency of a foreign country of great strategic or economic importance could force the President to cut off vital aid.

Answering the above objections, Representative Adair called attention to the provision in the subsection giving the foreign country six months to take appropriate steps to compensate American property owners. Contending that this clause provided sufficient flexibility, he asserted that "if a country cannot begin to do something in six months, then it will not do it in six years." Adair agreed with Representative Hays's statements that "as long as any negotiation is going on, there is no mandatory cutoff involved. . . ." If the foreign country is "willing to show any kind of good faith whatsoever," Hays explained, "they are not barred from foreign aid and the hands of the President are not tied at all." He called such an interpretation "implied and implicit" in the amendment.

Representative O'Hara disagreed with Hays's interpretation, contending that the requirement of "speedy compensation" precluded any flexibility on the President's part. In answer to Hays's argument that "speedy compensation could drag on for a long time," O'Hara replied:

> I do not know that the creditor is always going to give the debtor all the time he wants when he has back of him a law that says speedy compensation. He is going to make the law work for him. Negotiation on repayment of a loan has never in law or common sense been synonymous with speedy compensation.

Despite this opposition, the Hickenlooper Amendment was accepted by the House, which then passed the amended aid bill and sent it on to conference with the Senate. The conference report, submitted to the Senate on July 19, adopted the language of the House with a few minor exceptions. The revised bill passed the Senate by a 56–27 vote. When the conference report reached the House on July 24, Representative Adair, expanding on his earlier remarks, acknowledged that a good faith willingness to negotiate might for a time meet the requirements of the subsection. However, he warned that

> these negotiations must not be indefinitely prolonged. The provision calls for compensation in accordance with certain standards, not endless talk. And if the negotiations must be with a governmental authority that has admittedly no means to compensate as is true in one case in Latin America or with a government whose proposals show no intent to compensate as is true of Cuba, even a willingness to negotiate could not, in my opinion, meet the requirements of the statute.

The House then passed the revised bill by a 221–162 vote. The following day the Foreign Assistance Act of 1962 was sent to the President. *Id.* at 412-14 *passim.*

[19] 108 CONG. REC. 15187 (1962).

ernmental agency or subdivision within such country on or after January 1, 1962—

(1) has nationalized or expropriated or seized ownership or control of property owned by any United States citizen or by any corporation, partnership, or association not less than 50 per centum beneficially owned by United States citizens, or

(2) *has taken steps to repudiate or nullify existing contracts or agreements with any United States citizen or any corporation, partnership, or association not less than 50 per centum beneficially owned by United States citizens, or*

(3) has imposed or enforced discriminatory taxes or other exactions, or restrictive maintenance or operational conditions, *or has taken other actions*, which have the effect of nationalizing, expropriating or otherwise seizing ownership or control of property so owned,

and such country, government agency, or government subdivision fails within a reasonable time (not more than six months after such action, *or, in the event of a referral to the Foreign Claims Settlement Commission of the United States within such period as provided herein, not more than twenty days after the report of the Commission is received*) to take appropriate steps, which may include arbitration, to discharge its obligations under international law toward such citizen or entity, including speedy compensation for such property in convertible foreign exchange, *equivalent to the full value thereof*, as required by international law, or fails to take steps designed to provide relief from such taxes, exactions, or conditions, as the case may be; and such suspension shall continue until the President is satisfied that appropriate steps are being taken, and no other provision of this Act shall be construed to authorize the President to waive the provisions of this subsection.

Upon request of the President (within seventy days after such action referred to in paragraphs (1), (2), or (3) of this subsection), the Foreign Claims Settlement Commission of the United States (established pursuant to Reorganization Plan No. 1 of 1954, 68 Stat. 1279) is hereby authorized to evaluate expropriated property, determining the full value of any property nationalized, expropriated, or seized, or sub-

jected to discriminatory or other actions as aforesaid, for purposes of this subsection and to render an advisory report to the President within ninety days after such request. Unless authorized by the President, the Commission shall not publish its advisory report except to the citizen or entity owning such property. There is hereby authorized to be appropriated such amount, to remain available until expended, as may be necessary from time to time to enable the Commission to carry out expeditiously its function under this subsection.[20]

STATUTORY ANALYSIS

1. *Mandatory Character.* Under section 620(e), the President must suspend foreign aid if a recipient country expropriates American property, repudiates or nullifies existing contracts or agreements, or imposes or enforces discriminatory taxes, other exactions, restrictive maintenance or operational conditions, without taking appropriate steps to provide compensation or other relief as the case may be. In contrast to subsections (a) and (c) of section 620, which provide that aid shall not be furnished foreign countries *unless* the President finds such aid to be in the national interest,[21] subsection (e) specifically provides that "no other provision of this Act shall be construed to authorize the President to waive the provisions of this subsection." Therefore, regardless of the foreign country concerned or whether the taking of property was an isolated act of expropriation or part of a broad plan of nationalization, aid must be suspended when the President determines that the foreign country has violated the conditions of section 620(e).[22] The President has

[20] The italicized portions are amendments made during 1963 which are discussed in the text *infra*.

[21] 76 Stat. 260 (1962), 22 U.S.C. § 2370(a)(c) (Supp. V, 1964).

[22] Re noted in 1962 that "the amendment makes no provisions as to the determination of the facts of expropriation, the reasonableness under international law of the ensuing steps taken by the nation, or relief for the American property-owners." Re, *The Foreign Claims Settlement Commission: Its Functions and Jurisdiction*, 60 MICH. L. REV. 1079, 1096 n.90 (1962). In practice, the determination is left to the President, which means that it is made initially by the Agency for International Development, Department of State. For a brief discussion of the method and criteria that might be used by the Department, see LILLICH & CHRISTENSON, *International Claims: Their Preparation and Presentation* 90-92 (1962) [hereinafter cited as LILLICH & CHRISTENSON].

discretion, however, to lift the suspension when "he is satisfied that appropriate steps are being taken. . . ."

2. *Extent of Sanction.* The original amendment called for the suspension of aid "provided under this Act," namely, the Foreign Assistance Act of 1961, as amended. When the amendment first was invoked and aid to Ceylon suspended in 1963, the Department of State, "to avoid hardship to the people of Ceylon," decided to continue a Food for Peace program of school lunches for 1,847,000 children daily, plus a nutrition program for 70,000 mothers and preschool children. The Department argued that "suspension of Food for Peace programs is not legally required as these programs are authorized under legislation other than the Foreign Assistance Act."[23] Congress, noting that the Department had avoided the stringencies of section 620(e) by this strict interpretation, then inserted the phrase "or any other" before the word "Act." The intention of this 1963 amendment, according to the Senate Committee on Foreign Relations, was to "extend the sanctions of the section to such activities and agencies as Public Law 480, the Export-Import Bank,

---

See also Christenson, *International Claims Procedure Before the Department of State*, 13 SYRACUSE L. REV. 527, 533-34 (1962).

Senator Hickenlooper's draft bill originally gave the Foreign Claims Settlement Commission (FCSC) "*exclusive* jurisdiction to determine the extent and amounts of any losses sustained by a national of the United States for the purposes of this subsection." 108 CONG. REC. 7893 (1962). (Emphasis added.) This provision was allegedly included because the FCSC "already possesses the criteria, and has a history of evaluation of American property abroad seized by foreign countries." *Ibid.* Conceivably the mandatory referral to the FCSC was designed to prevent the President from side-stepping the full effect of the amendment by a liberal construction of the compensation requirement. The Senate rejected this aspect of the draft bill and sole discretion in determining the adequacy of compensation was left with the President.

The enacted amendment was amended itself in 1963 to provide the President, at his option, with the advisory services of the FCSC. See text at note 20 *supra*. In the event that the President utilizes the FCSC, he must do so within seventy days after the foreign country has taken the operative action. The FCSC then has only ninety days within which to make its determinations and submit an advisory report to the President, a period far too short for the FCSC to make the necessary findings. For this reason, and more importantly because the President would be unlikely to delegate to an "independent and permanent tribunal" even the initial step in a decision-making process which could terminate a multi-million aid program, presidential referral to the FCSC pursuant to the 1963 amendment is unlikely.

[23] Press Release issued Feb. 8, 1963, by the Agency for International Development, Department of State, reprinted in 2 INT'L LEGAL MATERIALS 386, 391 (1963).

and the Peace Corps."[24] A brief colloquy in the Senate between Senators Hickenlooper and Morse suggests that the Committee later excepted the Peace Corps and cultural exchanges from its blanket prohibition,[25] and a subsequent conference report states that the House agreed to the Senate provision with an amendment "specifically excepting assistance to any country through the Export-Import Bank in addition to the Peace Corps, assistance under the Mutual Education and Cultural Exchange Act of 1961, and famine or disaster relief under Public Law 480 from the provisions of the Foreign Assistance Act."[26] Although the bill, as enacted, follows the Senate's draft version and requires the suspension of aid "provided under this or any other Act . . . ," it also contains a new section 638 apparently making the Hickenlooper Amendment inapplicable to the above-mentioned types of assistance.[27]

3. *Responsibility of Foreign Country.* Under the amendment a cessation of aid to a foreign country may result from acts of the foreign country itself or "any governmental agency or subdivision within such country. . . ." The expropriation of the I. T. & T. subsidiary by the Brazilian state of Rio Grande do Sul undoubtedly generated support for the inclusion of this provision, which accords with Borchard's observation that:

> In international relations the national government is alone responsible for the proper safeguarding of the rights of foreigners, and aliens have the right to look to the central government in the case of violation of treaty rights and international obligations of the nation by its constituent parts.[28]

Although there may be good reason for retaining this rule in the law of international claims,[29] its use in the context of foreign assistance may well cause some difficulties in the future.[30]

---

[24] S. REP. No. 588, 88th Cong., 1st Sess. 30 (1963).

[25] 109 CONG. REC. 21763 (1963).

[26] H.R. REP. No. 1006, 88th Cong., 1st Sess. 27 (1963).

[27] 77 Stat. 389 (1963), 22 U.S.C. § 2398 (Supp. V, 1964).

[28] BORCHARD, THE DIPLOMATIC PROTECTION OF CITIZENS ABROAD 199 (1915). See also 5 HACKWORTH, DIGEST OF INTERNATIONAL LAW 593-97 (1943).

[29] RESTATEMENT, FOREIGN RELATIONS §§ 173-74 (Proposed Official Draft 1962) [hereinafter cited as RESTATEMENT].

[30] See President Kennedy's statement, note 14 *supra*. The effect of this portion of section 620(e) is to elevate particular grievances into serious international matters. The apparent abolition, for section 620(e) purposes, of the local remedies requirement also contributed to this result. See text accompanying note 63 *infra*.

4. *Operative Acts.* Section 620(e) becomes operative when the foreign country, governmental agency or government subdivision has: (1) nationalized, expropriated, or seized ownership or control of American property; or (2) taken steps to repudiate or nullify existing contracts or agreements with United States nationals; or (3) imposed or enforced discriminatory taxes, exactions, or conditions or taken other actions which have the effect of (1) above.

Under the first heading come the typical acts of nationalization and expropriation for which the United States has sought compensation by lump sum settlement since World War II.[31] In addition, depriving an owner of control of his property, which the Foreign Claims Settlement Commission (FCSC) has held constitutes a "taking" of property,[32] also is condemned. This assimilation of loss of control to expropriation is a recognition that "intervention in the management and control of a business, farm, or other property may constitute a constructive or an effective taking, depending upon the facts surrounding the intervention."[33]

The second heading, added in 1963, expressly provides for applying the amendment when a foreign government or one of its agencies or subdivisions "has taken steps to repudiate or nullify existing contracts or agreements" with United States nationals. This writer had suggested that such steps by a foreign government conceivably could lead to the invocation of the original amendment under what are now its first and third headings.[34] By expressly providing that section 620(e) applies when a foreign government takes steps to repudiate or nullify existing contracts or agreements with United States nationals, the Senate has removed any doubt as to its applicability under such circumstances.[35]

---

[31] A recent lump sum settlement recognizes the duty to pay compensation for such seizures. See Articles I(1)(a) and 2(a) of the Agreement With Bulgaria, July 2, 1963 [1963] 14 U.S.T. & O.I.A. 969, T.I.A.S. No. 5387. See also RESTATEMENT § 190.

[32] FCSC, FIFTEENTH SEMIANN. REP. 17 (1961); FCSC, FOURTEENTH SEMIANN. REP. 141 (1961); FCSC, TENTH SEMIANN. REP. 61 (1959).

[33] LILLICH & CHRISTENSON 60. See also RESTATEMENT § 197.

[34] Lillich, *supra* note 18, at 417-18.

[35] One must agree with Senator Morse's conclusion:

The language from the old act, with the previous Hickenlooper amendment, plus the new language in the bill that has come to the floor of the Senate from the committee, leaves no room for doubt that it covers nullification of contracts in which property values, as well as outright expropriation of property, are involved.

While this heading has been included to bring the section into operation when a foreign country has taken steps to repudiate or nullify existing contracts or agreements with United States nationals, section 620(c), a related provision whose coverage is limited exclusively to debt claims, should not be overlooked. This section, originally found in the Foreign Assistance Act of 1961 and expanded by 1962 amendments, provides that no assistance shall be given to a foreign country which is indebted to any United States citizen for goods or services furnished or ordered.[36] While section 620(c) does not cover the "taking" of all types of contracts—bondholder claims being an illustration[37]—it does cover certain types of contract breaches which would not constitute a "taking" for section 620(e) purposes.[38]

The third heading covers acts falling under the rubric of "creeping nationalization," a concept which also embraces the deprivation of control. "Creeping nationalization" may be defined as those acts of a foreign country, such as discriminatory taxes, exactions or conditions, which effectively deprive an alien of substantially all the benefit of his interest in property, even though his entire legal interest in the property is not taken.[39] Claims based upon such acts have been allowed by the FCSC[40] and specifically settled by lump

---

109 CONG. REC. 21762 (1963). Whether, as Senator Hickenlooper contends, it applies not only to the nullification of contracts "but also to the fruits of them" is a different matter. *Id.* at 21761.

[36] 76 Stat. 260 (1962), 22 U.S.C. § 2370(c) (Supp. V, 1964). The President may waive this provision if he finds that cutting off aid would be "contrary to the national security." Compare text accompanying notes 21 & 22 *supra.*

[37] "The phrase 'for goods or services furnished' was added to make clear that the debt must be for goods and services as distinguished from government bonds or similar obligations which may be in default." H.R. REP. No. 1088, 87th Cong., 1st Sess. 61 (1961). Bondholder claims conceivably could come under section 620(e). See LILLICH & CHRISTENSON 62 n.245.

[38] Compare RESTATEMENT §§ 198-99. See also H.R. REP. No. 1788, 87th Cong., 2d Sess. 30 (1962).

[39] "Among such measures may be mentioned sequestration and intervention . . . ; refusal of allowances for imports which are essential to the conduct of an established business; refusal to allow the entry of essential management personnel; refusal to allow repatriation in whole or in part of capital or yield; and taxation at a confiscatory or penal level." E. Lauterpacht, *The Drafting of Treaties for the Protection of Investment*, in THE ENCOURAGEMENT AND PROTECTION OF INVESTMENT IN DEVELOPING COUNTRIES, INT'L & COMP. L.Q. SUPP. No. 3, at 30 (1962). See also text at note 42 *infra.*

[40] FCSC, FOURTEENTH SEMIANN. REP. 136-67 (1961); FCSC, TENTH SEMIANN. REP. 53-54 (1959).

sum agreement.[41] "Creeping nationalization" is a subtle form of expropriation which is seeing increasing use, and its inclusion as a prohibited act under section 620(e) reflects the facts of international life. Gardner has warned:

> Property rights can be effectively destroyed in many ways short of an actual confiscation or expropriation—they can be taken indirectly by exchange controls, export and import regulation, taxation, labor regulation, limitations on the ownership and control of enterprises, price controls, even by runaway inflation. Indeed, the prospect of these indirect takings provides much more of a deterrent to private foreign investment in underdeveloped countries than the prospect of a direct taking via confiscation or expropriation.[42]

A 1963 amendment broadened section 620(e) insofar as "creeping expropriation" is concerned by adding "or has taken other actions," an open-end phrase designed to confirm that the amendment caught acts of so-called wealth deprivation,[43] to the other operative acts listed under the third heading. "The committee has added the phrase 'other actions'," states the Senate Report,

> because it has been concerned over recurring reports of actions which certain governments are either proposing or initiating and which can perhaps best be described as creeping expropriation. These other actions include, for example, unusually high taxes which are perhaps not discriminatory in a technical sense but which are tantamount to confiscation or which at least raise a serious question of their confiscatory effect. The committee intends for confiscation to be construed broadly and not in a narrow technical sense.[44]

5. *Definition of American Property.* Section 620(e) comes into play only if the property taken, or the contract repudiated or annulled, is owned or held by "any United States citizen or [by] any corpora-

---

[41] See Articles I(A) and II(b) of the Agreement With Poland, July 16, 1960 [1960] 11 U.S.T. & O.I.A. 1953-54, T.I.A.S. No. 4545. See also Rode, *The American-Polish Claims Agreement of 1960*, 55 AM. J. INT'L L. 452, 455 (1961).

[42] Gardner, *International Measures for the Promotion and Protection of Foreign Investment*, 53 A.S.I.L. PROCEEDINGS 255, 262 (1959).

[43] *Hearings on S. 1276 Before the Senate Committee on Foreign Relations*, 87th Cong., 1st Sess. 553-54 (1963) (Senator Hartke).

[44] S. REP. No. 588, 88th Cong., 1st Sess. 29 (1963). For a discussion of "creeping expropriation" and a dozen specific examples thereof, see the memorandum of Senator Hickenlooper printed in 109 CONG. REC. 21774-75 (1963).

tion, partnership, or association not less than 50 per centum beneficially owned by United States citizens. . . ." This standard, which is
a departure, at least in phraseology, from the eligibility requirements
under postwar international claims programs, deserves brief comment. Clearly a United States citizen falls under the standard if the
property in the foreign country, or the contract or agreement with it,
is owned or held directly by him. Suppose, however, his only claim
to ownership is an indirect one based upon stock ownership in a
juridical entity organized under the laws of a foreign country?[45]
Such interests have entitled claimants to compensation under postwar claims programs,[46] and they should suffice to invoke the sanctions of section 620(e), at least where there is a substantial American interest in the foreign juridical entity.[47]

When the property of legal entities is involved, the section requires that they be fifty percent owned by United States citizens.
This requirement reflects standard American claims practice.[48]
Somewhat surprising, however, is the omission of the usual requirement that they be entities organized under the laws of the United

---

[45] For purposes of section 620(e), it would make no difference whether the
juridical entity was organized under the laws of the foreign country which
expropriated the property or under the laws of a third state. Compare RESTATE-
MENT §§ 180-81.

[46] LILLICH & CHRISTENSON 17-20. See also LILLICH, INTERNATIONAL CLAIMS:
THEIR ADJUDICATION BY NATIONAL COMMISSIONS 90-94 (1962).

[47] Compare 5 HACKWORTH, DIGEST OF INTERNATIONAL LAW 840-45 (1943).
The traditional "substantial and bona fide interest" test has been abandoned in
recent claims programs, which have permitted claims of American stockholders
for their proportionate interest in foreign corporations regardless of the extent
of the total American interest therein. The test has retained its validity, however, with respect to claims based upon indirect interests in nationalized foreign
corporations, i.e., when an American stockholder has an interest in a foreign
corporation which in turn has an interest in a nationalized foreign corporation.
There the American stockholder is an eligible claimant only if 25% of the
nationalized corporation was owned, directly or indirectly, by United States
nationals. This double standard is found in the Czechoslovakian Claims Act of
1958, 72 Stat. 531 (1958), 22 U.S.C. § 1641j(b)(c) (1958), and in the Rumanian
Claims Agreement of 1960. See Article II(b)(c) of the Agreement With
Rumania, March 30, 1960 [1960] 11 U.S.T. & O.I.A. 318, T.I.A.S. No. 4451.
There is good reason to use the test in both instances when the extreme sanction
of cutting off foreign aid is involved.

[48] LILLICH & CHRISTENSON 15-17. Senator Hickenlooper has stated that this
requirement is not part of international law. 110 CONG. REC. APP. A5157 (daily
ed., Oct. 7, 1964). While this statement is technically correct, the requirement
certainly is consistent with international standards.

States or a constituent state or other political entity thereof.[49] The plain words of the section do not spell out such a requirement, although it may be presumed that the President, in construing the section, will imply it.[50]

6. *Appropriate Steps*. If a foreign country receiving aid commits an operative act, section 620(e) gives it six months to take appropriate steps to discharge its obligations under international law before aid is suspended. These steps, when property has been taken, may include arbitration.[51] However, the section specifically requires that eventually steps be taken to pay "speedy compensation equivalent to the full value thereof for such property in convertible foreign exchange, as required by international law. . . ." This provision was modified in 1963 to end speculation about the quantum of compensation required to satisfy the amendment's original "equitable" standard.[52] Although the Department of State in the Ceylon situa-

[49] LILLICH & CHRISTENSON 16.

[50] The House obviously intended such a reading. See H.R. REP. No. 1788, 87th Cong., 2d Sess. 30 (1962).

[51] 108 CONG. REC. 14131 (1962). A clause was added specifically stating that arbitration was one of the appropriate steps that a foreign country could take to discharge its obligations under international law. See Domke, *Arbitration Between Governmental Bodies and Foreign Private Firms*, 17 ARB. J. (n.s.) 129, 140 (1962).

[52] The House Committee on Foreign Affairs equated the original standard with the traditional Department of State view requiring the payment of prompt and adequate compensation. H.R. REP. No. 1788, 87th Cong., 2d Sess. 30 (1962). On the floor of the House, Representative Adair gave this perfunctory explanation of the new phraseology.

> As to the question of what is equitable and speedy compensation, the committee gave considerable thought to that, and was assured that those were words of particular meaning to international lawyers. They have been interpreted and do mean exactly what they say, that the compensation must bear a fair relation to the true value of the property, and it must be in some kind of money that can be used, and not, for example, in local currency which cannot be converted.

108 CONG. REC. 13152 (1962).

The above explanation is not overly helpful. In the first place, the requirement of "equitable and speedy compensation" has no particular meaning in international law. The international law requirement generally has been phrased in terms of "just compensation" (RESTATEMENT § 190[b]), but Cheng, after an exhaustive survey of the subject, has observed that "the quantum of compensation for expropriation, however in practice it may be computed, while it must always be 'just,' 'fair' or 'equitable,' need not necessarily be full." Cheng, *The Rationale of Compensation for Expropriation*, in 44 TRANSACT. GROT. SOC'Y

tion had interpreted the amendment to require "the prompt payment of compensation representing the full value of the property as required of international law,"[53] a construction in keeping with its usual approach to the question,[54] both the House and Senate sought to nail down this interpretation in 1963 by eliminating the word "equitable" and qualifying "compensation" by the clause "equivalent to the full value thereof."[55] The House Report assumed that this change, which was enacted into law, only "confirms that the term 'equitable' compensation means compensation 'equivalent to the full value' of the property taken. Compensation which is equivalent to the full value must include all elements or interest of value that make up the total worth of the property."[56] Thus Congress has clarified the original Hickenlooper Amendment on this score and deprived the President of any opportunity to take a more liberal attitude on the compensation question should a future situation so warrant.

Insofar as the requirement that the compensation be made "in convertible foreign exchange, as required by international law," Metzger accurately observes that "there is no such requirement of

---

267, 294 (1959). The Restatement, taking note of the position of Latin American states (RESTATEMENT, Explanatory Notes § 190, Reporters' Note 2, at 664) and recognizing the fact that "land reform programs may give rise to serious problems of state responsibility in cases in which the land holdings of aliens are affected if the requirement of just compensation is construed as calling for payment of full value," (id. at Explanatory Notes § 193, Reporters' Note at 673) finds American practice to require compensation equivalent to the full value of the property taken "unless special circumstances make such requirement unreasonable." Id. at § 193(2).

[53] 48 DEP'T STATE BULL. 328 (1963). The International Economic Policy Association patronizingly stated that "AID properly applied this statutory standard in suspending assistance to Ceylon under section 620(e). . . ." Hearings on H.R. 5490 Before the House Committee on Foreign Affairs, 88th Cong., 1st Sess. 1226 (1963).

[54] See, e.g., 3 HACKWORTH, DIGEST OF INTERNATIONAL LAW 656-57 (1943).

[55] H.R. REP. No. 646, 88th Cong., 1st Sess. 73 (1963) and S. REP. No. 588, 88th Cong., 1st Sess. 67 (1963).

[56] H.R. REP. No. 646, 88th Cong., 1st Sess. 31-32 (1963). Note the rather naive statement by the International Economic Policy Association that this change would "take valuation out of the vagaries of diplomatic negotiations and put it on some basis of fact." Hearings on S. 1276 Before the Senate Committee on Foreign Relations, 88th Cong., 1st Sess. 386 (1963). Most international lawyers familiar with valuation disputes would take the position that the nebulous concept of "full value" has very little factual basis indeed.

international law, and the [typical United States] friendship, commerce, and navigation treaty makes it clear that an expropriating country may delay transferability as long as exchange restrictions are permissible—as long as reserves are low—and it needs the money to satisfy the wants of its people."[57] While the Restatement provides that compensation be in convertible currency,[58] it also permits the delay of such conversion "to the minimum extent necessary to assure the availability of foreign exchange for goods and services essential to the health and welfare of the people of the taking state."[59] The President would seem free to adopt this flexible approach to the convertibility requirement, especially since its strict application would provoke severe foreign policy problems.[60]

One final aspect of the compensation question is worth comment. To prevent the equivalent of borrowing from Peter to pay Paul, section 620(g) provides that no *monetary* assistance shall be given to any foreign country if it is to be used to compensate owners for expropriated property.[61] Should the President find that such assistance has been so used, no further assistance shall be furnished to the country until "appropriate reimbursement" is made for sums so diverted.

If the operative act has been the imposition of discriminatory

---

[57] Metzger, *Multilateral Conventions for the Protection of Private Foreign Investment*, 9 J. PUB. L. 133, 142 (1960). See also Gardner, *supra* note 42, at 259 n.6.

[58] RESTATEMENT § 195(1). Compare E. Lauterpacht, *The Drafting of Treaties for the Protection of Investment*, in THE ENCOURAGEMENT AND PROTECTION OF INVESTMENT IN DEVELOPING COUNTRIES, INT'L & COMP. L.Q. SUPP. NO. 3, at 31 (1962).

[59] RESTATEMENT § 195(2).

[60] Metzger has demonstrated that a provision requiring prompt payment in transferable form is positively harmful.

[T]he quickest way to poison the atmosphere for private foreign investment is to attempt to secure a commitment from a country that it must be prepared to take food from the mouth of its people in order to pay compensation in foreign exchange for property taken in exercise of its eminent domain power, should it exercise such power. This proposition would be seen as either (a) a not-too-subtle attempt to preclude exercise of the eminent domain power itself, which it is known that no country is in a position to forego, or (b) an effort to erect "property rights" over the "human right" to eat the food necessary to have imported with scarce foreign exchange.

Metzger, *supra* note 57, at 142-43.

[61] 76 Stat. 261 (1962), 22 U.S.C. § 2370(g) (Supp. V, 1964).

taxes, exactions, conditions, or repudiation or nullification of existing contracts or agreements, the only steps which the statute suggests as "appropriate" are "arbitration, to discharge its [the foreign country's] obligations under international law," or "steps designed to provide relief from such taxes, exactions, or conditions, as the case may be." Notwithstanding the nebulous character of the latter provision, the President has discretion to lift the suspension when "he is satisfied that appropriate steps are being taken. . . ."

7. *Local Remedies.* In contrast to section 620(c), section 620(e) contains no requirement that the American investor have exhausted available legal remedies in the foreign country before the section becomes operative.[62] Nor can Congress be said to have thought such a requirement implied in the section, since one of the main points raised in the original debates in the House was the alleged failure of Brazilian courts to provide an adequate remedy to American owners of expropriated property.[63] The Department of State particularly objected to the short-circuiting of local courts and the consequent aspersions cast thereon.[64]

The Department's position reflects its usual approach to the local remedies requirement. Following this rule of international law,[65] it will not espouse the claim of an American for the taking of his property by a foreign country unless he has exhausted the remedies available under that country's law.[66] The rationale behind the rule

[62] 76 Stat. 260 (1962), 22 U.S.C. § 2370(c) (Supp. V, 1964). If the claim is denied or contested by the foreign country, the United States citizen must exhaust his available legal remedies, which shall include arbitration, before section 620(c) becomes operative. No exhaustion is required where the claim is not denied or contested or where the indebtedness arises under an unconditional guaranty of payment given by the foreign country, directly or indirectly, through any controlled entity. 108 CONG. REC. 9214-15 (1962).

[63] 108 CONG. REC. 3393 (1962) (Mr. Adair). With respect to the expropriation of I. T. & T.'s subsidiary, the *New York Times* originally reported that "the company is seeking to avoid carrying the dispute through the Brazilian courts, which it believes would be a long and uncertain process." N.Y. Times, Feb. 23, 1962, p. 8, col. 4.

[64] *Hearings on S. 2996 Before the Senate Committee on Foreign Relations*, 87th Cong., 2d Sess. 557-58 (1962). See text at note 16 *supra*.

[65] See generally RESTATEMENT §§ 211-15. See also Lillich, *The Effectiveness of the Local Remedies Rule Today*, 58 A.S.I.L. PROCEEDINGS 101 (1964).

[66] Department of State Memorandum entitled "Nationalization, Intervention or Other Taking of Property of American Nationals," March 1, 1961, reprinted in 56 AM. J. INT'L L. 167 (1962). "This, of course, does not mean that 'legal remedies' must be exhausted if there are none to exhaust or if the procurement

is "the desire to settle disputes between aliens and states on a domestic basis rather than on a state-to-state political basis, which involves added expense and may aggravate international relations."[67] Yet section 620(e), in contrast to the Investment Guaranty Program, which, as Metzger observes, tends "to de-politicalize the whole issue of expropriation,"[68] presupposes that the foreign country will not honor its international obligation and therefore elevates all disputes over foreign investments into matters of serious international concern. Clearly this is just what some American corporations wish.[69] Perhaps the President can temper the section's rigidity, at least for a reasonable period of time after an expropriation, by considering the availability of local remedies as the taking of "appropriate steps." In several instances, he apparently has taken notice of the availability of local remedies when failing to invoke the amendment, although he did terminate aid to Ceylon despite the fact that remedies were available and, indeed, still were being pursued.

AN EVALUATION OF THE AMENDMENT

There is no doubt today that "the fear of expropriation constitutes a serious deterrent to private foreign investment in underdeveloped countries."[70] The Cuban nationalizations and their aftermath, for instance, have given many American investors second thoughts about making new investments in Latin America.[71] As-

---

of justice would be impossible. . . ." *Ibid.* See RESTATEMENT, Explanatory Notes § 213, comments *a* & *b* at 719. See also LILLICH & CHRISTENSON 98-102 (obtaining Department assistance short of espousal).

[67] RESTATEMENT, Explanatory Notes § 211, comment *a* at 713-14.

[68] Metzger, *"Nations" and the Rules of International Law—A Commentary,* 8 How. L.J. 122, 126 (1962).

[69] See text at and accompanying note 62 *supra.*

[70] FATOUROS, *op. cit. supra* note 4, at 50.

[71] Although American investors were expected in 1962 to contribute $300 million of the $2 billion net annual inflow desired under the Alliance for Progress, N.Y. Times, Nov. 4, 1962, § 3, p. 9, col. 3, investments hit a low point that year when "Latin America actually suffered a net outflow of $32 million in capital back to the United States." N.Y. Times, Oct. 18, 1964, § 3, p. 1, col. 7. Recent statistics indicate a slight reversal of this trend. In 1963, for example, $64 million of new funds flowed into the area, N.Y. Times, Aug. 25, 1964, p. 45, col. 5, while the same amount "in new United States private direct investment entered Latin America in the first half of 1964." N.Y. Times, Oct. 18, 1964, § 3, p. 1, col. 7. Even if the total amount for 1964 exceeds $100 million, however, it will fall far short of the annual average of $150 million in the early 1950's and will be "nowhere near where it should be, considering the rise in costs and in population in Latin America in the last 10 years." *Ibid.*

suming the "necessity of encouraging private capital to invest in the developing countries,"[72] the question raised here is whether the threat to cut off foreign aid is a sound and effective method of protecting, and thereby encouraging, such investment. Experience to date suggests a negative answer. Before examining the facts in detail, however, several general criticisms of the Hickenlooper Amendment must be registered.

The main objection to section 620(e) is that it establishes an unnecessary and excessively heavy sanction against conduct which, at least in certain circumstances, the United States may wish to encourage. Should a foreign country nationalize the vast majority of American investments without paying fair compensation, as did Cuba, there is no doubt that the United States would cease its aid anyway, making the section mere surplusage. Should the foreign country expropriate only one or two American concerns, as several countries have done during 1965, cutting off all aid would be an act of disproportionate weight which ignores "the prime tenet that national self-interest is greater than the self-interest of a small group of American businessmen."[73] Granted that the United States should protect the rights of its citizens who invest abroad, it should not be required to pursue a fixed policy which, while it may offer those investors some protection, excludes all other factors from consideration.[74] As the Department of State noted in 1962, "the interests of single citizens in matters of eminent domain are among the factors to be evaluated in the decision in formulating our foreign policy, but these interests should not control it."[75]

The overemphasis on property protection at the price of other

[72] *Hearings on S. 2996 Before the Senate Committee on Foreign Relations*, 87th Cong., 2d Sess. 557 (1962) (Statement of the Department of State). This assumption has been questioned of late. See Drucker, Comment, in THE ENCOURAGEMENT AND PROTECTION OF INVESTMENT IN DEVELOPING COUNTRIES, INT'L & COMP. L.Q. SUPP. No. 3, at 15-17 (1962).

[73] Friedenberg, *Can the Alliance for Progress Work?* COMMENTARY, Aug. 1962, p. 101.

[74] Indeed, the law of international claims, by allowing a state to waiver or settle a claim of one of its nationals against a foreign state, permits the accommodation of conflicting intranational interests. RESTATEMENT § 218. See generally LILLICH, *op. cit. supra* note 46, at 23-36. Section 620(e), on the other hand, "may well commit our whole policy into the hands of one intransigent American citizen, whose actions could provoke expropriation and whose obstinacy could prevent a reasonable settlement. . . ." *Hearings on S. 2996 Before the Senate Committee on Foreign Relations*, 87th Cong., 2d Sess. 558 (1962).

[75] *Ibid.*

national objectives is apparent when one realizes that actions encouraged by the United States, such as land reform in Latin America, may serve at the same time to trigger section 620(e) and bring aid to an end.[76] Some countries, in the abundance of precaution, may fail to initiate needed land reform programs for fear that their inability to pay American owners in convertible foreign exchange might cause the United States to suspend assistance.[77] Other countries may view section 620(e) as an indirect attempt to restrict their powers of eminent domain[78] and thus consider it an unjustified interference in their internal affairs.[79] Furthermore, as the Department of State suggests, Communist countries are free to argue that

> our aid programs are substantially motivated by a desire to protect U.S. private investment and that they are, in effect, tools of U.S. capital. Since the Communists have long proclaimed that U.S. foreign aid is merely a strategem designed to facilitate the exploitation by Western capitalists, . . . [section 620(e)] would seem to play into their hands.[80]

[76] Senator Morse has suggested that "the foreign-aid program should be reoriented to require land reform by recipient nations." N.Y. Times, Oct. 18, 1962, p. 38, col. 3. Should such a provision ever be added to the Foreign Assistance Act, many countries receiving United States aid might find themselves on the horns of a dilemma. Presumably aid would cease unless they engaged in land reform. Yet should they do so they might run afoul of section 620(e).

[77] "The danger is that Latin American governments might avoid this type of reform, even though they intend to provide fair compensation, through fear that the United States would unilaterally determine the compensation inadequate or the procedures unfair and, hence, cut off all aid." *Hearings on S. 2996 Before the Senate Committee on Foreign Relations,* 87th Cong., 2d Sess. 558 (1962).

[78] See text accompanying note 60 *supra.*

[79] The reaction of foreign countries to other property protection devices indicates that many would take this attitude. Fatouros reports that "several underdeveloped states have been reluctant to conclude investment guaranty agreements with the United States because they regard the provisions calling for immediate compulsory arbitration and the by-passing of the usual requirement that local remedies be resorted to, as an infringement of their sovereignty." Fatouros, *Legal Security for International Investment,* in LEGAL ASPECTS OF FOREIGN INVESTMENT 710 (FRIEDMANN & PUGH EDS. 1959). For a thoughtful study of this general subject, see M. H. Cardozo, *Intervention: Benefaction as Justification,* in ESSAYS ON INTERVENTION 63 (1964).

[80] *Hearings on S. 2996 Before the Senate Committee on Foreign Relations,* 87th Cong., 2d Sess. 558 (1962).

Section 620(e) also plays into the hands of irresponsible leaders in recipient countries. In fact, it may "actually provoke further expropriations of American property by nationalist leaders who thrive on fighting 'Yankee imperialism'."[81] Since the section in effect makes the national government of a foreign country responsible for the acts of local officials,[82] expropriations may be occasioned by elements opposed to national governments which seek to rupture United States aid and thereby throw the foreign country into economic turmoil.[83]

Finally, the question of the section's ramifications on broader aspects of United States foreign policy must be considered. Several years ago Fatouros wrote that

> the exercise of direct or indirect pressure on the part of capital-exporting states, by means, for instance, of the refusal to give public loans or grants . . . , seems improbable, under present conditions. Capital-exporting countries are not at present prepared to jeopardize the political allegiance of underdeveloped countries. . . .[84]

Conditions have not changed radically since 1962; yet the United States by enacting section 620(e), a crude and heavy-handed sanc-

[81] Editorial, "Aid with Strings," The New Republic, Aug. 13, 1962, p. 8. Governor Brizola of the Brazilian State of Rio Grande do Sul obviously fell in this category. He once informed a news conference that his political mission was to fight for his country's liberation from the " 'process of plunder to which Latin America and Brazil are subjected by foreign capital.' " N.Y. Times, Nov. 16, 1962, p. 4, col. 5.

[82] See text at notes 28-30 *supra*. One Brazilian paper observed that the imposing of a sanction on the Brazilian people for what Governor Brizola did would have been the same as condemning all Americans as racists because of Governor Faubus. N.Y. Times, March 10, 1962, p. 8, col. 3.

[83] *Hearings on S. 2996 Before the Senate Committee on Foreign Relations*, 87th Cong., 2d Sess. 558 (1962):

> There are often elements within a country not representative of the sentiments of the country as a whole and hostile to the United States, that may appear to bring about inadequately compensated expropriation in any individual case. Generally, these are the very elements whose influence and power will be undermined if our aid program succeeds in promoting economic and social progress. Therefore, they seek every opportunity to obstruct the effective implementation of that program. Providing for the automatic termination of reduction of aid in case of an apparently inadequately compensated expropriation might well encourage them to attempt such expropriations.

[84] FATOUROS, *op. cit. supra* note 4, at 88.

tion differing only in degree from the use of the gunboat, has placed its good relations with a number of nations in jeopardy. Why should the United States use its economic might to impose upon another country a code of behavior which, insofar as it imposes a convertibility requirement and eliminates the necessity of exhausting local remedies,[85] is higher than the international law standard?[86] Why should the United States, a country which has always supported the concept of international arbitration, unilaterally seek to impose a self-determined international standard?[87] The additional protection which section 620(e) may afford the American investor is not worth jeopardizing the broader foreign policy objectives of the United States. As the Department of State argued in 1962, "the interest of the United States as a nation require the balancing of many factors, and the availability of our foreign assistance must depend on the same factors. . . ."[88]

The Hickenlooper Amendment, however, has been on the statute books for over three years. Debates during the past Congress indicate that the House,[89] the Senate,[90] and the business community[91]

[85] See text at notes 57-60 & 62-69 *supra*.

[86] Latin American countries would contend that the section 620(e) requirement of "full" compensation is higher than the standard required by international law. See text at and accompanying note 52 *supra*. They also might raise the question of the "Calvo Clause." See RESTATEMENT § 207.

[87] The futility of such an approach is made more apparent by the decision of the Supreme Court in Banco Nacional de Cuba v. Sabbatino 376 U.S. 398 (1964). As Metzger notes, "these congressional interpretations do not reflect existing international law, and . . . there is no likelihood that they will in the ascertainable future." Metzger, *Act-of-State Doctrine Refined: The Sabbatino Case*, [1964] SUP. CT. REV. 223, 246.

[88] *Hearings on S. 2996 Before the Senate Committee on Foreign Relations*, 87th Cong., 2d Sess. 558 (1962).

[89] "This requirement has been helpful in obtaining negotiated settlements of expropriations as well as preventing the taking of expropriatory actions in a number of countries. The more other nations are aware of this provision, the less likely it is that the provisions of Section 620(e) will have to be applied." H. REP. No. 646, 88th Cong., 1st Sess. 30 (1963).

[90] "The committee has been gratified by the experience under Section 620(e) since it was made a part of the law last year. At last one major expropriation case has been settled which, in the committee's judgment, probably would not have been settled in the absence of Section 620(e). Several other expropriations or discriminatory actions have been avoided. In only one case has the section operated to suspend assistance." S. REP. No. 588, 88th Cong., 1st Sess. 30 (1963).

[91] "In the brief period since its enactment, Section 620(e) has been respon-

believe the amendment to be a sound and effective method of protecting American foreign investment abroad. Former Senator Keating expressed what still appears to be the general consensus as follows:

> It is my belief—and I have heard this from many official sources—that the Hickenlooper amendment has substantially strengthened the hand of our Government in dealing with other nations which are prepared to accept out [sic] aid with one hand and confiscate our business with the other. Although there was some opposition from the Government to the Hickenlooper amendment last year, I believe it plays a most constructive role in our aid program and in our foreign policy generally.[92]

The strength of this sentiment, particularly at a time when the entire foreign aid bill was undergoing its heaviest attack in years, evidently caused the Administration in 1963 to change its position on the Hickenlooper Amendment. Whereas in 1962 both President Kennedy and Secretary Rusk had opposed the provision,[93] one year later the latter, agreeing that "the policy underlying the amendment is a very important one," concluded that "our experience thus far has meant that the amendment has been a good thing."[94] This unexpected change of view is surprising when one considers that almost simultaneously the Secretary was inveighing against Congressional attempts to "legislate foreign policy,"[95] and that President Johnson similarly assailed the foreign aid bill as reflecting, "unfortunately, the growing tendency to hamstring Executive flexibility with rigid legislative provisions wholly inappropriate and potentially dangerous in a world of rapid change."[96] Indeed,

---

sible for negotiated settlements in Brazil, and in the prevention of expropriatory actions in Honduras, Panama, and other countries. The United States suspended aid to Ceylon under Section 620(e), after exhaustive diplomatic efforts failed to achieve a settlement satisfying the standards required by the act and international law. General Clay's report commended Section 620(e) as 'especially helpful.' " *Hearings on S. 1276 Before the Senate Committee on Foreign Relations*, 88th Cong., 1st Sess. 405 (1963) (memorandum of International Economic Policy Association).

[92] *Hearings on S. 1276 Before the Senate Committee on Foreign Relations*, 88th Cong., 1st Sess. 348 (1963).

[93] See text accompanying notes 14 & 15 *supra*.

[94] *Hearings on S. 1276 Before the Senate Committee on Foreign Relations*, 88th Cong., 1st Sess. 30 (1963).

[95] N.Y. Herald-Tribune, Nov. 9-10, 1963, p. 1, col. 7 (Int'l ed.).

[96] N.Y. Herald-Tribune, Dec. 18, 1963, p. 1, col. 7 (Int'l ed.).

the President apparently singled out the Hickenlooper Amendment when he declared: "I wish to make clear now, for example, that—when a free and peaceful government is ever established in Cuba—I intend to exercise my authority to provide essential health, education and other assistance to the Cuban people, without waiting for a long and complex adjudication."[97]

What is so surprising about the Administration's sudden conversion is the fact that it apparently was based exclusively upon a reconsideration of the amendment's effectiveness in protecting private foreign investment.[98] Putting aside the above general objections to the amendment, if indeed that is possible, the Administration's position on this narrow point is open to question. What is the basis for its shared belief that, in the words of General Clay, "perhaps because of the Hickenlooper Amendment, compensation has been offered for the private property taken over without the consent of the U.S. companies concerned, and the compensation which was offered was acceptable to the companies"?[99] Although the legislative history of the 1963 revisions of the amendment is peppered with references to its beneficial effect with respect to actual or threatened expropriations in Chile,[100] Honduras,[101] Panama,[102] and Peru,[103] no facts to support these assertions were brought forth. Indeed, what facts are available concerning Argentina, Brazil, Ceylon, and Indonesia—the four major instances where the amendment theoret-

---

[97] *Ibid.* Actually, the amendment does not apply to the Cuban situation, since it only covers actions of foreign countries taken "on or after January 1, 1962. . . ." Moreover, the amendment permits the President to order the resumption of aid should he be satisfied that appropriate steps are being taken by the foreign country.

[98] It is worth noting that unlike Secretary of State Rusk, who was "happy" to endorse the amendment (*Hearings on S. 1276 Before the Senate Committee on Foreign Relations*, 88th Cong., 1st Sess. 29 [1963]), AID Administrator Bell refused to give it his personal blessing. The only statement on the amendment which Congress could extract from him was the neutral comment that "we are recommending no change in the present legislation." *Id.* at 274.

[99] *Id.* at 646.

[100] 109 CONG. REC. 21762-64 (1963).

[101] *Hearings on H.R. 5490 Before the House Committee on Foreign Affairs*, 88th Cong., 1st Sess. 1231 (1963).

[102] *Hearings on S. 1276 Before the Senate Committee on Foreign Relations*, 88th Cong., 1st Sess. 405 (1963).

[103] 109 CONG. REC. 21763 (1963).

ically should have been most effective—indicate that its effect varies from marginal to negligible.

In *Argentina,* seven American oil companies had their contracts with the government canceled on November 15, 1963, despite the efforts of then Under Secretary of State Harriman to prevent the annulment.[104] The Argentine government took the understandable position that "the companies could seek recourse in the courts if they disagreed with the decisions and actions taken."[105] The companies, estimating their investments at about three times the $70 million amount set by Argentina,[106] currently are seeking equitable compensation through negotiations and court actions.[107] Two companies, which had invested about $5 million in Argentina, reportedly have negotiated settlements with the government,[108] but negotiations concerning the larger claims of the remaining companies have reached a stalemate.[109] To date the President has not invoked the Hickenlooper Amendment,[110] although Argentina has charged that aid funds are being slowed down to force settlements.[111] These charges have kept the United States Ambassador busy clearing up "misunderstandings" between the two governments.[112]

[104] N.Y. Times, May 17, 1964, § 3, p. 1, col. 2.

[105] N.Y. Herald-Tribune, Nov. 12, 1963, p. 1, cols. 7-8 (Int'l ed.).

[106] See note 104 *supra.* The estimates by both sides were considerably higher at the time of the cancellation. See N.Y. Herald-Tribune, Nov. 5, 1963, p. 2, col. 7 (Int'l ed.) ($397 million and $200-300 million).

[107] N.Y. Times, May 17, 1964, § 3, p. 14, col. 5.

[108] N.Y. Times, Feb. 16, 1965, p. 47, col. 2. "The settlement was made out of court, and still has to be approved by the courts, although such approval appears to be taken for granted by all parties concerned." N.Y. Times, Feb. 16, 1965, p. 52, cols. 3-4.

[109] N.Y. Times, May 15, 1965, p. 35, col. 1. Two additional tentative settlements of $7 million were concluded recently. N.Y. Times, May 8, 1965, p. 35, col. 3.

[110] See text following note 69 *supra.* His failure to do so has provoked the charge from Senator Hickenlooper that "the executive department just has not obeyed the law on the books." *Hearings on S. 1837 Before the Senate Committee on Foreign Relations,* 89th Cong., 1st Sess. 23 (1965).

[111] N.Y. Times, Feb. 10, 1965, p. 53, col. 2. The Department of State has denied the charge. N.Y. Times, Feb. 11, 1965, p. 64, col. 2.

[112] N.Y. Times, Feb. 17, 1965, p. 61, col. 3. "Authoritative sources said that during a recent conversation with private business leaders, President Illia accused two oil companies not only of using pressure on the American Government but of having influenced ADELA, an organization of European investment concerns, against any major operation in Argentina." *Id.* at p. 67, col. 2.

The *Brazilian* expropriations, which generated the enactment of section 620(e), have been settled in a manner which at least avoided the necessity of its invocation. The I. T. & T. settlement, reportedly involving payment over a twenty-five-year period,[113] obviously resulted less from the threat to apply the amendment than from an over-all improvement in the Brazilian political situation.[114] Moreover, according to one authority on foreign investment, a Director and Vice President of the Standard Oil Company of New Jersey, the settlement's terms do not warrant congressional self-congratulation.[115] The agreement by which Brazil recently purchased the subsidiaries of the American and Foreign Power Company for $135 million, $10 million in cash down payment and the balance in notes payable over forty-five years, was achieved only after prolonged bargaining with the new Brazilian government.[116] Although the president of the company has called the settlement a "fair and reasonable agreement,"[117] he also admitted candidly that "anything we receive would be better than we've been getting."[118] Far from using section 620(e) as leverage, a $1 billion

[113] N.Y. Times, May 29, 1963, p. 3, col. 7 (Int'l ed.).

[114] N.Y. Times, Jan. 30, 1963, p. 4, col. 1 (Int'l ed.); N.Y. Times, June 19, 1964, p. 43, col. 4.

[115] Mr. Emilio Collado concluded that "the United States Government has probably acted to the long-run detriment of both private investment and economic development by its exaggerated acclaim for the settlements reached by several U.S. companies for properties in Brazil which had been seized or seemed likely to be acquired by governmental authorities. The managements of the companies concerned apparently felt that acceptance of the compensation offered was better than the practical alternatives facing them. But it should be remembered that these alternatives seemed to involve at best unreasonable governmental restraints which were likely to make profitable operation impossible; and the terms of compensation—which provide low valuation, partial down payment and decades for payment of the remainder—can only serve to incite the interest of nationalistic groups in other countries." Collado, *Economic Development Through Private Enterprise*, 41 FOREIGN AFFAIRS 703, 714 (1963). See text at notes 117-18 *infra*.

[116] The agreement is reprinted in 4 INT'L LEGAL MATERIALS 72 (1965). The company also agreed to invest 75% of the payments in nonutility operations in Brazil.

[117] N.Y. Times, Nov. 13, 1964, p. 48, col. 3. "The purchase price was agreed upon after a study by an independent European engineering concern." *Ibid.*

[118] N.Y. Times, June 25, 1964, p. 42, col. 8. See text accompanying note 115 *supra*.

aid program concluded within a month of this settlement indicates that it was the incentive of additional assistance from the United States rather than the threat to terminate existing aid commitments that produced the eventual settlement.[119]

Insofar as *Ceylon* is concerned, the very fact that aid to that country had to be suspended demonstrates the Hickenlooper Amendment's failure to achieve its prime objective: the effective protection of private foreign investment.[120] Ceylon refused to bow to diplomatic pressure to settle the claims of two American oil companies for the taking of their installations,[121] pointing out that local remedies were available to the companies and that "the U.S. Government's decision [to suspend aid] cannot fail to impair the prospects of successful negotiation of a lump sum settlement."[122] Furthermore, the termination of aid did not cause Ceylon to change its attitude, for as Mr. Bell told Congress shortly thereafter, "there is no forward progress whatever on the settlement of the claim of the oil companies."[123] Indeed, once the United States had retaliated massively (and ineffectively), Ceylon proceeded to expropriate additional assets of the very same companies.[124] As in the case of Brazil, a recent improvement in the Ceylonese political situation may foreshadow an acceptable compensation agreement,

[119] N.Y. Times, Dec. 15, 1964, p. 11, col. 1.

[120] The attitude of certain members of Congress seems confused on this point. The Administrator of the Agency for International Development, for instance, had to remind Representative Adair that the objective was "not to take AID out of Ceylon but to get an appropriate settlement . . . ." *Hearings on H.R. 5490 Before the House Committee on Foreign Affairs*, 88th Cong., 1st Sess. 118 (1963).

[121] See text at and accompanying note 23 *supra*.

[122] Public Communiqué issued Feb. 8, 1963, by the Government of Ceylon, reprinted in 2 INT'L LEGAL MATERIALS 393, 394 (1963). The communiqué notes that "experience in this instance shows the reliance on foreign aid could entail some measure of surrender of a country's freedom of action in regard to the adoption of policies which receive the full endorsement of its own nationals." *Ibid.* The Prime Minister put it more forcefully. It has been reported that "Mrs. Bandaranaike angrily accused the American Government of trying to dictate terms and said, 'Ceylon is not prepared to dance to the tune of the capitalist countries to obtain aid.'" The Observer (London), Feb. 24, 1963, p. 38, col. 3. See also N.Y. Times, May 3, 1964, p. 4, col. 2.

[123] *Hearings on S. 1276 Before the Senate Committee on Foreign Relations*, 88th Cong., 1st Sess. 274 (1963).

[124] The Daily Telegraph (London), June 6, 1963, p. 20, col. 3.

for which the Hickenlooper Amendment can claim little if any credit.[125]

Finally, the negotiations with *Indonesia* over new oil concessions in 1963 involved a situation where section 620(e) could have become operative. Informed of a report that the United States might terminate aid if Indonesia expropriated the properties of American oil companies,[126] the Indonesian Minister of Basic Industries rejoined that "if it were true and it contains a threat, then Indonesia is prepared to face it."[127] In fact, according to Mr. Wilson Wyatt, the special representative of the President for these negotiations, the amendment was mentioned to President Sukarno only in the context of its being a political fact of life.[128] Whether one agrees with the Department of State that the eventual settlement bestows "great benefits" upon both the oil companies and Indonesia,[129] or sides with the *New York Times* which characterized it editorially as another example of "what Sukarno wants, it seems, Sukarno gets,"[130] it is difficult to single out the effect of the amendment, or

---

[125] Before the recent general elections, the new Finance Minister declared that "he would settle the question of compensation for Western oil distributors for their expropriated property within 24 hours of taking office." N.Y. Times, March 26, 1965, p. 3, col. 1. On June 22, 1965, Ceylon signed an agreement with three oil companies providing for the payment of about $11 million in compensation spread over a five-year period. N.Y. Times, June 23, 1965, p. 9, col. 3 (Int'l ed. 1965). See also The Times (London), June 23, 1965, p. 11, col. 6. The same official noted that the "restoration of the aid would more than offset the amount to be paid in compensation." N.Y. Times, March 22, 1965, p. 12, col. 3. Latest reports indicate that the United States will resume its program of economic aid to Ceylon shortly. N.Y. Times, July 5, 1965, p. 1, col. 6 (Int'l ed.).

[126] See, *e.g.*, N.Y. Times, May 29, 1963, p. 1, col. 2 (Int'l ed.).

[127] N.Y. Herald-Tribune, June 1-2, 1963, p. 2, col. 5 (Int'l ed.). President Sukarno's observations, of course, have been much more colorful. See text accompanying note 140 *infra*.

[128] *Hearings on H.R. 5490 Before the House Committee on Foreign Affairs*, 88th Cong., 1st Sess. 1584 (1963).

[129] *Id.* at 1589 (statement of Mr. Abram Chayes, then Legal Adviser, Department of State).

[130] N.Y. Times, June 4, 1963, p. 6, col. 2 (Int'l ed.). "Faced with the possibility of complete expropriation, the companies have signed an agreement which nationalizes their refining, distribution and marketing facilities in Indonesia within the next 15 years under a complicated compensation plan. In return, they retain their right to continue their $250 million-a-year crude-oil production and export business for at least 20 years under a contract giving Indonesia 60 per cent of their profits." *Ibid.* Reports of the contracts signed in September, 1963, stress the fact that they permit Indonesia to nationalize

to understand how it could have been more effective than a firm diplomatic reminder of Congress' attitude made in the absence of such a statute. Moreover, the fact that Indonesia recently seized the holdings of three oil companies valued at around $300 million less than two years after the conclusion of the above settlement,[131] plus American rubber plantations valued at $80 million[132] and a tire factory valued at $5 million,[133] demonstrates that the Hickenlooper Amendment has failed to deter the taking of American property in this important Asian nation.

One may conclude from this brief survey that the amendment has played a marginal, and perhaps even negative, rôle during its three years of existence.[134] In addition, from a broader perspective than property protection alone, it contains the potential germs to infect United States relations with many foreign countries. The possibility of the outright repeal of section 620(e) is remote, however, since from a political standpoint a Congressman's vote for repeal would be tantamount to a vote against God or motherhood. What, then, can be done to remedy its many defects? This writer believes that at present the only remedial change in the amendment which could possibly obtain congressional approval would be one making its application discretionary and not mandatory. This single change would eliminate many, if not all, of the problems discussed above. True, there are members of Congress who lay great stress upon the amendment's automatic character, believing that its binding effect on the President actually strengthens his hand in negotiating with foreign countries.[135] However, some members, at

---

the local facilities of the companies after twelve years without paying compensation. See, *e.g.*, N.Y. Herald-Tribune, Sept. 28-29, 1963, p. 6, col. 4 (Int'l ed.). While technically accurate, such reports do fail to give sufficient weight to other aspects of the "package" which favor the companies involved.

[131] N.Y. Times, March 20, 1965, p. 1, col. 3.

[132] N.Y. Times, Feb. 27, 1965, p. 1, col. 5.

[133] N.Y. Times, March 24, 1965, p. 1, col. 2.

[134] There have been other instances where the amendment appears to have had little effect, the most recent being the nationalization by Syria of two American oil companies. See, *e.g.*, N.Y. Times, March 5, 1965, p. 1, col. 3.

[135] "My impression has been that as long as you had the discretion to say that our national interests required that aid be continued countries just waited until they found you tied on a vote in the United Nations or in some important international matter and put the pressure on you to back down.

"I heard both business people and your [AID] representatives in the field feel this way about it—that if you had no discretion about the matter, you had

least in 1962, took a different view,[136] and other sections of the Foreign Assistance Act calling for the termination of aid in certain situations permit a waiver by the President if he finds such aid to be in the national interest.[137] Revision of the Hickenlooper Amendment in this way would not seriously weaken either the belief abroad that the United States is determined to protect its foreign investments or their actual protection. Yet it would restore to the President the flexibility he needs to balance this objective along with others in formulating over-all United States foreign policy toward countries which are embroiled in social, economic, and political change.[138]

Then Under Secretary of State Harriman, one of the few administration spokesmen to voice a frank opinion of the Hickenlooper Amendment recently, stated bluntly that "you can't dictate to people. If the United States threatens to take away aid under these conditions there is not a country in the world that would not tell us to go to hell."[139] His admonition already has been borne out literally.[140] If not heeded in the near future, it may well come back to haunt the halls of Congress. While Americans who have invested abroad deserve their government's protection in the fullest, it can be achieved by sounder and more effective methods than the approach taken by the Hickenlooper Amendment.

---

to tell them: 'If you expropriate this property the President can't continue this aid, Congress won't let him. Here is a law that says that'." *Hearings on S. 1276 Before the Senate Committee on Foreign Relations*, 88th Cong., 1st Sess. 275 (1963) (Senator Long).

[136] See Lillich, *supra* note 18, at 411-13.

[137] See, *e.g.*, 76 Stat. 260 (1962), 22 U.S.C. § 2370(c) (Supp. V, 1964).

[138] There has been very little comment by international lawyers on the Hickenlooper Amendment. Compare Metzger, *Property in International Law*, 50 VA. L. REV. 594, 618-22 (1964) (criticizes amendment), with Olmstead, *Foreign Aid As an Effective Means of Persuasion*, 58 A.S.I.L. PROCEEDINGS 205 (1964) (supports amendment). For an excellent article by an experienced diplomat which supports the thesis of this Chapter, see Brown, *The Use of Foreign Aid As an Instrument to Secure Compliance with International Obligations*, 58 A.S.I.L. PROCEEDINGS 210 (1964).

[139] N.Y. Herald-Tribune, Jan. 7, 1964, p. 10, col. 8 (Int'l ed.).

[140] N.Y. Times, March 26, 1964, p. 2, col. 4. "To hell with your aid!" (Statement of President Sukarno.) He recently repeated this observation. N.Y. Times, Feb. 26, 1965, p. 2, col. 1.

IV.

The Investment Guaranty Program

BACKGROUND AND LEGISLATIVE HISTORY

THE POLICY of the United States since World War II has been to encourage American business to invest abroad.[1] One of the government's first efforts to stimulate increased foreign investments was the Investment Guaranty Program (IGP), established by the Economic Cooperation Act (ECA) of 1948[2] and now administered by the Agency for International Development (AID).[3] This program, "designed to encourage private U.S. capital and know-how to participate in furthering the economic development and increasing the productive capacities of underdeveloped countries or areas,"[4] attempts to overcome investor reluctance by providing for "what are essentially insurance contracts between the American investor and the United States insuring the investor against loss due to certain risks."[5] These specific risks now include: (1) the inability to convert foreign currency holdings into dollars; (2) the loss due to expropriation or confiscation; and (3) the loss from damage to tangible property caused by war, revolution, or insurrection.[6]

An interesting self-help device of great potential, the IGP has developed from a modest program into one providing substantial protection to many Americans making investments abroad.[7] More-

[1] Foreign Assistance Act of 1961, § 601(a), 75 Stat. 438, 22 U.S.C. § 2351 (Supp. V, 1964).

[2] Economic Cooperation Act of 1948, ch. 169, § 111(b)(3), 62 Stat. 144 (1948).

[3] INVESTMENT GUARANTIES DIVISION, AID, INVESTMENT GUARANTY HANDBOOK 1 (prelim. draft 1964) [hereinafter cited as HANDBOOK]. For ease of reference, this writer has numbered the unpaginated HANDBOOK beginning with page 1 on the reverse side of the Table of Contents headed by the word "Foreword."

[4] Ibid.

[5] Comm. on Foreign Law, N.Y.C.B.A., The Guaranty Program of the International Cooperation Administration, 14 RECORD OF N.Y.C.B.A. 270 (1959).

[6] FAA of 1961, § 221(b)(1), 75 Stat. 429 (1961), 22 U.S.C. § 2181(b)(1) (Supp. V, 1964).

[7] The total number of specific risk guaranties issued through December 1,

over, the number of countries for which guaranties are available may increase in the near future. Congress, at the same time that it was strengthening and broadening the Hickenlooper Amendment, wrote a provision into the Foreign Assistance Act of 1963 terminating aid to any less developed country which, by December 31, 1965, has not signed an agreement to institute the IGP insofar as the risks of inconvertibility and expropriation are concerned.[8] Although this provision is subject to criticism on other grounds,[9] it certainly cannot lessen the availability of guaranties to American investors. Before describing these guaranties, however, a brief sketch of the IGP's origin and development would be useful.

The IGP had its origin in the Marshall Plan, that imaginative postwar effort devised to assist Europe's economic recovery. The proposal for such a guaranty program to insure private investors against the nonbusiness risks involved in foreign investment was made by a committee of the American Bar Association.[10] The com-

---

1964, was 1261. INVESTMENT GUARANTIES DIVISION, AID, *Cumulative Report of Guaranties Issued by Country through Dec. 31, 1964.* The face amount of all such guaranties was in excess of $2.2 billion. *Ibid.*

[8] Foreign Assistance Act of 1963, § 301(l), 77 Stat. 388 (1963), 22 U.S.C. § 2370(l) (Supp. V, 1964):

> No assistance shall be provided under this Act after December 31, 1965, to the government of any less developed country which has failed to enter into an agreement with the President to institute the investment guaranty program under section 221(b)(1) of this Act, providing protection against the specific risks of inconvertibility under subparagraph (A), and expropriation or confiscation under subparagraph (B), of such section 221(b)(1).

[9] "Was an economy-minded Congress perhaps intent upon attempting to increase the financial risks of the United States, knowing that such surely would ensue from guaranteeing investments in countries which did not really welcome them? Was Congress aware that even if a host country agrees to institute the program, nothing in the agreement requires the country to approve any investments for guaranty purposes? Was Congress aware of the fact that what had hitherto been a successful, voluntary, and cooperative program was being portrayed by this provision, in the eyes of underdeveloped countries, as a device to regulate the management of their affairs, which the program itself had never done before? It is almost incredible that the Administration could have permitted the 1963 foreign aid bill to get away from it so far as to be unable to secure the defeat of that section, and it is trusted that it will be eliminated from the foreign aid legislation at the earliest possible opportunity." Metzger, *Property in International Law,* 50 VA. L. REV. 594, 625 (1964). Indications are that this Congress will extend the deadline for at least one year. See, *e.g.,* H.R. REP. No. 321, 89th Cong., 1st Sess. 32, 56 (1965).

[10] *Hearings on United States Assistance to European Economic Recovery*

mittee, acknowledging that the revival of the continent's economy required vast sums of capital, pointed out that such a program would encourage private capital to flow into Europe despite otherwise unfavorable circumstances. Moreover, using private capital as a recovery tool would cost the government less than direct government assistance and also would permit an earlier termination of the latter. Following the committee's advice, Congress wrote into the ECA of 1948 a *convertibility* guaranty for funds invested in new projects.[11] This guaranty protects the investor against future happenings which might preclude him from converting his foreign currency holdings into United States dollars.[12] "Under these contracts," explain two former AID attorneys:

> AID agrees to exchange dollars for local currency where the local government has prohibited transfer or where the transfer can only be made at a rate less advantageous to the investor than the rate assured by the guaranty contract.[13]

Amendments to the ECA in 1950 authorized, for the first time, a guaranty against *expropriation and confiscation*.[14] Under this guaranty "American investors may assure themselves that they will be compensated by the United States Government in the event of expropriation, in dollars, in accordance with an agreed upon formula for determining loss set forth in the contract."[15] The "investment" which could be guarantied also was broadened to include, in addition to direct equity investments in the foreign economy, capital contributions in the form of loans, shares, and participation in royalties, earnings, profits and the like.[16] The Mutual Security Act (MSA) of 1951 extended the IGP by making it applicable to new investments in all areas to which assistance was authorized, *e.g.*, Europe, the

Before the Senate Committee on Foreign Relations, 80th Cong., 2d Sess., pt. 111, at 1080-1101 (1948); *Hearings on H.R. 2362 Before the House Committee on Foreign Affairs*, 81st Cong., 1st Sess., pt. II, at 631-70 (1949); *Hearings on S. 2197 Before the Senate Committee on Banking and Currency*, 81st Cong., 1st Sess. 75-111 (1949).

[11] European Cooperation Act of 1948, ch. 169, § 111(b)(3), 62 Stat. 144 (1948).

[12] HANDBOOK 14.

[13] Clubb & Vance, *Incentives to Private U.S. Investment Abroad Under the Foreign Assistance Program*, 72 YALE L.J. 475, 492 (1963).

[14] European Cooperation Act of 1950, ch. 220, § 103(c), 64 Stat. 199 (1950).

[15] HANDBOOK 18.

[16] ECA of 1950, ch. 220, § 103(b), 64 Stat. 198 (1950).

Near East, Africa, Asia and the Pacific, and the American Republics,[17] while two years later the MSA of 1953 widened its geographic coverage to all countries with which the United States had agreed to institute the program.[18]

Finally, after the MSA of 1954 had codified the guaranty provisions of all previous acts,[19] the MSA of 1956 rounded out the non-business risk guaranties by providing for a guaranty against war,[20] later expanded to include *war, revolution, or insurrection.*[21] Three years later Congress excluded economically developed countries from the program, thus bringing the IGP full circle from exclusive application to Europe to that area's exclusion from the program's coverage.[22] Today one or more of the above three specific risk guaranties are available for new American investments in over sixty less developed countries.[23]

The Foreign Assistance Act (FAA) of 1961, which contained the last major statutory overhaul of the IGP, strengthened the specific risk guaranties and created a new "all risk" guaranty program. This program permits guaranties against the loss of any loan investment for housing projects,[24] especially in Latin American countries,[25] and against the loss "of any other investment due to such risks as the President may determine. . . ."[26] With many possible risks not covered by the specific risk guaranties,[27] "it was intended that the 'all risk' authority would allow AID to write a guaranty

[17] Mutual Security Act of 1951, ch. 479, § 520, 65 Stat. 384 (1951).

[18] Mutual Security Act of 1953, ch. 195, § 706(b), 67 Stat. 158 (1953).

[19] Mutual Security Act of 1954, ch. 937, § 413, 68 Stat. 846 (1954).

[20] Mutual Security Act of 1956, ch. 627, § 8(k)(3), 70 Stat. 558 (1956).

[21] FAA of 1961, § 221(b)(1)(C), 75 Stat. 429 (1961), 22 U.S.C. § 2181(b)(1)(C) (Supp. V, 1964).

[22] Mutual Security Act of 1959, § 2, 73 Stat. 246-47 (1959).

[23] INVESTMENT GUARANTIES DIVISION, AID, *Countries Where Investment Guaranties Are Available* (Jan. 1, 1965).

[24] FAA of 1961, § 221(b)(2), 75 Stat. 430 (1961), 22 U.S.C. § 2181(b)(2) (Supp. V, 1964).

[25] FAA of 1961, § 224, 75 Stat. 432 (1961), 22 U.S.C. § 2184 (Supp. V, 1964).

[26] See note 24 *supra.*

[27] "These include all the regulatory and revenue producing measures which may appear reasonable to a young nationalistic government, but which make it exceedingly difficult for an investor to continue making profits. Other risks, such as riots and general strikes, which are virtually unknown in the United States, but which occur frequently in less developed countries, also are not covered." Clubb & Vance, *supra* note 13, at 494.

contract in which the covered risks did not have to be defined because 'all risks' would be covered."[28] To be eligible for all risk coverage, whether of "housing" or "extended risk" variety, the investment must "emphasize development projects furthering social progress and the development of small independent business enterprises. . . ."[29]

Despite the IGP's shortcomings, which will be considered in the final Section of this Chapter, the program always has been popular with Congress. As the following table shows, there has been a steady annual increase in the total amount of guaranties which Congress has authorized it to issue.

	Specific Risk	L.A. Housing	Extended Risk
1961	$1 billion	$10 million	$90 million
1962	$1.3 billion	$60 million	$180 million
1963	$2.5 billion	$150 million	$180 million
1964	$2.5 billion	$250 million	$300 million[30]

This increase in the total amount of authorized guaranties also reflects the increased use of the IGP by investors. For instance, applications pending for specific risk guaranties at the end of September, 1963, amounted to $4.7 billion.[31] By the end of March, 1964, pending applications had swelled to $5.6 billion, a jump of $900 million in just six months.[32] During calendar year 1964 AID approved $707.8 million worth of specific risk guaranties: $316

[28] *Id.* at 495.

[29] FAA of 1961, § 221(b)(2), 75 Stat. 430 (1961), 22 U.S.C. § 2181(b)(2) (Supp. V, 1964). While the Senate Report on the Foreign Assistance Act of 1961 mentions "small independent business enterprises, credit unions, cooperatives, low cost housing projects and other similar activities," Congress has not indicated elsewhere what business enterprises it envisages as being within the purview of this provision. S. REP. No. 612, 87th Cong., 1st Sess. 15 (1961).

[30] *Specific Risk*: § 221(b)(1), 75 Stat. 429 (1961); § 104(a)(1), 76 Stat. 256 (1962); § 104(a)(2), 77 Stat. 381 (1963), 22 U.S.C. § 2181(b)(1) (Supp. V, 1964). *Latin American Housing*: § 224(b), 75 Stat. 432 (1961); § 104(c)(1), 76 Stat. 257 (1962); § 104(g)(1), 77 Stat. 382 (1963); § 103(b), 78 Stat. 1010 (1964), 22 U.S.C. § 2184(b) (Supp. V, 1964). *Extended Risk*: § 221(b)(2), 75 Stat. 430 (1961); § 104(a)(3), 76 Stat. 256 (1962); § 103(a)(1), 78 Stat. 1010 (1964), 22 U.S.C. § 2181(b)(2) (Supp. V, 1964).

[31] INVESTMENT GUARANTIES DIVISION, AID, *Quarterly Report of Applications in Process* (Sept. 30, 1963).

[32] INVESTMENT GUARANTIES DIVISION, AID, *Quarterly Report of Applications in Process* (March 31, 1964).

million against expropriation; $261.1 million against inconvertibility; and $130.7 million against war, revolution, or insurrection.[33]

The above statistics demonstrate that the IGP is a going concern playing an important role in the foreign investment picture. They also reveal that foreign investors are most concerned about the non-business risk of expropriation and, to a lesser degree, inconvertibility. While the war risk guaranty took on added importance with the inclusion of revolution and insurrection within its coverage, the chief problem which investors face in the event of revolution or successful insurrection is postrevolutionary expropriation or imposition of restrictive exchange controls. Thus the investor generally has little interest in the war risk guaranty, which protects his investment only from direct damage caused by war, revolution, or insurrection.[34] For this reason the balance of this Chapter will describe and evaluate the specific risk guaranties against expropriation and inconvertibility, by number and size the most important guaranties under the program.

SPECIFIC RISK GUARANTIES

1. *In General.* Since specific risk guaranties only insure against the nonbusiness risks involved, they offer the investor no protection "against failure to make a profit, general devaluation of a foreign currency, inability or failure of a borrower to repay due to commercial losses, or against other normal business risks that attend any investment."[35] Moreover, guaranties against expropriation and inconvertibility are available only in those less developed countries which have agreed to institute this type of coverage under the guaranty program,[36] and even then the specific project must be approved for guaranty purposes by the foreign country before a guaranty contract will be issued.[37] Furthermore, "since the program's

---

[33] INVESTMENT GUARANTIES DIVISION, AID, *Specific Risk Guaranties Issued by Month, Calendar Year 1964.*

[34] HANDBOOK 22-23.

[35] *Id.* at 2.

[36] *Ibid.*

[37] *Id.* at 5. "This approval is in addition to any other approvals an investor must ordinarily obtain from a host country before entering a business venture in that country. It is the responsibility of the investor to obtain this approval

purpose is to facilitate and increase private enterprise's participation in the economic development of less developed countries and areas, these guaranties are not available for existing investment or investment which has been irrevocably committed before an application for guaranties has been filed."[38] However, recognizing that an investor may be unable to delay making or committing himself to an investment, AID in response to a proper application for a guaranty will issue a "waiver" or "no prejudice" letter, valid for one year and renewable for successive one-year periods, which permits the investor to go forward with the investment and still obtain a guaranty if the investment is found to satisfy the other eligibility requirements.[39] Lastly, the proposed investment must meet certain general standards.

> To be eligible for a guaranty, an investment must be approved by A.I.D. as furthering the development of the economic resources and productive capacities of less developed countries and areas. This would include most projects which promote trade, provide economic development, increase production, raise standards of living, or improve technical efficiency. Investments which have a significantly adverse effect upon the U.S. economy or violate national policy objectives will not be eligible for investment guaranties.[40]

The above standards, which are exceedingly vague, give AID almost unchecked discretion in passing upon applications for guaranties.[41]

If the investment meets the above criteria, the investor then must demonstrate that he is eligible for a guaranty under the terms of the FAA.[42] Persons eligible to secure investment guaranties are United States citizens or corporations, partnerships, or other associations created under the laws of the United States or of any state

---

and the U.S. Embassy and A.I.D. Mission in the country are available to assist the investor in obtaining all approvals necessary." *Ibid.*

[38] *Id.* at 3. "However, guaranties are available for new additions, expansions or major changes to existing investment. In order to be covered, the project which is the object of the investment must be new—not the enterprise in which the investment is made." *Ibid.* See also *id.* at 6-7.

[39] *Id.* at 10.

[40] *Id.* at 4.

[41] See generally Note, *The Investment Guaranty Program: Problems of Administration*, 64 COLUM. L. REV. 315, 323-26, 336-37 (1964).

[42] FAA of 1961, § 221(b), 75 Stat. 429-30, 22 U.S.C. § 2181(b) (Supp. V, 1964).

or territory which are "substantially beneficially owned by citizens of the United States."[43] Foreign corporations which are wholly owned subsidiaries of eligible United States corporations also are eligible to secure investment guaranties.[44] The eligibility requirements are reasonable, self-explanatory, and generally productive of no difficulty.

Finally, the nature of the investment deserves careful consideration. Section 223 of the FAA of 1961 defines the term "investment" to include:

> any contribution of capital commodities, services, patents, processes, or techniques in the form of (1) a loan or loans to an approved project, (2) the purchase of a share of ownership in any such project, (3) participation in royalties, earnings, or profits of any such project, and (4) the furnishing of capital commodities and related services pursuant to a contract providing for payment in whole or in part after the end of the fiscal year in which the guaranty is made. . . .[45]

The investment contribution, according to the AID *Handbook*, may take any of the following forms: (1) cash;[46] (2) materials or equip-

---

[43] *Ibid.* "Ordinarily, a company organized under United States law will be considered an eligible investor if more than one-half of the total value of each of the classes of its stock is owned by United States citizens. However, even though stock ownership may meet this mechanical test, the statute may require that a guaranty be denied if a corporate applicant is in fact not substantially beneficially owned by citizens of the U.S. For example, a U.S. corporation whose indebtedness to foreign creditors is so disproportionately large when compared to the size of the U.S. owned equity as to give stockholders only a minimal beneficial ownership interest may be deemed ineligible. Unusual ownership arrangements of the stock of corporate investors which might affect eligibility should be brought to the attention of the Investment Guaranties Division because the penalty for failure of eligibility is loss of coverage even though a contract may be issued." HANDBOOK 6.

[44] A 1963 amendment to the FAA provides that a "foreign subsidiary will be deemed 'wholly' owned by the American corporate parent if less than 5% of the subsidiary's total issued and subscribed share capital is held by persons other than the parent corporation pursuant to the laws of the host country." HANDBOOK 6. See FAA of 1963, § 104(a)(1), 77 Stat. 381 (1963), 22 U.S.C. § 2181(b) (Supp. V, 1964), amending FAA of 1961, § 221(b), 75 Stat. 429-30 (1961).

[45] FAA of 1961, § 223(a), 75 Stat. 431 (1961), 22 U.S.C. § 2183(a) (Supp. V, 1964). The types of investment eligible for coverage are spelled out at HANDBOOK 7.

[46] "If cash is to be invested, it must be dollars or credits in dollars, or foreign currency either (i) purchased with dollars for the purpose of the investment,

ment;[47] (3) patents, processes, or techniques;[48] (4) services;[49] and in some instances (5) loan guaranties.[50]

2. *Expropriation Guaranty*. The most popular guaranty administered by the IGP is the one against the "loss of investment, in whole or in part, in the approved project due to expropriation or confiscation by action of a foreign government. . . ."[51] AID defines "expropriatory action" in its contract of guaranty to mean:

> any action, other than an exchange control action, which is taken, authorized, ratified or condoned by the Government of the Project Country . . . with or without compensation therefor, and which for a period of one year directly results in preventing:
>
> (a) the Investor from receiving payment when due in the currency specified of the principal amounts of or interest on debt Securities, or amounts, if any, which the Foreign Enterprise owes the Investor in connection with the Securities; or
>
> (b) the Investor from effectively exercising its fundamental rights

---

or (ii) otherwise acquired or owned by the investor and transferable into dollars." HANDBOOK 8.

[47] "Both new and used materials may be eligible as investment contributions. If the material or equipment is new, it will ordinarily be valued at its cost to the investor, including transportation and installation costs. If used, it will ordinarily be valued on the basis of depreciated original cost to the investor not exceeding fair market value in the United States in accordance with generally accepted principles of valuation, plus freight and insurance, etc." *Ibid.*

[48] "Congress had made these intangible assets eligible under certain circumstances for guaranty because of the desirability of encouraging the spread of advanced technological methods. However, the licensing of trade names, trademark and good will, often closely associated with the licensing of patents, processes and techniques, is not eligible for guaranty. It should also be understood that, to be eligible for guaranty, the patents, processes and techniques included in the investment should represent predominantly a body of information and experience already in existence." *Ibid.*

[49] "Contributions of engineering and management services will usually be considered an eligible investment when these costs, borne by the investor, are included as a part of the capital contribution to the foreign enterprise and when performed for the purpose of transmitting other eligible investment such as equity capital, processes and techniques, or if such contributions are a part of an investment in the form of a construction contract. However, when these services are to be separately and currently paid for, they are not eligible for the guaranty." *Ibid.*

[50] "Guaranties of repayment given by investors on behalf of the foreign enterprise on loans made by financial institutions to the foreign enterprise may be considered to be eligible investments. Because this type of investment raises special problems, guaranties may not be available in every case." *Ibid.*

[51] FAA of 1961, § 221(b)(1)(B), 75 Stat. 429 (1961), 22 U.S.C. § 2181(b) (1)(B) (Supp. V, 1964).

with respect to the Foreign Enterprise either as shareholder or as creditor, as the case may be, acquired as a result of the Investment; or

(c) the Investor from disposing of the Securities or any rights accruing therefrom; or

(d) the Foreign Enterprise from exercising effective control over the use and disposition of a substantial portion of its property or from constructing the Project or operating the same; or

(e) the Investor from repatriating amounts received in respect of the Securities as Investment Earnings or Return of Capital, which action commences within the eighteen (18) months immediately succeeding such receipt. . . .[52]

Moreover, Congress adopted a broad definition of the term "expropriation" in the FAA of 1961, under which the term "includes but is not limited to any abrogation, repudiation, or impairment by a foreign government of its own contract with an investor, where such . . . [action] is not caused by the investor's own fault or misconduct, and materially adversely affects the continued operation of the project."[53] This definition expands the concept of expropriation to protect "the investor from losses caused by the foreign government's actions which would repudiate its own contracts with the investor, if such action materially affects the continued operation of the project and is not attributable to the investor's own fault or misconduct."[54]

The maximum amount of the guaranty for equity investments generally is 200 percent of the dollar value of the actual amount invested.[55] Guaranties for loan investments are limited to the total

---

[52] AID, *Contract of Guaranty*, para. 1.15 (221 K GT 8-64 Revised).

[53] FAA of 1961, § 223(b), 75 Stat. 432 (1961), 22 U.S.C. § 2183(b) (Supp. V, 1964).

[54] HANDBOOK 18. The definition enables the investor to make "an agreement with the host government relating to the treatment of the investment. If this contract is breached by the host government and the effect of the breach is to prevent operation of the enterprise, the investor may collect under his expropriation guaranty." Clubb & Vance, *supra* note 13, at 494. See also Note, *supra* note 41, at 321.

[55] HANDBOOK 19. "If there are extenuating circumstances which indicate a need for greater protection they will be given consideration. In such cases the investor may request protection for the amount originally invested plus future earnings which the investor can reasonably justify as being retained in the foreign enterprise and which will not completely alter the character of the proposed project." *Ibid.*

value of the principal amount plus a reasonable local rate of interest provided for by the loan instrument.[56] The cost of the expropriation guaranty for either type of investment is one-half of one percent per annum of the current amount of the guaranty.[57] The current amount of the guaranty is the coverage in force during a given year. If an investor previously has stipulated for a maximum amount in excess of the current amount, he must pay a "standby" fee of one-quarter of one percent per annum on the difference between the current and maximum amounts.[58] While the current amount may be raised or lowered each annual contract period, the maximum amount may only be lowered.[59] Flexibility in establishing the current amount of coverage is needed since "guaranty contracts may be written for a maximum term of twenty years from the date of issuance,"[60] and the value of the investment may fluctuate during the contract period.

The expropriation guaranty affords protection against expropriatory or confiscatory actions taken by the foreign government, or by any governmental subdivision thereof, while the contract is in force.

> The nature of the protection offered varies with the form of the investment. In *equity investments*, expropriation will be deemed to have occurred if, for a period of one year, the foreign government prevents the exercise of substantial control over the investment property. . . . In *loan investments*, expropriation will be deemed to have occurred if, for a period of one year, the foreign government directly prevents any repayment of principal or any payments of interest or causes a prevention of such payments as a direct consequence of expropriation of the rights of the investor or of the property of the foreign enterprise.[61]

During the one-year period, "the investor must take all reasonable measures available to pursue and preserve his claims against the

[56] *Ibid.*

[57] *Id.* at 20.

[58] *Ibid.*

[59] "For any contract year the investor has the option to increase up to the maximum amount or decrease the current amount of coverage, or to terminate the contract or reduce the maximum amount of protection by written notice prior to the anniversary date, thereby reducing the fee payable." *Ibid.* "The maximum amount, once reduced, may not be increased in any subsequent contract year." *Id.* at 3.

[60] *Id.* at 9.

[61] *Id.* at 18-19.

expropriating government."[62] These measures "include pursuing judicial as well as administrative remedies."[63]

Assuming that the above measures bear no fruit, the investor after one year may seek reimbursement from AID, which determines whether he is entitled to collect under his guaranty and, if so, the amount to which he is entitled.[64] Any dispute about the decision is to be settled by arbitration in accordance with the rules of the American Arbitration Association,[65] with the award rendered by the arbitrator being final and binding upon the investor and the United States.[66] Once the amount of compensation due under the guaranty is ascertained, the investor assigns his right, title and interest in the investment to AID, whereupon AID shall make immediate payment to the investor of the amount of compensation due.[67]

3. *Inconvertibility Guaranty.* The oldest guaranty under the IGP, and certainly a most important one in the eyes of investors, is the guaranty against inconvertibility.[68] This guaranty protects the investor against the "inability to convert into United States dollars other currencies, or credits in such currencies, received as earnings or profits from the approved project, as repayment or return of the investment therein, in whole or in part, or as compensation for the sale or disposition of all or any part thereof. . . ."[69] Since many potential investors "are seriously concerned that a shortage of foreign exchange may develop which would preclude them from obtaining dollars from dividends, interest, principal or other payments from their investment," this guaranty seeks to alleviate their fears by insuring that

> a means, available at the time the contract is *executed* [,] of converting into U.S. dollars foreign currency representing earnings on, or a return of, capital will continue for the life of the contract. Thus, A.I.D. will not guaranty convertibility in the face of exchange regula-

[62] *Id.* at 21.

[63] Comm. on Foreign Law, N.Y.C.B.A., *supra* note 5, at 273.

[64] HANDBOOK 19.

[65] FAA of 1961, § 635(i), 75 Stat. 457 (1961), 22 U.S.C. § 2395(i) (Supp. V, 1964); AID, *Contract of Guaranty*, para. 10.01 (221 K GT 8-64 Revised).

[66] See AID, *Contract of Guaranty*, para. 10.01 (221 K GT 8-64 Revised).

[67] AID, *Contract of Guaranty*, para. 19.04 (221 K GT 8-64 Revised).

[68] See text at notes 11-13 *supra.*

[69] FAA of 1961, § 221(b)(1)(A), 75 Stat. 429 (1961), 22 U.S.C. § 2181(b)(1)(A) (Supp. V, 1964).

tions and practices under which it would be clear at the time a contract was issued that conversion could be effected only through the guaranty.[70]

However, it does not guaranty against the effects of devaluation or inflation.[71]

While much that has been said in the above sections applies with equal force to the inconvertibility guaranty, it nevertheless has some unique features which warrant separate treatment.[72] The maximum amount of coverage for an equity investment generally is an amount equal to 200 percent of the dollar amount of the original investment.[73] For a loan investment, "the maximum that can be guarantied is the amount (stated in dollars) of the principal, plus the total accruable interest, at a rate considered reasonable in the light of prevailing rates for comparable loans in the foreign country."[74] As with the guaranty against expropriation, the investor must select both a maximum and a current amount of coverage. Irrespective of the type of investment or the maximum amount of coverage purchasable, the investor's recovery is limited to 95 percent of his loss up to the current amount of his guaranty.[75] The cost of the guaranty

[70] HANDBOOK 14.

[71] *Ibid.* This fact has been considered one of the most serious flaws in the IGP. Note, *supra* note 41, at 331.

[72] "Before any guaranty is issued, the investor must secure an approval of the investment by the government of the foreign nation pursuant to the investment guaranty agreement between that nation and the United States. . . .

"Applicants for guaranties against inconvertibility of currency must also show foreign government approval for the remittances of earnings and/or repatriation of capital. In most cases, this approval may take the form of general regulations of the country under which the applicant would qualify; in other cases, a special approval by the foreign government may be required. It is necessary to know what arrangements have been made because the extent of the protection offered under convertibility guaranties will partly depend upon the kinds of currency transfers available in the foreign nation at the time of the contract." HANDBOOK 11-12.

[73] "The additional 100% of the original investment is to allow coverage of accumulated earnings up to the amount of the original investment." *Id.* at 15.

[74] *Ibid.*

[75] AID, *Contract of Guaranty*, para. 13.01 (221 K GT 8-64 Revised). "The 5% margin is to allow for minor fluctuations and such ordinary expenses as transfer commissions, mail or cable transfer charges, transaction stamp taxes, etc., usually borne by foreign investors transferring local currency into dollars." HANDBOOK 14. "This is an administative decision; the statute does not require it." Note, *supra* note 41, at 318 n.26.

against inconvertibility is the same as the cost of an expropriation guaranty, *i.e.*, one-half of one percent per annum of the current amount of the guaranty, plus a "standby" fee of one-quarter of one percent per annum on the difference between the current and maximum amounts.[76]

To establish his right to compensation under the guaranty, the investor must show to AID's satisfaction that he has encountered substantive transfer difficulties and that the adverse situation has existed for thirty consecutive days. "In the case of passive blocking, e.g., where the governing authorities fail either to grant or deny an application for transfer, the contracts provide that after 60 days of such inaction (and in some cases perhaps longer) the investor can invoke the guaranty protection."[77] After AID determines whether and to what extent the investor is entitled to collect under the guaranty, the latter is paid in dollars at the free-market rate or its equivalent on the date of his application for payment.[78] Prior to payment, the investor must transfer his title to the local currency to AID. Once again, disputes are subject to binding arbitration.[79]

AN EVALUATION OF THE PROGRAM

Three years ago the General Counsel of AID stated that "the guaranty technique seems to have been sufficiently proved so that little doubt remains—as did exist some years ago—of its usefulness."[80] One year later a prominent international lawyer affirmed that,

> from the standpoint of providing the investor with an instrument readily available which will reduce or remove the non-economic risks inherent in his investment, the national bilateral guarantee programs are clearly the most effective investment incentive device in the field.[81]

Nevertheless, a number of factors have caused the IGP to be less than a complete success. Reasons advanced for this state of affairs

---

[76] HANDBOOK 16.

[77] *Id.* at 15.

[78] *Ibid.* See AID, *Contract of Guaranty*, paras. 1.33, 13.01 (221 K GT 8-64 Revised).

[79] See note 65 *supra.*

[80] Rubin, *The Investment Guaranty Program of the United States*, 56 A.S.I.L. PROCEEDINGS 77, 81 (1962).

[81] Spofford, Comment, 57 A.S.I.L. PROCEEDINGS 134, 137 (1963).

include administrative hesitancy,[82] foreign policy considerations,[83] the high cost of coverage,[84] the wariness of investors to subject themselves to administrative scrutiny,[85] and the reluctance of foreign countries, many of which equate private investment by foreigners with neo-colonialism, to enter into the agreements which are the condition precedent to the institution of the program in a given country.[86] Gradually, however, the program has become more popular with foreign investors and foreign countries.[87] Even its critics, who complain that "the investment guaranty program so far has achieved only the most limited success,"[88] acknowledge that it "is potentially one of the most effective tools for promoting private investment in underdeveloped countries. . . ."[89]

Weighing the importance of the IGP to the foreign investor presents certain problems. A former Associate General Counsel has pointed out that "it is difficult to assess with precision the achievements of a Program which by its very nature is designed to interact with many other factors to help bring about an environment conducive to private U.S. investment in less developed areas of the world."[90] There is no doubt that the IGP has contributed to bringing capital, technical knowledge, and management experience into many foreign countries which badly need them. However, as in any program where the "basic criterion is the extent to which the project will further American foreign policy objectives,"[91] the interests of investors and AID do not always coincide. The major political limitation is the fact that guaranties are available only in less developed countries, and only in some of these countries at that. True, "if the Investment Guaranty Program is viewed as a specialized tool for

---

[82] See, e.g., Clubb & Vance, supra note 13, at 475-78.

[83] See, e.g., Spofford, note 81 supra.

[84] See, e.g., Hammond, An Evaluation of the Investment Guaranty Program, 15 MAINE L. REV. 67, 83 (1963).

[85] See, e.g., Note, Government Guaranties of Foreign Investments, 66 HARV. L. REV. 514, 518 (1953).

[86] FAA of 1961, § 221(a), 75 Stat. 429 (1961), 22 U.S.C. § 2181(a) (Supp. V, 1964). But see Note, supra note 41, at 330.

[87] See text at and accompanying note 7 supra. See also Appendix E.

[88] Clubb & Vance, supra note 13, at 490.

[89] Id. at 488.

[90] Rivkin, Investment Guaranties and Private Investment, 19 FED. B.J. 357, 364 (1959).

[91] Note, supra note 41, at 324.

facilitating the flow of U.S. investment to less developed areas of the world, it must be judged a useful device,"[92] although its usefulness would be enhanced if guaranties were available in more countries. But why should the IGP be viewed in such limited perspective? Why, as one writer contends, is it "a mistake to view the Program from any other vantage point or as a general-purpose instrument"?[93] Surely the IGP offers fruitful possibilities for expansion into just such a general instrument for the protection of American investment abroad.

Even from the limited viewpoint of the above writer, areas where administrative procedures of the present program need revision are visible. Thus, while the IGP is to be administered "under broad criteria,"[94] AID has refused to define its standards for the issuance of guaranties in any meaningful way.[95] Moreover, a notewriter recently revealed that according to AID "a project's contribution to the economy of the host country is not, as the statute intimates, the sole or even primary criterion."[96] Since the necessity for government approval of a project enables AID "to exercise regulatory supervision over United States investment abroad,"[97] at least in less developed areas of the world, strict adherence to statutory standards should be required. In light of the present balance-of-payments problems of the United States, which caused Congress in 1963 to insert a clause in the FAA requiring AID to consider "the possible adverse effect of the dollar investment under such guaranty upon the balance of payments of the United States,"[98] foreign investors may experience greater difficulties in obtaining guaranties in coming years.

A basic question which must be answered in evaluating the long-range desirability of the IGP is whether it shifts "the burden of fulfilling the capital-importing states' obligations to the capital-exporting states . . . [so as] to encourage them in the wrong direc-

[92] Rivkin, *supra* note 90, at 365.
[93] *Ibid.*
[94] FAA of 1961, § 221(a), 75 Stat. 429 (1961), 22 U.S.C. § 2181(a) (Supp. V, 1964).
[95] See Note, *supra* note 41, at 323-26.
[96] *Id.* at 336.
[97] FATOUROS, GOVERNMENT GUARANTIES TO FOREIGN INVESTORS 107 (1962).
[98] FAA of 1963, § 104(f), 77 Stat. 382, 22 U.S.C. § 2182(g) (Supp. V, 1964.)

tion"?[99] Spofford, while supporting the IGP concept, believes that it "operates by shielding the investor from unwise or illegal acts of the host state rather than deterring such action or encouraging the contrary."[100] Fatouros, on the other hand, concludes that the program has not had unfortunate side effects.[101] What little evidence there is bears him out. Though over $2,200,000,000 worth of specific risk guaranties had been written from the IGP's inception through December 31, 1964,[102] only four claims have been made so far, all by the same company under its guaranty against inconvertibility for investments made in the Congo. The four claims in the amount of $77,175.77 have been paid, and the Congolese francs obtained by AID later were sold for $80,837.98, resulting in a net gain to the IGP of $3,662.21.[103] The requirement of the bilateral agreement and the foreign government's prior approval of the specific project may well serve to screen out investments which otherwise might generate potential claims.[104] Proposals to expand IGP coverage in depth or in geographical area, while desirable on other grounds, undoubtedly would increase such claims.[105] Yet at present a reserve in excess of $250,000,000 exists to pay for any losses which might occur.[106]

In sum, the IGP is not a panacea for the problems created by countries which expropriate or otherwise hamper private United States investments abroad. However, the program certainly is a step in the right direction, and all developments point to its increasing use and probable expansion.[107] While government control over

[99] FATOUROS, op. cit. supra note 97, at 117-18.

[100] Spofford, supra note 81, at 138.

[101] FATOUROS, op. cit. supra note 97, at 117-18.

[102] INVESTMENT GUARANTIES DIVISION, AID, Cumulative Report of Guaranties Issued by Country through Dec. 31, 1964.

[103] AID Press Releases of Feb. 24, 1962, Feb. 20, 1963, Feb. 25, 1964, and Nov. 27, 1964. AID sold the local currency to another government agency needing Congolese francs at the legal rate of exchange.

[104] See text at notes 36-37 supra.

[105] See text accompanying note 9 supra.

[106] HANDBOOK 4. "The contracts of guaranty represent a contingent obligation backed by the full faith and credit of the Government of the United States of America. . . ." Ibid. See FAA of 1963, § 104(e), 77 Stat. 382 (1963), 22 U.S.C. § 2182(e) (Supp. V, 1964). On March 31, 1965, the amount of fees collected was $22.5 million. Letter from V. Lucile Sanders, Records and Reports Section, Investment Guaranties Division, AID, to Richard B. Lillich, May 18, 1965.

[107] On March 31, 1965, AID had 1,262 applications on record having a total

foreign investments has not been appreciable in the past, restrictions against new investments abroad may be in the offing should the present balance of payments situation continue. Since prudent investors increasingly demand guaranty contracts before investing anyway, the time may come when Congress will deem it advisable to compel all prospective United States investors in foreign economies to insure their investments. This step would assure just compensation to the American investor and allow the United States, as subrogee, to pursue claims against foreign countries through diplomatic channels or by arbitration, satisfying them in many cases through lump sum settlements.

value of $9.8 billion. *Ibid.* Both House and Senate committees have recommended doubling the amount of authorized specific risk guaranties from $2.5 to $5 billion. See H.R. REP. No. 321, 89th Cong., 1st Sess. 11, 41 (1965); S. REP. No. 157, 89th Cong., 1st Sess. 10, 46 (1965). See text at notes 30-33 *supra.*

Part Three

PROTECTION FOR THE FUTURE

The self-help measures described in the previous two Chapters represent in order poor and promising methods for protecting Americans whose foreign properties have been taken. Neither one, however, protects the American claimant from his own government when it decides, for unrelated foreign policy reasons, to compromise his claim under an executive agreement. Nor does international law or the Constitution come to his aid. The two Chapters in this Part discuss the promising device of preadjudicating claims before settlement and suggest that if claims are later settled for less than their worth the burden should not fall exclusively on the shoulders of the American business community.

V.

Preadjudication of International Claims

Lump Sum Settlement Agreements

A UNITED STATES NATIONAL whose property is taken by a foreign country traditionally looks to the Department of State for assistance in obtaining redress.[1] As the Department of State pointed out in 1961, it has handled such claims:

> (1) by submitting individual claims through the diplomatic channel to the foreign government concerned and obtaining restitution or compensation; (2) by obtaining a lump sum in settlement of all claims, with the amount paid distributed by an agency of the United States Government; or (3) by an agreement submitting all claims to an international arbitral tribunal for adjudication.[2]

The first alternative, Department of State espousal of a claim, is often the only remedy available to a claimant, especially if his claim is based upon an isolated occurrence.[3] However, beginning with the Jay Treaty of 1794,[4] which provided for the establishment of three international claims commissions,[5] the United States generally opted for the third alternative whenever a large number of claims arose against a foreign country. While this method of claims settlement contributed to the development of international law by

[1] Portions of this Section of the Chapter are taken from Lillich, *International Claims: A Comparative Study of American and British Postwar Practice*, 39 IND. L.J. 465, 468-70, 477-79 (1964).

[2] Department of State Memorandum entitled "Nationalization, Intervention or Other Taking of Property of American Nationals," March 1, 1961, reprinted in 56 AM. J. INT'L L. 166 (1962).

[3] See generally LILLICH & CHRISTENSON, INTERNATIONAL CLAIMS: THEIR PREPARATION AND PRESENTATION ch. VI (1962) [hereinafter cited as LILLICH & CHRISTENSON]. Of course, the claimant may be able to invoke an effective nonlegal sanction, such as the Hickenlooper Amendment, against the foreign country. Also, under the Investment Guaranty Program he may have a remedy against the United States. See Chapters III & IV.

[4] 8 Stat. 116, T.S. No. 105 (effective Feb. 29, 1796).

[5] See Lillich, *The Jay Treaty Commissions*, 37 ST. JOHN'S L. REV. 260 (1963).

substituting a legal for a political determination,[6] it also must be recorded that many international claims commissions during the nineteenth and twentieth centuries failed to function smoothly.[7] Indeed, one of the original Jay Treaty Commissions broke down completely,[8] whereupon the United States resorted to the second alternative and paid a lump sum to the United Kingdom,[9] which in 1803 established the first national claims commission to distribute the fund.[10] Thus, the lump sum settlement–national claims commission device is not an innovation of recent years, but a device dating back to the earliest days of modern international arbitration.[11]

From 1803 until 1941 the United States concluded at least seventeen lump sum claims settlements with foreign countries.[12] These settlements generally were followed by legislation establishing *ad hoc* national commissions, the last of which, the so-called American-Mexican Claims Commission, completed its functions in 1947.[13] By this time, of course, the vast postwar nationalization programs instituted in Eastern Europe were in full swing.[14] The wholesale claims of this period, coupled with the disinterest in international claims commissions shown by the nationalizing countries, brought their immediate usefulness to an end.[15] The United States has utilized

[6] STUYT, SURVEY OF INTERNATIONAL ARBITRATIONS vii (1939).

[7] See generally LILLICH, INTERNATIONAL CLAIMS: THEIR ADJUDICATION BY NATIONAL COMMISSIONS 5-15 (1962) [hereinafter cited as LILLICH].

[8] Lillich, *supra* note 5, at 268-76.

[9] Convention With Great Britain, Jan. 8, 1802, 8 Stat. 196, T.S. No. 108 (effective April 27, 1802).

[10] 43 Geo. 3, ch. 39 (1803). See 3 MOORE, INTERNATIONAL ADJUDICATIONS, MODERN SERIES 349-433 (1931).

[11] See Coerper, *The Foreign Claims Settlement Commission and Judicial Review*, 50 AM. J. INT'L L. 868, 877 (1956).

[12] See LILLICH 8-9. See also LITMANS, THE INTERNATIONAL LUMP-SUM SETTLEMENTS OF THE UNITED STATES 4-45 (1962).

[13] See AMERICAN-MEXICAN CLAIMS COMM'N, REPORT TO THE SECRETARY OF STATE (1948). See generally Wilson, *Some Aspects of the Jurisprudence of National Claims Commissions*, 36 AM. J. INT'L L. 56 (1942).

[14] See generally Drucker, *The Nationalisation of United Nations Property in Europe*, 36 TRANSACT. GROT. SOC'Y 75 (1951); Doman, *Compensation for Nationalized Property in Post-War Europe*, 3 INT'L L.Q. 323 (1950); Doman, *Postwar Nationalization of Foreign Property in Europe*, 48 COLUM. L. REV.. 1125 (1948). See also Gutteridge, *Expropriation and Nationalization in Hungary, Bulgaria and Roumania*, 1 INT'L & COMP. L.Q. 14 (1952); Herman, *War Damage and Nationalization in Eastern Europe*, 16 LAW & CONTEMP. PROB. 498 (1951).

[15] A member of Parliament observed in 1950 that "it has become more and

this method of settlement only twice since World War II,[16] validating
the old War Claims Commission's 1950 prediction that "the trend
of international conditions may direct current national policy to
continue to afford redress in the domestic forum and not through
bilateral tribunals."[17]

This prediction came just when the United States had committed
itself to the use of a semipermanent national commission to distribute
funds received under a 1948 lump sum settlement with Yugoslavia
and under future settlement agreements. The $17 million Yugoslav
Agreement,[18] by far the most successful postwar settlement concluded
by the United States,[19] was aided by the fortuitous fact that, with
Yugoslavia desperately needing foreign exchange, the United States
held $47 million of blocked Yugoslav assets, mostly gold bullion
on deposit with the Federal Reserve Bank in New York. This fact
both induced Yugoslavia to settle its American claims expeditiously
and provided a fund from which they could be paid. Thereupon,
Congress enacted the International Claims Settlement Act of 1949,[20]
which established the International Claims Commission[21] with jurisdiction:

> to receive, examine, adjudicate, and render final decisions with respect
> to claims of the Government of the United States and of nationals
> of the United States included within the terms of the Yugoslav Claims

---

more difficult to get foreign governments to agree to the use of the Mixed
Claims Commission procedure. In fact, the countries with whom we have had
to deal in this matter since the end of the war have in all cases, I think, refused to accept the procedure." 475 H.C. DEB. (5th ser.) 40 (1950) (Mr.
Younger).

[16] These instances were the United States-Italian Conciliation Commission,
established under the Treaty of Peace With Italy, Feb. 10, 1947, art. 83, 61
Stat. 1410, T.I.A.S. No. 1648, and the United States-Japanese Property Commission, established under the Agreement With Japan, June 12, 1952, art. 2,
[1952] 3 U.S.T. & O.I.A. 4054, T.I.A.S. No. 2550. See Summers & Fraleigh,
The United States-Japanese Property Commission, 56 AM. J. INT'L L. 407
(1962). See also text accompanying note 58 *infra*.

[17] WCC REPORT, H.R. DOC. No. 580, 81st Cong., 2d Sess. 9 (1950).

[18] Agreement With Yugoslavia, July 19, 1948, 62 Stat. 2658, T.I.A.S. No.
1803. See Clay, *Aspects of Settling Claims Under the Yugoslav Claims Agreement of 1948*, 43 GEO. L.J. 582 (1955).

[19] See text at notes 25-34 *infra*.

[20] 64 Stat. 12 (1950), as amended, 22 U.S.C. §§ 1621-27 (1958).

[21] See ICC, FIRST-EIGHTH SEMIANN. REPS. (1950-1954). See also Rode,
The International Claims Commission of the United States, 47 AM. J. INT'L L.
615 (1953).

Agreement of 1948, or included within the terms of any claims agreement . . . concluded between the Government of the United States and a foreign government . . . similarly providing for the settlement and discharge of claims of the Government of the United States against a foreign government arising out of the nationalization or other taking of property, by the agreement of the Government of the United States to accept from that government a sum in en bloc settlement thereof.[22]

Although the Commission was renamed the Foreign Claims Settlement Commission (hereinafter FCSC) in 1954, when it also assumed the functions of the War Claims Commission,[23] adjudication of nationalization claims under the above statute still "constitutes the Commission's greatest area of current and potential activity."[24]

The success of the lump sum settlement–national claims commission device, at least from the perspective of the American investor whose property has been taken, depends almost exclusively upon one fact: the adequacy of the compensation obtained from the foreign country.[25] In the case of the Yugoslav Claims Agreement of 1948, awards were made in the amount of $18,817,904.89, ex-

---

[22] 64 Stat. 13 (1950), 22 U.S.C. § 1623(a) (1958).

[23] The President's Reorganization Plan No. 1 of 1954, 19 Fed. Reg. 3985 (1954) abolished the War Claims and International Claims Commissions and transferred their functions, officers, and employees, as well as the functions of the commissioner provided for in Joint Resolution No. 36, Aug. 4, 1939, ch. 421, 53 Stat. 1199, to distribute funds to claimants from the Litvinov Assignment collections, to the FCSC. The War Claims Commission had been established by the War Claims Act of 1948, 62 Stat. 1240 (1948), as amended, 50 U.S.C. app. §§ 2001-16 (1958). See WCC, FIRST-TENTH SEMIANN. REPS. (1950-1954). For a brief survey of the war claims programs completed by the FCSC after its establishment in 1954, see Re, *The Foreign Claims Settlement Commission: Completed Claims Programs*, 2 VA. J. INT'L L. 101, 115-19 (1963).

[24] *Id.* at 104.

[25] The FCSC's Chairman rightly emphasizes the distinction between the two phases of the device: (1) the negotiation of the settlement agreement, which is "the responsibility of the Department of State"; and (2) the adjudication of claims filed thereunder, which is "the precise responsibility of the Foreign Claims Settlement Commission. . . ." Re, *Domestic Adjudication and Lump-Sum Settlement as an Enforcement Technique*, 58 A.S.I.L. PROCEEDINGS 39, 40-41 (1964). While the Commission is not to be held accountable for inadequate lump sum settlements, neither should it place undue value upon its activities when the "enforcement technique" of which it is a part provides only partial compensation for American claimants.

clusive of interest, against a fund of $17,000,000.[26] Thus claimants received compensation for approximately 90 percent of the principal amount of their adjudicated awards. After the lump sum settlement with Panama in 1950,[27] a fund of $400,000 provided compensation for awards aggregating $441,891.84.[28] Excluding interest once again,[29] claimants received approximately 90 percent on their awards. Of the 10,929 claims filed with the FCSC following the $40,000,000 settlement agreement with Poland in 1960,[30] the Commission already has decided more than 3,700 with awards aggregating approximately $22,000,000.[31] Assuming that this amount includes interest,[32] a rough estimate indicates that about 65 percent of the principal *and* interest on Polish awards will be paid.[33] It is too early to judge the adequacy of the compensation payable to claimants under the Claims Agreement with Yugoslavia concluded on November 5, 1964.[34]

If the above lump sum settlements covered all countries which had taken American property since World War II, one might possibly agree with the statement, made by the United States in its amicus curiae brief in *Banco Nacional de Cuba v. Sabbatino,* that "the efforts of the Executive Branch to achieve general compensation for claims of all United States nationals affected by foreign national-

---

[26] FCSC, Settlement of Claims by the Foreign Claims Settlement Commission of the United States and Its Predecessors 4 (1955) [hereinafter cited as FCSC 1955 Rep.]. See text accompanying note 29 *infra.*

[27] Convention With Panama, Jan. 26, 1950 [1950] 1 U.S.T. & O.I.A. 685, T.I.A.S. No. 2129.

[28] FCSC 1955 Rep. 217.

[29] The Commission apparently refused to award interest on Panamanian claims on the ground that it "could not be satisfied from the proceeds of such a fund." *Id.* at 226. Nevertheless, it had allowed interest on Yugoslav claims despite the fact that the principal amount of the awards exceeded the lump sum. *Id.* at 18-20, 53-54. See text accompanying note 32 *infra.*

[30] Agreement With Poland, July 16, 1960 [1960] 11 U.S.T. & O.I.A. 1953, T.I.A.S. No. 4545. See Rode, The *American-Polish Claims Agreement of 1960,* 55 Am. J. Int'l L. 452 (1961).

[31] Re, *supra* note 25, at 42.

[32] The FCSC has held that awards are entitled to interest under the Polish claims program. FCSC, Seventeenth Semiann. Rep. 47-49 (1962).

[33] This percentage compares favorably with the 90% return on Yugoslav and Panamanian awards, where the FCSC's computation of amounts awarded excluded interest.

[34] Agreement With Yugoslavia, Nov. 5, 1964, 51 Dep't State Bull. 830 (1964), T.I.A.S. No. 5750.

izations . . . have in the past met with success."[35] Unfortunately, where the United States neither has leverage over the foreign country, as it once had in the case of Yugoslavia, nor wishes to make economic concessions as an inducement to settle claims, as it did in the case of Poland,[36] American claimants have not been able to look to lump sum settlements. Instead, they have had to rely upon the FCSC's "preadjudication" of their claims, with the Commission's awards often paid in part from the vested assets of the foreign country.[37]

THE PRACTICE OF PREADJUDICATION

The technique of preadjudicating claims, which gradually is supplanting the traditional lump sum settlement–national claims commission device, dates back ten years. In 1955, realizing that Bulgaria, Hungary, and Rumania had no intention of negotiating satisfactory settlements compensating American claimants for the nationalization of their property, Congress enacted Title II of the International Claims Settlement Act, providing for the vesting and liquidation of the blocked assets of these countries.[38] Simultaneously, Congress added a new Title III which authorized the FCSC to preadjudicate the amount and validity of claims by United States nationals against the three countries.[39] During the four-year

[35] Brief for the United States as Amicus Curiae, p. 30, Banco Nacional de Cuba v. Sabbatino, 376 U.S. 398 (1964), 2 INT'L LEGAL MATERIALS 1019 (1963).

[36] See LILLICH 108. The economic factors underlying lump sum settlements are the subject of an extensive study under the research program on Procedural Aspects of International Law being conducted by the International Legal Studies Program of the Syracuse University College of Law.

[37] The term "preadjudication," first used by this writer in *The Foreign Claims Settlement Commission and the Protection of Foreign Investment*, 48 IOWA L. REV. 779 (1963), refers to the FCSC's unilateral determination of claims against a foreign country before the conclusion of a lump sum settlement with it. The term has been accepted by the Commission and the Department of State. See *Hearings Before the Subcommittee on Inter-American Affairs of the House Committee on Foreign Affairs*, 88th Cong., 2d Sess. 32, 142 (1964) [hereinafter cited as *Hearings*].

[38] 69 Stat. 562 (1955), 22 U.S.C. § 1631 (1958).

[39] 69 Stat. 570 (1955), 22 U.S.C. § 1641 (1958). See Ujlaki, *Compensation for the Nationalization of American-Owned Property in Bulgaria, Hungary and Rumania*, 1 N.Y.L.F. 265 (1955). Title III also authorized the adjudication of certain claims against Italy and the Soviet Union, awards being paid from funds received under the Lombardo Agreement and the Litvinov Assignment. See Agreement With Italy, Aug. 14, 1947, 61 Stat. 3962, T.I.A.S. No. 1759, and Roosevelt-Litvinov correspondence reprinted in 28 AM. J. INT'L L. 10 (Supp. 1934). See generally FCSC, TENTH SEMIANN. REP. (1959).

period ending August 9, 1959, the Commission rendered awards in 1,868 of 4,189 claims in the amount of $171,597,163, including interest, against funds totaling about $26,823,415.[40] Depending upon the country involved, claimants receiving varying percentages of their adjudicated awards: Bulgarian claimants, 47.8 percent; Hungarian claimants, 2.1 percent; and Rumanian claimants, 26 percent.[41]

The above statute specifically provided that the partial payment received by claimants was not to "extinguish such claim[s], or to be construed to have divested any claimant, or the United States on his behalf, of any rights against the appropriate foreign government or national for the unpaid balance of his claim or for restitution of his property."[42] Thus, while the claims were to be adjudicated prior to lump sum settlements with the foreign countries, Congress clearly envisaged the negotiation of such agreements after the FCSC had concluded its functions. That Congress actually thought preadjudication would facilitate the conclusion of satisfactory settlements is apparent from Title IV of the International Claim Settlement Act, enacted in 1958 to provide for the preadjudication of Czech nationalization claims and their partial payment from vested Czech assets.[43] The Act hopefully provided for the contingency of a settlement agreement "within one year following the date of enact-

[40] See FCSC, THIRTEENTH SEMIANN. REP. 7 (1960), and FCSC, ELEVENTH SEMIANN. REP. 1 (1959). The three funds broke down as follows: *Bulgarian* $3,143,398 (see Article II[a] of the Agreement With Bulgaria, July 2, 1963 [1963] 14 U.S.T. & O.I.A. 970, T.I.A.S. No. 5387); *Hungarian*, $1,653,647 (see *Staff Memorandum on Claims Programs Administered by the Foreign Claims Settlement Commission*, Senate Committee on Foreign Relations, 88th Cong., 1st Sess. 5 [1963]); and *Rumanian*, $22,026,370 (see Article III[a] of the Agreement With Rumania, March 30, 1960 [1960] 11 U.S.T. & O.I.A. 318, T.I.A.S. No. 4451).

[41] The FCSC rendered awards in 217 of 391 *Bulgarian* claims in the amount of $6,571,825; in 1,153 of 2,725 *Hungarian* claims in the amount of $80,296,047; and in 498 of 1,073 *Rumanian* claims in the amount of $84,729,291. FCSC, THIRTEENTH SEMIANN. REP. 7 (1960). For the funds available to pay these awards, see note 40 *supra*. The percentages given in the text are rough ones, since the statute's provision calling for payment in full of the principal amount of each award of $1,000 or less and the payment in the amount of $1,000 on account of the principal of each award of more than $1,000 worked a slight distortion in the distribution picture. 69 Stat. 573 (1955), 22 U.S.C. § 1641i(a) (1958). Also, the United States deducts 5% of each claims fund to cover the FCSC's administrative expenses. 69 Stat. 571 (1955), 22 U.S.C. § 1641a (1958). See text accompanying note 46 *infra*.

[42] 69 Stat. 574 (1955), 22 U.S.C. § 1641l (1958).

[43] 72 Stat. 527 (1958), 22 U.S.C. § 1642 (1958).

ment of this title. . . ."[44] Final figures on Czech claims, which the Commission had finished adjudicating by September 15, 1962, show that the FCSC made 2,630 awards in 3,976 claims in the amount of $113,645,205.41, including interest, against an $8,540,768.41 fund.[45] Thus, Czech claimants received compensation for approximately 7.5 percent of their awards.[46]

About the time the Commission completed the Czech program, Congress enacted an overlooked piece of legislation which, to quote the FCSC's Chairman in another context, "indicates in a striking manner the extent to which the Commission's broad experience in claims adjudication may be effectively utilized in new areas."[47] The legislation did not concern nationalization claims, but rather claims by United States property owners against Canada for damage caused by the Gut Dam in the St. Lawrence River. Following the institution of several actions in the United States District Court for the Northern District of New York in 1952 and 1953, the Canadian government had made an offer to representatives of the property owners to submit the matter to arbitration. The claimants were unable to conclude an agreement with Canada, however, and on May 10, 1954, they requested the Department of State's assistance.[48] Negotiations between the two governments on an agreement to arbitrate the claims progressed smoothly until the district court ordered hearings in the above actions. Canada then broke off negotiations pending the final disposition of the actions, which occurred on April 22, 1957, when the United States Supreme Court refused to review the district court's dismissal of the actions for want of jurisdiction over Canada.[49]

[44] 72 Stat. 527 (1958), 22 U.S.C. § 1642a(c) (1958).

[45] See FCSC, SEVENTEENTH SEMIANN. REP. 143 (1962). See also *Staff Memorandum on Claims Programs Administered by the Foreign Claims Settlement Commission*, Senate Committee on Foreign Relations, 88th Cong., 1st Sess. 8 (1963).

[46] This percentage also is a rough one for the reasons given in note 41 *supra*. Actually, "the percentage of the amount of awards in excess of $1,000 to be paid under this program was 5.3." FCSC, SEVENTEENTH SEMIANN. REP. 143 n. 16 (1962).

[47] Re, *The Foreign Claims Settlement Commission: Its Functions and Jurisdiction*, 60 MICH. L. REV. 1079, 1097 (1962).

[48] The facts given in this and subsequent paragraphs are taken from a Department of State letter to the House Committee on the Judiciary. H.R. REP. No. 2089, 87th Cong., 2d Sess. 5-7 (1962) (letter from Hon. Frederick G. Dutton).

[49] Oster v. Canada, 144 F. Supp. 746 (N.D.N.Y. 1956), *aff'd sub nom.*

Although the Department of State continued to press Canada for a settlement of the claims or for their submission to a tribunal for adjudication, its efforts were unavailing. Negotiations were at an impasse when a bill was introduced in 1962 authorizing the FCSC to investigate the claims and submit a detailed report thereon to the President for such action as he might deem appropriate. The Department of State expressed no objection to the enactment of such legislation. Indeed, in view of a 1958 engineering investigation made by the International Joint Commission at the direction of the United States and Canada, which concluded that the operation of Gut Dam was only one of various factors contributing to the property damage, it admitted that it did not have

> sufficient information to determine the amount of the damage which is attributable to Gut Dam. Such information could be obtained from an investigation and analysis of the several factors which caused the changes and fluctuations in the water level of Lake Ontario and from evidence furnished by those who sustained damage. . . .[50]

The Department noted, however, that the draft bill "could be interpreted as stating the conclusion that Gut Dam caused damage. It is believed that the Foreign Claims Settlement Commission should be authorized to determine whether Gut Dam caused damage and if it did, the amount of such damage."[51]

The Gut Dam Claims Act,[52] which incorporated the above suggestion and two other minor amendments,[53] authorized and directed the FCSC "to accept" claims of United States citizens for damages caused during 1951 and 1952 by Gut Dam and "to determine" their validity and amount.[54] As soon as practicable after this determination, the Commission was to submit to the President, for such

Clay v. Canada, 238 F.2d 400 (2d Cir.), *cert. denied*, 353 U.S. 936 (1957). See Griffin, *Adjective Law and Practice in Suits Against Foreign Governments*, 36 TEMP. L.Q. 1, 10-11 (1962).

[50] HOUSE REPORT, *supra* note 48, at 7.
[51] *Ibid.*
[52] Pub. L. No. 87-587, 76 Stat. 387 (1962).
[53] HOUSE REPORT, *supra* note 48, at 4, 7.
[54] Pursuant to its statutory authority, the FCSC gave notice that claims were to be filed with it on or before October 15, 1963. FCSC Reg. § 560.1, 27 Fed. Reg. 11229 (1962). See also FCSC Reg. § 560.2, 27 Fed. Reg. 11229-30 (1962). If Canada and the United States reached an agreement providing for arbitration or adjudication of the claims, the FCSC was to terminate its investigation and determination of them. Pub. L. No. 87-587, § 5, 76 Stat. 388 (1962).

action as he might deem appropriate, a list of claims determined to be valid and their amount, as well as a list of claims determined to be invalid.[55] The statute expressly provided that nothing contained therein "shall be construed as authorizing the Commission to pay or certify for payments any claim filed hereunder."[56] Since the vesting of Canadian assets to make partial payments was out of the question, the statute thus represented Congress' first attempt to have claims preadjudicated with no compensation fund at hand. The FCSC's Chairman rightly noted:

> The rôle of the Commission under the Lake Ontario [Gut Dam] Program represents a valuable innovation in the field of international claims adjudication. Significantly, investigation and adjudication of international claims now precede negotiations designed to effect settlement.[57]

The Objectives of Preadjudication

The preadjudication of international claims with or without compensation represents a promising approach to the problem of compensating American claimants that bears more examination than it has received to date. From the point of view of prompt compensation, of course, it has little to offer. Viewed from a wider perspective, however, it may well aid the United States in its efforts to obtain more adequate compensation from recalcitrant foreign countries. The Senate Committee on the Judiciary, evaluating the Gut Dam Claims Act, explained that

> while this legislation is in no way a substitute for a negotiated settlement with Canada, it does seem to the committee to be a step in the right direction. Apparently additional investigation is necessary to determine the amount of damage which is attributable to Gut Dam, inasmuch as the total damage is described as having resulted from a combination of factors. This legislation would make it possible for such investigations to go forward and, it is hoped, would contribute to reopening negotiations with Canada.[58]

[55] Pub. L. No. 87-587, § 3, 76 Stat. 387 (1962).
[56] Pub. L. No. 87-587, § 4(c), 76 Stat. 387 (1962). Reasons for the inclusion of such a provision are given in the text at notes 110-14 *infra*.
[57] Re, *supra* note 25, at 46. See text accompanying note 58 *infra*.
[58] S. Rep. No. 1750, 87th Cong., 2d Sess. 5 (1962). On March 25, 1965, the United States and Canada signed an agreement providing for the establishment of a three-member international arbitral tribunal, known as the Lake

These purposes have been inherent in previous claims programs administered by the FCSC, although not always in conjunction and never in the fact situation involved here.

The problem of investigating and evaluating claims prior to a settlement agreement is an old one.[59] Since the Department of State has no formal method of receiving and registering claims, much less preadjudicating them,[60] "the cases are usually in an undeveloped stage and trustworthy evidence of their soundness and of the amount of damage sustained may be lacking."[61] Attempts to remedy the same problem were made in England during the 1950's. Section 3(a) of the Foreign Compensation Act of 1950[62] provides that when the British government contemplates a compensation agreement with a foreign country, it may, by Order in Council, require its Foreign Compensation Commission (the FCSC's counterpart)[63] to register claims to participate in such compensation and make a report thereon.[64] Three such Orders were made in 1954

Ontario Claims Tribunal—United States and Canada, to adjudicate the Gut Dam claims. Agreement with Canada, March 25, 1965, 52 DEP'T STATE BULL. 643 (1965), T.I.A.S. No. ————. After the Senate has given its advice and consent to the ratification of the agreement by the President, the claimants will be informed about the procedures for filing claims with this tribunal. Department of State Press Release No. 60, March 25, 1965. Pursuant to Section 5 of the Gut Dam Claims Act, the FCSC will terminate its investigation and determination of these claims and transfer its records to the Secretary of State for use by the Agent for the United States in the forthcoming arbitration. Pub. L. No. 87-587, § 5, 76 Stat. 388 (1962).

[59] See LILLICH 110-11.

[60] See LILLICH & CHRISTENSON 89-90. Congressman Fascell, who introduced the bill which became the Cuban Claims Act of 1964, argued that "the present system of filing with the State Department and at some time in the future allowing the Department to negotiate with a new Government of Cuba and then determining pro rata payment to claimants, who may or may not exist, is too loose a system, we feel, in view of the extent of the losses which American businessmen have suffered. Therefore, we think it is time to formalize the procedure for recording claims. . . ." *Hearings* 8. The Department of State agreed. *Id.* at 141-42 (remarks of Hon. Leonard C. Meeker). See text following note 89 *infra*.

[61] 3 WHITEMAN, DAMAGES IN INTERNATIONAL LAW 2067 (1943).

[62] Foreign Compensation Act, 1950, 14 Geo. 6, c. 12, § 3(a).

[63] For a brief description of the Foreign Compensation Commission, see Lillich, *supra* note 1, at 479-88. See also Lillich, *International Claims: A Comparative Study of United Kingdom and United States Practice*, in 17 CURRENT LEGAL PROBLEMS 157 (1964).

[64] Under § 3(b) the government may require the Commission "to determine" the claims. Apparently this section has not been utilized yet. Brooks,

authorizing the registration of claims against Bulgaria, Hungary, and Rumania.[65] Drucker correctly predicted the advantages of such registration when he observed that the Commission's report of the above claims would

> no doubt be of great value to the United Kingdom representatives in their discussions for compensation with the various governments, as it will enable them to present a closely examined and verified statement as to British claims against the countries concerned. The previous practice of presenting merely general estimates as to British claims on the basis of insufficient information proved no doubt detrimental to British interests, as is shown by the low dividends which are expected in the Czechoslovak and Yugoslav cases.[66]

That the above registration assisted British negotiators has been attested to by a Foreign Office official.[67] Whether it has resulted in more satisfactory settlements is still, for want of sufficient statistical data, an open question.[68] Awards against Czechoslovakia and Yugoslavia, which negotiated lump sum settlements of £8,000,000[69] and £4,500,000[70] prior to the institution of registration, totaled £89,768,175 and £25,120,582, respectively.[71] Thus a Czech claimant received 8.9 percent and a Yugoslav claimant 17.9 percent of his award.[72] On the other hand, claimants against Bulgaria, which

---

Registration of International Claims Under the Foreign Compensation Act, 1950, 44 TRANSACT. GROT. SOC'Y 187, 197 (1959).

[65] [1954] 1 Stat. Instr. 915 (No. 220), 921 (No. 219), 929 (No. 221). See FCC, FOURTH REPORT, CMD. No. 9241, at 6-7 (1954).

[66] Drucker, *Compensation for Nationalized Property: The British Practice,* 49 AM. J. INT'L L. 477, 485-86 (1955).

[67] Brooks, *op. cit. supra* note 64, at 197. Backing up this attestation is the fact that the Commission has been authorized to register additional claims against Czechoslovakia and the Soviet Union. [1960] 2 Stat. Instr. 1560 (No. 849), as amended, [1961] 1 Stat. Instr. 1302 (No. 585); [1959] 1 Stat. Instr. 1407 (No. 1968).

[68] Martin, *The Distribution of Funds Under the Foreign Compensation Act,* 1950, 44 TRANSACT. GROT. SOC'Y 243, 249 (1959).

[69] British-Czech Agreement, Sept. 28, 1949, CMD. No. 7797 (T.S. No. 60 of 1949).

[70] British-Yugoslav Agreement, Dec. 23, 1948, CMD. No. 7600 (T.S. No. 2 of 1949).

[71] FCC, SIXTH REPORT, CMD. No. 9849, at 4 (1956).

[72] In fact they received a slightly larger percentage, since both funds were increased by income derived from the investment of incoming instalments. See FCC, TWELFTH REPORT, CMND. No. 1834, at 3 (1962). Otherwise, the percentages given in the text are accurate, since the FCC normally pays the same

negotiated a £400,000 settlement agreement[73] after the Foreign Compensation Commission had registered claims, received payments amounting to 32.6 percent of their adjudicated awards.[74] The Bulgarian experience cannot be considered conclusive evidence of the usefulness of registration, of course, for as Martin has observed, "the size of a compensation fund obtainable from an expropriating Government is determined neither exclusively nor predominantly by the particulars which can be presented of the claims put forward."[75] Nevertheless, it establishes a prima facie case for the effectiveness of the registration device, which now appears to be a permanent fixture on the British scene.[76]

In 1957, several years after the initial registration Orders and after Drucker's suggestion that "the new British practice of registering and examining claims as a preliminary step to negotiations for lump-sum settlements should be adopted generally,"[77] the FCSC, at the request of the Department of State, began the registration of 17,000 Polish claims.[78] This informal registration had as its purpose the collection of data for use by United States negotiators of the Polish Claims Agreement of 1960.[79] Once again, want of statistical information precludes a conclusion about the registration's effectiveness.[80] It is safe to say, however, that the registration plus actual adjudication of the Gut Dam claims would not have lessened the bargaining position of the United States had negotiations with Canada proceeded to a lump sum settlement.[81]

---

percentages to all claimants who have received awards. Compare the FCSC's practice in the text accompanying note 41 *supra*.

[73] British-Bulgarian Agreement, Sept. 22, 1955, Cmd. No. 9625 (T.S. No. 79 of 1955).

[74] FCC, THIRTEENTH REPORT, CMND. No. 2175, at 8 (1963). Moreover, the classes of claims settled by this agreement and the eligibility requirements contained therein were both wider than those contained in the Czech and Yugoslav settlements, with a resultant lowering of the percentage payable on awards. See Articles 1 & 3 of the British-Bulgarian Agreement, note 73 *supra*.

[75] Martin, *op. cit. supra* note 68, at 249-50.

[76] See text accompanying note 67 *supra*.

[77] Drucker, *supra* note 66, at 486. (Emphasis omitted.)

[78] FCSC, THIRTEENTH SEMIANN. REP. 4 (1960).

[79] FCSC, FOURTEENTH SEMIANN. REP. 17 (1961). See note 30 *supra*.

[80] But see text at notes 32-33 *supra*.

[81] "After we determine what the damages are, if any, that have been sustained by these American citizens, the law provides that we make a report to the President of the United States, who will then take such action as he may

The problem of securing adequate compensation from the foreign country, already raised by the above two paragraphs, is a difficult one. Certainly the second purpose behind the Gut Dam Claims Act, equally as important as the investigation and evaluation of claims, was to put pressure upon Canada to settle them. The Senate Report, for instance, speaks of its hope that the Act will "contribute to re-opening active negotiations with Canada,"[82] a wish which fortunately came true in relatively short order.[83] Among the various self-help measures that the United States has used in its efforts to achieve larger settlements, though, the device of preadjudicating claims has met with less success than expected. Of the four countries—Bulgaria, Czechoslovakia, Hungary, and Rumania—against which the FCSC has rendered awards from vested assets, only Rumania and Bulgaria have reached subsequent settlements with the United States, settlements which under the circumstances were less than adequate.[84] Rumanian claimants received 28.9 percent of their preadjudicated claims following a 1960 lump sum agreement with that country, but 26 percent came from vested assets and only 2.9 percent from additional funds payable under the agreement. Bulgarian claimants, who had received 47.8 percent of their awards from vested assets, obtained an additional 6.1 percent under a 1963 settlement with that country, giving them a total recovery of 53.9 percent. Thus, in concluding the first two claims agreements to follow FCSC preadjudication, the Department of State thought it necessary to waive 71.1 and 46.1 percent of the amount of the Commission's awards. Settlements now in the process of negotiation with Czechoslovakia and Hungary promise no better results.[85]

Granted that Canada might have had more respect for the FCSC's determinations than the above Communist countries, and

---

deem appropriate. Clearly, what is intended here is that negotiations with Canada will result, but the advantage is that we will then know precisely what the damages are." *Hearings* 19 (remarks of Hon. Edward D. Re). See text accompanying note 58 *supra*.

[82] S. REP. No. 1750, 87th Cong., 2d Sess. 5 (1962).

[83] See text accompanying note 58 *supra*.

[84] See text at and accompanying notes 40 & 41 *supra*. See generally Christenson, *The United States-Rumanian Claims Settlement Agreement of March 30, 1960,* 55 AM. J. INT'L L. 617 (1961), and Lillich, *The United States-Bulgarian Claims Agreement of 1963,* 58 AM. J. INT'L L. 686 (1964).

[85] Indeed, they may be even less satisfactory. In this regard, see the discussion of the "Keating Resolution" in Chapter VI.

therefore have been more amenable to a satisfactory lump sum settlement if other procedures had not been devised, there is no reason to expect any foreign country to acquiesce automatically in the United States' unilateral determination of the extent of its international liability. Nevertheless, presumably foreign countries will pay more attention to preadjudicated claims than they would to the Department of State's unsubstantiated allegations concerning the number and amount of claims.[86] Therefore, the Gut Dam Claims Act, besides contributing to the speedy settlement of a decade-old dispute with Canada, represents a promising new precedent for the FCSC. Heretofore its work has been with war and nationalization claims, for which compensation has come from lump sum settlements and vested assets. Even more important than the ultilization of the Commission to handle a different category of claims, however, is the fact that for the first time Congress instructed the FCSC to preadjudicate claims with no compensation fund at hand.[87] This new approach reflects a change in legislative policy,[88] a change which raises some problems to be considered in the next section of this Chapter. These problems can be evaluated in better perspective after a brief description of how Congress, in the Cuban Claims Act of 1964, applied the Gut Dam precedent to the claims of United States nationals against Cuba.

The Problems of Preadjudication

When a lump sum settlement cannot be negotiated and assets to vest are not in the United States, Americans who have had property taken by foreign countries have been almost remediless.[89]

---

[86] One reason being that the FCSC will have had the opportunity to narrow down both the number and amount of these claims. For example, in the case of the Gut Dam claims, "although it was originally estimated that approximately 1,300 property owners had suffered damages, actually only 540 filed claims with the Commission." Re, *supra* note 25, at 45.

[87] The Polish claims, it will be recalled, were only registered. See text at notes 77-80 *supra*.

[88] "The question of the utilization of the existing personnel and facilities of the Commission in carrying out the provisions of H.R. 10955 prior to the conclusion of any claims settlement with the Government of Canada or the enactment of legislation providing for a final settlement of such claims, is, of course, a matter of legislative policy." HOUSE REPORT, *supra* note 48, at 5 (letter from Hon. Edward D. Re).

[89] The remedies discussed in Parts One and Two of this book have been available to relatively few claimants.

The recent Cuban nationalizations are a case in point. Beginning on May 17, 1959, the Castro government seized all properties owned by United States nationals in violation of the principles of international law.[90] Although it has been "estimated that 4,000 U.S. nationals have claims against the Government of Cuba totalling more than $1.5 billion,"[91] to date they have received no compensation for the taking of their property.[92] True, the Department of State had established procedures for receiving claims,[93] but "claimants are naturally discouraged from spending time and money in preparing and documenting claims against a country like Cuba when they discover that the only method available for presenting those claims is unlikely to be fruitful."[94] This observation is supported by the fact that, while the majority of large corporate claimants have filed their claims with the Department of State, hundreds of smaller claimants have made no effort to do so.[95]

The Cuban Claims Association, an organization representing United States citizens who suffered losses in Cuba, sought to remedy this situation in 1962. With the cooperation of Congressman Dante B. Fascell of Florida, the Association instituted a campaign for legislation applying the Gut Dam approach to Cuban nationalization claims.[96] In a letter to prospective members, the Association

[90] For a brief survey of the Cuban nationalizations, see the *Report of the Committee on International Law*, 84 N.Y.S.B.A. REP. 151 (1961).

[91] H.R. REP. No. 1759, 88th Cong., 2d Sess. 2 (1964) [hereinafter cited as HOUSE REPORT]. "This represents the most sizable uncompensated taking of American private property in our history and affects hundreds of companies and hundreds of thousands of American citizens and stockholders located all over the United States." *Hearings* 40 (remarks of Mr. Cecil J. Olmstead).

[92] 110 CONG. REC. 4888 (1964) (Mr. Fascell).

[93] *Hearings* 141-42.

[94] LILLICH & CHRISTENSON 93-94.

[95] *Hearings* 151:

Mr. MEEKER. I might recapitulate very briefly what we have here on the existing claims. We have received claims in the State Department from 83 claimants. Of that number, about nine-tenths of them are corporate entities rather than individuals. The claims of the corporate entities I would say would be for the greater part of the $524 million, but we can't be sure that this pattern would necessarily be repeated in exactly the same way.

Mr. FARBSTEIN. Will you break that down to amounts besides percentage of claimants? That should be very simple to break down.

Mr. MEEKER. Probably about 95 percent of the $524 million is corporate claims, about 95 percent.

[96] Letter from Nancy E. Hubbard, Secretary to Hon. Dante B. Fascell, to Richard B. Lillich, Dec. 12, 1962.

advanced its reasons for an early investigation and evaluation of these claims as follows:

> We feel that we should seek an immediate adjudication of claims, rather than see them shelved indefinitely in the U.S. State Department. Whereas the Department now "permits" the filing of claims without suggesting any further action concerning them, we feel that these matters should be resolved without further delay.
>
> The United States at the present time does not have the slightest calculation as to what U.S. losses in Cuba might be. Thus, if the moment should arrive for our country to bargain concerning these losses as a lump sum, the U.S. would be necessarily negotiating from unnecessary ignorance. This is true for two obvious reasons: (1) Since filing is permissive rather than obligatory, there is no possible way of knowing what percentage of claims have been filed, and (2) since claims have been accepted without comment, there is no way of separating the frivolous claims from those based on actual and sustained losses.
>
> There is one simple way to change this: resolve the claims now.[97]

Two years ago this writer, agreeing with this aspect of the Association's proposal,[98] urged Congress to enact legislation providing for the immediate preadjudication of claims against Cuba, recognizing

[97] Letter from John H. Parker, Secretary of Cuba Claims Association, to Prospective Members, Oct. 29, 1962. The Association's General Counsel reiterated this view in 1963, stating that

> the parties most affected here have been lulled into self hypnosis by filing their claims with the State Department—a procedure that has really no probative effect whatsoever.
>
> It is certain that no one will be denied the right to have his claim adjudicated for failure to file with the State Department; it is equally certain that filing will give no advantage. Probably, on some future date, when the machinery of compensation is activated, the proper commission will simply request the State Department to send over the files it has. This will be done.
>
> If this be true, then the present filing with the State Department is a formality without any basis in value for the claimant. It gives him a feeling of false security, not based on any real protection. This policy . . . precludes the U.S. from ever dealing realistically with the Cuban government about losses: it has no idea what the losses are, since filing is only permissive, and since the wildest claims are accepted with a quiet acknowledgement.

Letter From Clarence W. Moore, General Counsel of Cuba Claims Association, to Richard B. Lillich, Jan. 24, 1963.

[98] The second and more novel aspect of its proposal, involving loans to claimants secured only by the uncompensated portion of adjudicated claims, will be mentioned again in Chapter VI.

that "it would be the first time in the history of the United States that nationalization claims were determined before the conclusion of a lump-sum settlement with the foreign country or at least the vesting of its assets."[99] The Cuban Claims Act of 1964 writes the essentials of this preadjudication program into law.[100]

For present purposes it is unnecessary to describe in detail the above statute, which provides for the preadjudication of nationalization, debt, disability, and death claims against Cuba.[101] Rather, the intention here is to raise and consider two of the problems inherent in preadjudication, both of which also were present under the Gut Dam Act. For, while it is hard to find fault with the concept of registering claims, as was done in the case of Poland and is being done in the United Kingdom, going one step further and actually adjudicating them may cause difficulties. The pros and cons of pre-adjudication were discussed in great detail in the early 1950's by the old War Claims Commission, whose reversal of opinion on the question is some indication of its complexity. In its initial report on war claims in 1950, the Commission recognized that "an accurate and comprehensve résumé of the total number, types, and value of property claims cannot be ascertained unless alleged losses are substantiated by proof."[102] Furthermore, the Commission noted that

> a long postponement of the adjudication of international claims results in increasing difficulties in obtaining indemnification. Such delays also have a tendency to result in the exaggeration of amounts, the filing of unfounded claims, and the ultimate inability to substantiate just claims because of the loss of proof or the death of important witnesses.[103]

Therefore, the Commission strongly urged, "despite the fact that immediate payment cannot be made, that authority be granted to receive and adjudicate claims. . . ."[104]

[99] Lillich, *supra* note 37, at 787. Indeed, the Association acknowledged that "the pre-adjudication of [Cuban] claims would be unique." Letter From Clarence W. Moore, General Counsel of Cuba Claims Association, to Richard B. Lillich, Jan. 24, 1963.

[100] Cuban Claims Act of 1964, 78 Stat. 1110 (1964), 22 U.S.C.A. § 1643 (Supp. 1964).

[101] This task was attempted in Lillich, *The Cuban Claims Act of 1964*, 51 A.B.A.J. 445 (1965).

[102] WCC REP., H.R. Doc. No. 580, 81st Cong., 2d Sess. 53 (1950).

[103] *Id.* at 54.

[104] *Id.* at 53.

Three years later this same Commission reversed its position on preadjudication and concluded that:

> . . . the possible unrewarded burden to claimants and the cost to the Government which this method would involve militate against its use. It is the view of the Commission that claimants should not be required to incur the cost and effort involved in the preparation and presentation of their claims unless there is assurance that the claims will, in a reasonable measure, be compensated. Moreover, regardless how clear and precise the legislative language might be, calling for the advance adjudication of the claims without any commitment as to payment, claimants will construe the invitation to present and prove their claims as containing the implied promise to honor the awards.[105]

These two difficulties, in the Commission's reconsidered judgment, precluded legislation by Congress authorizing preadjudication.

There is, of course, a burden upon claimants when their claims are preadjudicated with no lump sum settlement in sight. Moreover, the burden on Cuban claimants is appreciably heavier than that imposed by Titles III and IV of the International Claims Settlement Act, where claimants against Bulgaria, Hungary, Rumania, and later Czechoslovakia received at least partial compensation from vested assets.[106] This burden, however, is no greater in the long run than that shouldered by a claimant seeking to establish his right to share in a lump sum settlement. The filing of claims is always burdensome. Yet to achieve the objective of ascertaining the exact

---

[105] WCC REP., H.R. Doc. No. 67, 83d Cong., 1st Sess. 160-61 (1953).

[106] See text at notes 38-46 *supra*. The financial burden of filing would have been eased somewhat and one objection raised by the War Claims Commission eliminated, see text at note 105 *supra*, had Congress enacted the original draft bill permitting the partial payment of adjudicated claims from vested Cuban assets. H.R. 10327, 88th Cong., 2d Sess. §§ 511-20 *passim* (1964). The bill as passed provides for the vesting of the assets of the government of Cuba, but it limits the use of the proceeds thereof to the payment of the FCSC's administrative expenses. 78 Stat. 1113 (1964), 22 U.S.C.A. § 1643j (Supp. 1964).

Since even such use has been questioned, the Departments of Justice, Treasury, and State, at the President's request, have recommended amendatory legislation with regard to the vesting provision. 51 DEP'T STATE BULL. 674-75 (1964). Compare Letter From Arthur S. Miller to the Editor, N.Y. Times, Nov. 5, 1964, p. 44, col. 5, with Letter From Monroe Karasik to the Editor, N.Y. Times, Nov. 15, 1964, § 4, p. 8, col. 5. The Acting Legal Adviser for the Department of State has taken the position that "international law does not require that we refrain from vesting property, but I think good judgment and policy do require it." *Hearings* 155 (remarks of Hon. Leonard C. Meeker).

number and amount of the claims, desired by claimants[107] and the executive[108] alike, surely the filing must be made obligatory and not, as in the case of the Polish claims, merely a voluntary process.[109] This reason retains its validity even when no funds to compensate claimants are available.

There is also, of course, a strong possibility (if not a certainty) that claimants, despite what the plain words of a statute may say, will construe legislation authorizing preadjudication as placing a moral obligation upon the United States to see that compensation is forthcoming. The Cuban claims bill passed by the House, while it made no provision for compensating claimants, failed to preclude the possibility of future compensation.[110] The House Report, although noting that "the adjudication of these claims will be for evaluation only," left the question open by adding that "this measure contains no provision *relating to any decision* as to the time, form, or manner of payment of eventual compensation."[111] The Senate eliminated any possible ambiguity by inserting a sentence in the Act specifically stating that "this title shall not be construed as authorizing an appropriation or as any intention to authorize an appropriation for the purpose of paying such claims."[112] As the Senate Report explained:

[107] In addition to the Cuba Claims Association (*id.* at 106), the bill providing for the preadjudication of Cuban claims received strong support from the American Claims in Cuba Committee. *Id.* at 47 (statement of Mr. Cecil J. Olmstead).

[108] The Department of State (*id.* at 141), of the Treasury (*id.* at 164), and of Commerce (*id.* at 172) all supported the concept of the prompt determination of Cuban claims.

[109] Although the Cuba Claims Association recognized the necessity of mandatory filing, see text accompanying note 97 *supra*, the statute does not specifically preclude non-filers from sharing in any eventual lump sum settlement. Nevertheless, while filing may not be compulsory as a matter of form, presumably it is imperative as a matter of practice. *Cf.* Martin, *op. cit. supra* note 68, at 247-49. In order to insure compliance with the statute's filing requirements, late filers undoubtedly will be denied compensation from any subsequent agreement with Cuba. *Cf.* Brooks, *op. cit. supra* note 64, at 195. To allow them to share in such a settlement would undercut the main reason for preadjudication and penalize diligent claimants by reducing the fund available to pay their awards. Since the FCSC must certify to the Secretary of State the amount determined to be the loss or damage suffered by claimants, 78 Stat. 1112 (1964), 22 U.S.C.A. § 1643f(a) (Supp. 1964), there appears to be no need for a refiling and readjudication of claims after any future settlement with Cuba.

[110] H.R. 12259, 88th Cong., 2d Sess. (1964).

[111] HOUSE REPORT 3. (Emphasis added.)

[112] 78 Stat. 1110 (1964), 22 U.S.C.A. § 1643 (Supp. 1964). See also 78 Stat.

This language should not require a detailed explanation; however, the committee wishes to make it abundantly clear that at no time in the future does it expect to authorize an appropriation of Federal funds to pay any claims of U.S. nationals against the Government of Cuba. In other words, if the claims in question are to be paid at all, the money will have to come from some source other than U.S. tax dollars.[113]

Nevertheless, should no settlement be reached with Cuba, or should any eventual settlement only partially compensate claimants, pressures undoubtedly will be brought to bear upon Congress to have the awards, or the balance due thereon, paid from appropriated funds.[114] Arguments for and against such congressional action will be considered in Chapter VI.

An Evaluation of Preadjudication

From the above discussion of the two objections to preadjudication raised by the War Claims Commission a dozen years ago, it is fair to conclude that the device's benefits outweigh its disadvantages. In the first place, as the Senate Report points out, preadjudication enables claimants to establish their claims "while the means of documenting and supporting such claims are still available."[115] Second, "the prompt receipt and determination of the amounts and validity of the claims will provide the Department of State with an accurate record for use in any future negotiations."[116] True, certain practical problems arise with respect to the Cuban Claims Act: it is much more difficult, for instance, to secure evidence from within a foreign country when claims are decided prior to settlement.[117] Moreover,

---

1112 (1964), 22 U.S.C.A. § 1643h (Supp. 1964), incorporating by reference an analogous provision found in Title I. 64 Stat. 17 (1950), 22 U.S.C. § 1626(f) (1958). This writer, urging the inclusion of some such disclaimer, had suggested that the Title I provision "would serve as a good model." Lillich, *supra* note 37, at 789. The Gut Dam Claims Act contained a less explicit provision. See text at note 56 *supra*.

[113] S. Rep. No. 1521, 88th Cong., 2d Sess. 2 (1964).

[114] One need look no further than the history of the advisory opinions of the Court of Claims on the French spoliation claims to become convinced of this likelihood. See WCC Rep., H.R. Doc. No. 67, 83d Cong., 1st Sess. 65-69 (1953). See also Toelle, *The Court of Claims: Its Jurisdiction and Principal Decisions Bearing on International Law*, 24 Mich. L. Rev. 675, 686-97 (1926).

[115] S. Rep. No. 1521, 88th Cong., 2d Sess. 8 (1964).

[116] *Ibid.*

[117] Compare the difficulties claimants are experiencing under the Czech program (FCSC, Fifteenth Semiann. Rep. 5 [1961]) with the access to records

certain theoretical problems also are present: Congress and the FCSC, a federal "administrative agency,"[118] in effect are impinging upon a traditionally executive function, the negotiation of claims settlements, with the possible consequence of putting the Department of State in a disadvantageous position in its future attempts to secure the best possible over-all settlement. Nevertheless, these and other problems, none of which were germane to the War Claims Commission's study and hence were not considered by it, are outbalanced by the need for a prompt adjudication of the claims for present negotiating and eventual distribution purposes, an adjudication which takes place before witnesses die and proof is lost. If the Gut Dam Claims Act opened up a new area of responsibility to the FCSC, the Cuban Claims Act will enable the Commission to make yet another modest contribution to the protection of foreign investment. To quote Congressman Fascell, "after 5 long years, it can be called the first effective step toward obtaining compensation for our American citizens whose property was arbitrarily taken pursuant to [Castro's] Communist design."[119] The Chapter that follows will consider the need for additional steps and the direction they should take.

---

and inspection of properties available to Polish claimants (FCSC, FOURTEENTH SEMIANN. REP. 18 [1961]). Chairman Re noted that "the difficulties [of proof] are more apparent in countries such as Czechoslovakia and Hungary where there was a total lack of cooperation or access to documents and witnesses." *Hearings* 18. These two countries, of course, have not concluded lump sum agreements with the United States. See text at note 85 *supra*. Poland, on the other hand, reached such a settlement, Article V of which requires it to furnish information or evidence needed by the FCSC. Agreement With Poland, July 16, 1960 [1960] 11 U.S.T. & O.I.A. 1954, T.I.A.S. No. 4545.

[118] American & European Agencies v. Gillilland, 247 F.2d 95, 100 (D.C. Cir.) (Miller, J., dissenting), *cert. denied*, 355 U.S. 884 (1957). See also Herman v. Dulles, 205 F.2d 715, 716 (D.C. Cir. 1953).

[119] 110 CONG. REC. 18587 (daily ed. Aug. 12, 1964).

VI.

A New Look at Old Problems

THE FORMULATION of a comprehensive program which will protect American investments abroad while at the same time avoiding results incompatible with the over-all foreign policy objectives of the United States must be based upon a realistic appraisal of the actual rights and remedies of a foreign investor under international law today.[1] Substantively, the so-called international law standards of the Hickenlooper Amendment,[2] now incorporated by reference into the Sabbatino Amendment,[3] could not conceivably be maintained in an international adjudication. Procedurally, the government's "ample powers to effect compensation," about which the Supreme Court waxed so lyrical in *Sabbatino*,[4] often prove to be a mirage. If the "bad man" approach of Mr. Justice Holmes be applied,[5] it is readily apparent that the amount and degree of protection available to a foreign investor whose property is taken generally is much less than he has been led to believe.

The initial task, therefore, is to examine with care and without national bias the present state of foreign investment law and the prospects of securing a greater measure of compliance with this body of law in the years ahead.[6] On the substantive side, one must

---

[1] Timberg rightly notes that "the mere opportunity to assert and claim substantive legal rights is a futile exercise, unless accompanied by effective legal remedies and procedures. As international lawyers, however, we have been too prone to confuse ethical and moral judgments with legal victories, and too inclined to be satisfied with the enunciation of abstract legal rights, divorced from tangible legal remedies and appropriate administrative procedures." Timberg, *Wanted: Administrative Safeguards for the Protection of the Individual in International Economic Regulation*, 17 AD. L. REV. 159, 166-67 (1965) [hereinafter cited as Timberg].

[2] See Chapter III.

[3] See Chapter II.

[4] Banco Nacional de Cuba v. Sabbatino, 376 U.S. 398, 436 (1964).

[5] Holmes, *The Path of the Law*, 10 HARV. L. REV. 457 (1897).

[6] "Accurate descriptions of the emperor's state of dress are rarely unhealthy, since the occasions when a myth is to be preferred to reality seldom occur. . . ." Metzger, *Act-of-State Refined: The Sabbatino Case*, [1964] SUP. CT. REV. 223, 232.

agree with Metzger's conclusion that "the effort to secure legal commitments to an international standard of treatment higher than national treatment, whether by growth of customary international law or through treaty, has fared poorly."[7] Moreover, as he goes on to state, "the forces and currents of our world do not indicate a change for the better in the foreseeable future. . . . Thus, codes of treatment for investments, arbitration conventions, and all the rest of the devices resting expressly or tacitly upon the assumption of such commitments appear to be atmospheric exercises."[8] The present writer, agreeing with Metzger on this score, also believes that more substantial progress can be made along other paths for the time being.

Lack of agreement on substantive norms, moreover, has had its effect on the procedural side too. Last year, for instance, the Latin American countries unanimously voted against a plan, proposed by the International Bank for Reconstruction and Development and strongly backed by the United States, which would have established new machinery for the conciliation and arbitration of international investment disputes.[9] The spokesman for these countries maintained that they

> already offered full legal protection for private foreign investments, including a guarantee against expropriation without fair compensation. The new convention . . . would give an unfair special advantage to foreign investors over domestic investors.[10]

This attitude has prevented not only the conclusion of a multilateral investment convention but also bilateral Friendship, Commerce and Navigation treaties which would offer protection to United States overseas investment.[11] Since there is little expectation of an immediate change of view, further efforts along these lines appear pointless at present.[12]

This brief examination of the attempts to firm up and render enforceable the international law rules regulating the protection of

[7] Metzger, The Individual and International Law: Property Interests (unpublished paper).

[8] *Ibid.*

[9] N.Y. Times, Sept. 10, 1964, p. 47, col. 3.

[10] N.Y. Times, Sept. 10, 1964, p. 55, col. 4.

[11] See text at notes 7 & 8 *supra.*

[12] For a more optimistic appraisal see Hynning, *The World Bank's Plan for the Settlement of International Investment Disputes,* 51 A.B.A.J. 558 (1965).

foreign investment, while showing that "we are effectively at the end of the road so far as the creation of international legal commitments in these areas is concerned, should not call for hand-wringing, nostalgia for an older and better world (for some only), or even dirges for the demise of international law."[13] Rather, it requires continued efforts by the United States to aid in the formulation of an acceptable body of international law concerning the taking of property,[14] coupled with new and redoubled efforts on the national level to revise and coordinate the various patchwork provisions and programs which the United States has established to protect its citizens who invest abroad. This all-important latter task can be accomplished satisfactorily only if the interrelated problems discussed in the preceding Chapters are considered collectively and not singly.[15]

A comprehensive study of these problems must start with the unenviable position of the American investor whose property is taken by a foreign country. Under the traditional rule holding that only states have rights under international law, the individual or corporate investor may not present an international claim directly to the foreign country.[16] Instead, under the theory that whoever wrongs a person indirectly injuries his state, the investor must seek redress by demonstrating to the Department of State that it should adopt his private grievance and espouse it as an international claim against the taking country.[17] Although the investor may satisfy all the formal conditions precedent, such as the exhaustion of local remedies in the foreign country,[18] the Department nevertheless

[13] Metzger, The Individual and International Law: Property Interests (unpublished paper).

[14] See generally Lillich, *Toward the Formulation of an Acceptable Body of Law Concerning State Responsibility*, 16 SYRACUSE L. REV. 721 (1965).

[15] The hearings this session on whether to extend the Sabbatino Amendment offered Congress the opportunity to examine the interrelationships between these various problems, but once again Congress adopted the piecemeal approach and limited its inquiry to the act of state doctrine alone. See the last two Sections of Chapter II.

[16] 1 OPPENHEIM, INTERNATIONAL LAW § 155b (8th ed., Lauterpacht 1955). See also RESTATEMENT, FOREIGN RELATIONS, Explanatory Notes § 175, comment *a* at 624 (Proposed Official Draft 1962) [hereinafter cited as RESTATEMENT].

[17] RESTATEMENT, Explanatory Notes § 217, comment *a* at 727.

[18] Department of State Memorandum entitled "Nationalization, Intervention or Other Taking of Property of American Nationals," March 1, 1961, re-

asserts an absolute (and judicially unreviewable) discretion as to whether it will "espouse" such claims against the foreign government, and claims complete (and judicially unreviewable) authority to waive or settle such claims without the consent of the claimant. Yet, it has no effective administrative procedure pursuant to which the claimant can set forth his case.[19]

Suppose, however, the American investor whose property is taken does not want government espousal of his claim, but prefers to negotiate a settlement himself with the foreign country or seek redress against it in municipal courts. Here the executive branch has it two ways. Although normally the investor retains control over his claim,[20] this control is subject to the executive's power to adopt the claim as its own and waive or settle it without the investor's consent.[21] In taking such action the government does not incur any liability under the Fifth Amendment since "it does not take away any material thing—the other country did that."[22] Thus, while the investor cannot compel espousal, often he may have it forced upon him to his detriment.[23]

---

printed in 56 AM. J. INT'L L. 167 (1962). See also Lillich, *The Effectiveness of the Local Remedies Rule Today*, 58 A.S.I.L. PROCEEDINGS 101 (1964).

[19] Timberg 160. "Whether to lend support to the claim of an American national by making it the claim of the United States is traditionally within the ultimate discretion of the Secretary of State. A claimant cannot compel espousal and . . . has no right to be accorded a formal hearing on his claim. Once the Department of State espouses a claim, it acquires exclusive control over it both under traditional international law and United States practice. Consequently, it may waive or settle the claim without the claimant's consent. Thus the claimant, after his claim is adopted by the United States, theoretically has little or no control over it. However, except in unusual circumstances, the Department will give great weight to the wishes of the claimant." LILLICH & CHRISTENSON, INTERNATIONAL CLAIMS: THEIR PREPARATION AND PRESENTATION 95 (1962).

[20] RESTATEMENT § 216. Since the magic wand of espousal has not been waved over his injury at this point, the claimant technically possesses only a private grievance and not an international claim.

[21] RESTATEMENT § 218(1).

[22] Oliver, *Executive Agreements and Emanations from the Fifth Amendment*, 49 AM. J. INT'L L. 362, 365 (1955). He adds, however, that "we should not expect that due process problems could be avoided by the simple expedient of adverting to the old dogma that the international reclamation is the sovereign's cause of action, not the individual's. Despite this theory, the fact remains that something is being done by executive agreement to diminish or change the citizen's legal relationship to property." *Id.* at 364. See text at notes 24-32 *infra*.

[23] The legal position of private foreign investors in other countries may be

The international law "dogma"[24] outlined above permits the private rights of American individuals and corporations investing abroad to be obliterated, limited or altered by governmental action unchecked by legal rules and unattended by adequate administrative safeguards.[25] Several court of claims cases have acknowledged that the government's actions with respect to the claims of its citizens may constitute the taking of property for a public use. In *Meade v. United States*,[26] involving an 1819 settlement agreement with Spain,[27] the court asked:

> Was the release and cancellation of Meade's claim against Spain such an appropriation of private property to public use as comes within the rule of law and the provision of the Constitution? A man's *choses* in action, the debts due him, are as much property and as sacred in the eye of the law as are his houses and lands, his horses and cattle. And when taken for the public good, or released or cancelled to secure an object of public importance, are to be paid for in the same manner.[28]

The court then went on to state that "while the right cannot be destroyed, the remedy may be denied, or an inadequate one supplied."[29]

In a subsequent decision, *Gray v. United States*,[30] the court held that the release of the French spoliation claims entitled the claimants to compensation for the taking of their property. Acknowledging the government's power to take action at the expense of the individual when such action is beneficial to the country at large, the court added:

---

the same, but at least in Great Britain the government gives their wishes greater consideration, even to the point of excluding specific claims from lump sum compensation agreements when such action promises to afford the claimants eventual higher recoveries. See the Schedule to the British-Rumanian Agreement, Nov. 10, 1960, CMND. No. 1232 (T.S. No. 82 of 1960), 385 U.N.T.S. 114.

[24] See text accompanying note 22 *supra*.

[25] Timberg 159.

[26] 2 Ct. Cl. 224 (1866), *aff'd on other grounds*, 76 U.S. 691 (1869).

[27] Treaty With Spain, Feb. 22, 1819, 8 Stat. 252, T.S. No. 327.

[28] 2 Ct. Cl. at 275.

[29] *Ibid*. The Supreme Court did not reach the question whether the release of a claim is a taking of private property. See note 26 *supra*. The question was raised in Petition for Certiorari, pp. 10-14, Haas v. Humphrey, 246 F.2d 682 (D.C. Cir.), *cert. denied*, 355 U.S. 854 (1957).

[30] 21 Ct. Cl. 340 (1886).

> Nevertheless, the citizen whose property is thus sacrificed for the safety and welfare of his country has his claim against that country; he has a right to compensation, which exists even if no remedy in the courts or elsewhere be given him. A right often exists where there is no remedy, and a most frequent illustration of this is found in the relation of the subject to his sovereign, the citizen to his Government.
>
> ... [The release of these claims] falls within the intent and meaning of the Constitution, which prohibits the taking of private property for public use without just compensation.[31]

The court then reiterated its view that an individual whose claim is released has been deprived of a compensable right, but that such right is enforceable only if the United States provides a remedy.[32]

Any doctrine which grants a government complete discretion to take or limit the property rights of its citizens deserves careful and continued examination. At a time when all efforts are being bent to accord individuals greater rights and remedies under international law, persons concerned with its development should be especially alert for such areas where the application of old fictions to new fact situations may harm the rights of many individuals. Permitting the executive complete freedom in the settling of claims perhaps could be justified when they were relatively few in number,[33] when the Department of State was uncertain as to their amount and validity,[34] and when the prime *raison d'être* of lump sum agreements was the settlement of international claims.[35] However, it becomes much

[31] *Id.* at 392-93.

[32] *Id.* at 406. Subsequent cases taking this view are Cushing v. United States, 22 Ct. Cl. 1 (1886) and The Schooner Betsey, 44 Ct. Cl. 506 (1909). It is only fair to say that the Department of State regards all these cases as completely outmoded.

[33] Originally the United States espoused most claims individually. Even when the number of claims against a foreign country warranted the establishment of a national or international claims commission, they generally were very few by today's standards. For instance, the national commission set up under the Convention With Peru, March 17, 1841, 8 Stat. 570, 9 Stat. 815, T.S. No. 275, rendered 26 awards and denied 7 claims. See 5 MOORE, INTERNATIONAL ARBITRATIONS 4603-07 (1898). See text at and accompanying note 36 *infra*.

[34] See generally 3 WHITEMAN, DAMAGES IN INTERNATIONAL LAW 2067 (1943).

[35] Of course, diplomatic factors always have entered into the settlement of international claims, but until recently they rarely were the paramount consideration. For instance, although Article VII of the Convention With France, July 4, 1831, 8 Stat. 432, T.S. No. 88, did provide that the United States would lower the duties on French wines for ten years, neither this nor other early lump

harder to support this position when thousands of claims are involved,[36] when they have been preadjudicated by the Foreign Claims Settlement Commission,[37] and when it is common knowledge that Cold War political considerations weigh more heavily on the minds of United States negotiators of settlement agreements than do the interests of American claimants.[38]

The pending claims agreement with Czechoslovakia serves to illustrate the problem. The Foreign Claims Settlement Commission, which completed the preadjudication of Czech claims in 1962, rendered 2,630 awards in the amount of $113,645,205.41.[39] These awards have been partially paid from an $8,540,768.41 fund derived from vested Czech assets.[40] The United States, for political reasons which appear quite sound, wishes to expand its trade with Czechoslovakia and other countries of Eastern Europe,[41] while Czech-

---

sum settlements attempted to tie foreign countries economically to the United States at the expense of American claimants. See text at and accompanying note 38 *infra*.

[36] Writing in 1962, the Chairman of the Foreign Claims Settlement Commission estimated that in twelve years the commission and its predecessors had processed 600,000 claims and issued nearly 400,000 awards exceeding $500 million. Re, *The Foreign Claims Settlement Commission: Its Functions and Jurisdiction*, 60 MICH. L. REV. 1079, 1089 (1962). See text at and accompanying note 33 *supra*.

[37] See generally Chapter V.

[38] It is no secret that during the negotiation of lump sum compensation agreements with Communist countries the wishes of the claimants often are subordinated to the desire of the executive branch to expand trading ties and to obtain cultural concessions. See text at and accompanying note 36 of Chapter V. For example, the Agreement With Rumania, March 30, 1960 [1960] 11 U.S.T. & O.I.A. 317, T.I.A.S. No. 4451, in which the Department of State waived 71.1% of the claimants' preadjudicated awards, laid the groundwork for expanded trade by that country with the United States. 42 DEP'T STATE BULL. 670 (1960). Rumania's Director of Planning Coordination chanced to note recently that "the trend that began shifting Rumania's trade from East to West four years ago would continue." N.Y. Times, Nov. 25, 1964, p. 51, col. 2. Similarly, Hungary, which recently expressed a desire to settle outstanding financial and property claims against it, hopes to convince the United States "to exchange commercial benefits in the West for a degree of cultural and ideological penetration." N.Y. Times, Nov. 27, 1964, p. 9, col. 1. See also N.Y. Times, Dec. 3, 1964, p. 54, col. 3; N.Y. Times, Jan. 7, 1965, p. 8, col. 5. *Quaere*: will such "benefits" include the waiver of a substantial percentage of the preadjudicated claims against Hungary? See text at and accompanying note 41 of Chapter V.

[39] FCSC, SEVENTEENTH SEMIANN. REP. 143 (1962).

[40] See text at and accompanying note 45 of Chapter V.

[41] "From the political viewpoint, the Administration holds that the greater the trade ties with the West, and particularly the United States, the more

oslovakia, for her part, "wants to sign a trade agreement with the United States, carrying a settlement of outstanding American claims."[42] The only obstacle blocking agreement is the fact that Czechoslovakia wants these claims discharged for about $15 million, almost $100 million less than their adjudicated value.[43] Now $100 million may or may not be a reasonable amount to pay for the political advantages that conceivably could flow from a Czech settlement. This question is debatable. What is less debatable is the fact that the 2,630 American citizens who hold Czech awards should not be required to pay the entire price themselves.[44] Yet the Department of State, without even according these claimants a hearing, may soon conclude an agreement with Czechoslovakia having just this effect.[45]

The same determination to protect American property abroad that caused Congress to respond to the Brazilian expropriations and the *Sabbatino* decision by enacting the Hickenlooper and Sabbatino Amendments may soon manifest itself again in legislation placing practical, if not legal, limitations upon the absolute discretion of the executive branch with respect to the settlement of international claims. In late 1963, then Senator Keating and Senator Douglas introduced a bill "to require Senate ratification of any claims agreement made with foreign nations for claims adjudicated by the

---

independent the Eastern European countries can become within the Communist sphere." N.Y. Times, Jan. 7, 1965, p. 8, col. 4. See text accompanying note 38 *supra*.

[42] *Ibid.*

[43] N.Y. Times, Jan. 7, 1965, p. 8, col. 5.

[44] See text at notes 28 & 31 *supra*. Former Senator Keating, strongly opposed to the pending Czech settlement, aptly remarked during the last Congress that he regarded "an agreement to accept less than 10 percent on a dollar of adjudicated claims as a form of foreign aid at the expense of [certain] U.S. taxpayers." 109 CONG. REC. 25149 (1963).

[45] Commenting upon the Supreme Court's rather naive endorsement of the efficacy of diplomatic remedies argument made by the government in *Sabbatino*, Timberg correctly observes that, "in actual practice, the redress obtained for claimants in State Department negotiations with the expropriating government is frequently only a small fraction of the actual losses caused by the expropriation, and the amounts ultimately paid to claimants only a negligible portion of the awards made by the Foreign Claims Settlement Commission. Yet, as a general rule, claimants are not informed either of the objectives or of the progress of the Department's negotiations, and consequently have no effective opportunity for a hearing in this connection." Timberg 160-61.

Foreign Claims Settlement Commission."[46] S. 2405 was designed to amend Section 4 of Title I of the International Claims Settlement Act by adding the following subsection:

> (k) It is the sense of the Congress that any agreement hereafter entered into between the Government of the United States and any foreign government, relating to the settlement of claims, determined or in the process of determination by the Foreign Claims Settlement Commission, by nationals of the United States against such foreign government shall be submitted to the Senate for its advice and consent.[47]

Reviewing recent instances where the United States has settled preadjudicated claims against foreign countries for a small percentage of their value, Senator Keating noted that these agreements

> have not been limited to claims settlements, but have included other points at issue and frequently trade agreements have been the quid pro quo to get agreement by the Communist governments on the claims owed.
>
> The result of these actions by the Department of State has been to deprive U.S. citizens of property, in the form of validated claims, without due process of law and with no further appeal to any agency of the Government.[48]

Pointing out that "a settlement of the Czech claims for roughly 10 percent would constitute a very dangerous precedent" in future negotiations,[49] the Senator also argued the need to make clear

> to the State Department through this and other methods that we will not tacitly accept the seizure of U.S. property overseas and then settle

---

[46] 109 CONG. REC. 25148 (1963).

[47] S. 2405, 88th Cong., 1st Sess. (1963). The bill applies only when Congress has authorized the Foreign Claims Settlement Commission to preadjudicate the particular claims for which settlement is sought. Thus it would not have covered the lump sum settlement with Poland in 1960, which was concluded before the Commission adjudicated the Polish claims.

[48] 109 CONG. REC. 25148-49 (1963). See also *id.* at 21592.

[49] *Id.* at 21591. "In other words, if an agreement of roughly 10 percent is concluded with Czechoslovakia, we can expect no better terms from Hungary or the U.S.S.R. and a total value of close to $300 million of validated U.S. claims may be simply junked." *Ibid.* Senators Douglas and Hickenlooper expressed similar sentiments. *Id.* at 21594. See generally LILLICH, INTERNATIONAL CLAIMS: THEIR ADJUDICATION BY NATIONAL COMMISSIONS 105-06 (1962).

for a mere pittance of the true value. This measure should appreciably strengthen the hand of our Government in all such negotiations, by giving the Senate an opportunity to pass on claims settlements before they go into effect.[50]

Since, as we have seen, the settlement of international claims is one of those areas where the executive has demonstrated "a reluctance to expose pending issues to the catalyzing influence of a formal public record,"[51] Senator Keating probably was right in anticipating Department of State opposition to his bill.[52] Moreover, as the Senator acknowledged, the bill was only a "sense of the Congress" resolution and hence not binding upon the President,[53] who certainly possesses the inherent power to settle international claims by executive agreement and thus avoid the necessity of securing Senate consent.[54] Nevertheless, the bill if passed would constitute a strong affirmation of congressional policy which scarcely could be ignored by an Administration dependent upon Congress for the authorization and appropriation of foreign assistance funds. Cer-

[50] 109 Cong. Rec. 25149 (1963). "What is more, even the Czechs, who now plead poverty, might think twice if they expected such an argument to be weighed by the Senate, which is well aware of Czech foreign aid to Cuba and other nations around the world." Id. at 21592.

[51] Timberg 168.

[52] "I am sure that the State Department is opposed to the amendment, because it does not want any interference in regard to the amount for which it can settle such claims of U.S. citizens against other countries. But there is precedent for the amendment." 109 Cong. Rec. 21593 (1963), citing Convention With Panama, Jan. 26, 1950 [1950] 1 U.S.T. & O.I.A. 685, T.I.A.S. No. 2129. Moreover, almost all lump sum compensation agreements concluded by the United States before World War II were in the form of conventions or treaties rather than executive agreements. See Lillich, op. cit. supra note 49, at 7-9. Compare McDougal & Associates, Studies in World Public Order 491 n.167 (1960): "The notion that the Executive has exclusive control over the settlement of international private claims has, however, yielded in favor of a doctrine of coordinate control, with primary presidential responsibility."

[53] "Mr. PASTORE. Would the Senator's amendment require a two-thirds vote for ratification of the agreement?

"Mr. KEATING. Yes, it would, except I wish to point out that the amendment, like so many others, is one which the State Department would have a right to ignore if it wished to do so. It is a sense-of-Congress amendment. . . .

"Mr. PASTORE. What if the Administration chose not to do it?

"Mr. KEATING. There is very little that we could actually do about it." 109 Cong. Rec. 21593 (1963).

[54] See McDougal & Associates, op. cit. supra note 52, at 512-15. See also text accompanying note 53 supra.

tainly Congress has the power to adopt such a measure,[55] the enactment of which would be unnecessary if the Department of State
possessed the initiative to adopt some-imposed standards of its
own.[56]

The international law doctrine which prevents American investors whose property abroad is taken from enforcing their rights
internationally, leaving them instead to wait for whatever compensation the executive branch may achieve by way of settlement, also
permits the executive branch to control the outcome of related actions brought in municipal courts in the United States. As the classic case of *United States v. Pink*[57] demonstrates, "when the State
Department executes an overall claims settlement . . . a not infre-
quent consequence is to deprive actual or prospective litigants of
rights and remedies which they have been seeking in other judicial
forums."[58] Moreover, by intervening in sovereign immunity and act
of state cases when negotiations are pending or have not even begun,

---

[55] "I do not think this amendment interferes improperly with the responsibilities of the Department of State. We do not ask for a 100 percent settlement,
merely for Senate review of the settlement the State Department asks that we
accept. Perhaps a case can be made that other considerations among the issues
at stake justify a less than 100 percent settlement. But in a case in which the
decision of the responsible agency [the Foreign Claims Settlement Commission]
is threatened with almost complete contradiction by another agency, I think we
can properly insist on Senate review to provide an opportunity for the protection of legitimate interests of citizens." 109 CONG. REC. 21594 (1963) (Senator
Douglas).

[56] Timberg, who believes it desirable to hold the executive branch to some
standard of administrative accountability when its foreign relations operations
impinge on the rights of private persons, cautions that "such accountability
should not be secured by placing the Executive Branch under restraints not
contemplated by the Federal Constitution, and subordinating it to the Legislative
Branch. Greater administrative accountability need not involve any infringement of the constitutional doctrine of separation of powers, such as was inherent in the Bricker Amendment. It can be secured by the easier route of
replacing, wherever possible, the Department's present informal procedures
with formal administrative procedures incorporating the maximum feasible
amount of public notice, statement of applicable standards, public hearing and
explanation of the grounds of agency decision." Timberg 168. Unfortunately, if
the history of the new administrative safeguards in connection with revocation
of passports is a fair example, the Department appears content to eschew procedural reforms unless prodded from the outside. *Id.* at 165.

[57] 315 U.S. 203 (1942). See M. H. Cardozo, *The Authority in Internal Law
of International Treaties: The Pink Case*, 13 SYRACUSE L. REV. 544 (1962).

[58] Timberg 161.

the Department of State attempts, very successfully one may add, to impose the *Pink* rationale on American courts in the absence of an overriding executive agreement.[59] Relying upon the doctrine that when American property overseas is taken "the claim of the individual merges in the right of the offended sovereign,"[60] the Department seeks to "internationalize" the claim from the start, and thus effectively close down American courts in the interest of an eventual over-all claims settlement.[61]

To the American who invests abroad, then, the practical thrust of the doctrine discussed above is to deprive him of effective control over the disposition of his rights in property when that property is taken by a foreign country. The Department of State, in effect, assumes residual control over all property acquired and investments made beyond American shores, such control becoming nearly absolute should the property or investment be taken. Thus when property is taken abroad the Department achieves the same power over American investors that it would have if a federal marshaling of assets statute dealing with such situations were on the books. Ironically, since its stated policy is "to facilitate and increase the participation of private enterprise in furthering the development of the economic resources and productive capacities of less developed friendly countries and areas,"[62] the United States, far from coming forth with a comprehensive program protecting such investors, has approached the problem on a piecemeal basis, content to obtain the political advantages of such investment without assuming any firm commitments to American investors which might limit its discretionary political power in such matters.

At a time when Congress is deeply concerned with the protection

[59] See text at notes 230-33 of Chapter II.

[60] The United States Attorney made this argument in The Schooner Exchange, 11 U.S. (7 Cranch) 116, 122 (1812).

[61] See text at notes 20-23 *supra*. No one has accepted the executive's claim to paramountcy more wholeheartedly than did Mr. Justice Stone in *Ex parte Peru*, 318 U.S. 578, 587 (1943): "When the Secretary elects . . . to settle claims . . . by diplomatic negotiations between the two countries rather than by continued litigation in the courts, it is of public importance that the action of the political arm of the Government taken within its appropriate sphere be promptly recognized, and that the delay and inconvenience of a prolonged litigation be avoided by prompt termination of the proceedings in the district court."

[62] Foreign Assistance Act of 1961, § 221(a), 75 Stat. 429 (1961), 22 U.S.C. § 2181(a) (Supp. V, 1964).

of private foreign investment,[63] and when the President for balance of payments reasons is attempting to regulate such investment informally,[64] both branches of government would do well to rethink their objectives in this area and then cooperate in preparing a program designed to achieve these objectives in the years ahead. While future policy choices undoubtedly will influence the degree and method of protection to be accorded American investors, thus rendering unprofitable any attempt to set forth a definitive program now, it may be useful in summary to catalogue the various problems which would have to be considered and to suggest alternative and sometimes preferred choices for their resolution.

Problem I: Municipal Courts. Enough has been said in Part One of this book to indicate this writer's belief that courts in the United States, under congressional mandate if need be, should assume a more active role in those cases where American investors seek relief for the taking of their property. The Sabbatino Amendment, preferably without the provision permitting the executive to order the application of the act of state doctrine, should be retained,[65] and Congress should consider enacting a bill, along the lines of the one introduced by Senator Erwin,[66] prohibiting the Department of State from short-circuiting the judicial process in sovereign immunity cases.[67] If the executive branch can justify its present right to intervene in act of state cases or its supposed right to issue "conclusive" suggestions in cases involving sovereign immunity, either on grounds of an equitable marshaling of assets or otherwise, then perhaps Congress should create a limited right of intervention in truly exceptional cases. In these instances, considerations of public policy if not technical due process would require a provision holding the particular investor harmless,[68] by permitting him either to sue in

---

[63] See Chapter II, Section on "The Sabbatino Amendment."

[64] N.Y. Times, Feb. 11, 1965, p. 57, col. 5.

[65] For a critique of the amendment see the last Section of Chapter II.

[66] See Appendix A.

[67] For an analysis of Senator Erwin's bill see the last Section of Chapter I.

[68] *Cf.* Brief of the North American Sugar Industries, Inc. & the Cuban American Sugar Mills Co., as Amici Curiae, p. 25, Banco Nacional de Cuba v. Sabbatino, 376 U.S. 398 (1964): "If now the United States wishes to marshal the proceeds of the property of C.A.V. and other particular interests for 'all American interests,' it should then ask that proceedings be stayed until enactment of legislation authorizing the Government to expropriate the property of these

the Court of Claims[69] or to have his claim adjudicated and paid for by the Foreign Claims Settlement Commission.[70] The heavy burden of proving the necessity of such right of intervention, it must be reiterated, rests with the executive.

Problem II: Established Government Programs. While no country should expect the United States to continue its foreign assistance in the face of uncompensated takings of American property, the Hickenlooper Amendment, making "full" compensation the *sine qua non* of continued aid, is a political mistake which has not lived up to the expectations of its supporters in practice.[71] Abolition of the statute would not lessen appreciably the protection available to Americans who invest abroad, although the impossibility of securing its repeal might dictate a compromise measure permitting the President to waive its application. Moreover, the positive approach of the Investment Guaranty Program, in marked contrast to the Hickenlooper Amendment, represents a far better way of protecting American investment abroad. Congress, which undoubtedly will continue to expand the program in any event, may want to give serious consideration to requiring prospective United States investors in foreign economics to insure their investments under the IGP.[72]

Problem III: Developing Government Programs. The Cuban Claims Act, which authorizes the preadjudication of nationalization and other claims against Cuba, is a laudable first step in the direction of according American investors a measure of formal due process before as well as after the conclusion of lump sum settlement agree-

---

particular business interests for the public purpose of dividing it amongst 'all American interests.' Such legislation would, of course, provide for just compensation. Without this, to deprive despoiled owners of their defenses, even for a high public purpose, would constitute a deprivation of property without due process of law. *Home Ins. Co.* v. *Dick*, 281 U.S. 397. This Court has held that when such a deprivation by Executive action occurs, just compensation is owing. *Cities Service Co.* v. *McGrath*, 342 U.S. 330." See also text at notes 28 & 31 *supra*.

[69] This suggestion was advanced in a Note, 50 CALIF. L. REV. 559, 564-66 (1962).

[70] It is understood that a bill seeking to amend the Sabbatino Amendment in this fashion may be introduced during this Congress.

[71] For a critique of the amendment see the last Section of Chapter III.

[72] This step, of course, would require making the IGP's coverage world-wide. "Old" investments might be made insurable too. See a critique of the program in the last Section of Chapter IV.

ments.[73] Unfortunately, American claimants who obtain adjudicated awards will receive no compensation at this time, and if past practice is any guide their awards will be paid only in part under an eventual Cuban settlement. The enactment of a bill along the lines suggested by Senator Keating, while constitutionally no bar to a disastrous settlement such as the Czech agreement appears to be, certainly would have a salutory effect on all future lump sum settlements, since the Department of State would be faced with the alternatives of ignoring the statute, and therefore calling attention to the possibly poor terms of the agreement, or of having to justify the settlement if it sought Senate approval.[74] However, while the Keating Resolution undoubtedly would assure claimants of a better dividend once a settlement was negotiated, it would offer them little consolation in the meantime.

It now may be time, as Metzger contends, for the United States and other capital-exporting countries to assume greater obligations for their citizens who invest abroad. As he astutely observes, "until fifteen years ago this was avoided both because of the potential costs involved and because there was deemed to be a limited national interest in his venture in any event."[75] The growth of the Investment Guaranty Program reflects a marked change in congressional sentiment, and if this change continues it conceivably could lead to the compensation of award holders, to the extent that they are not covered by the IGP, through loans[76] or from appropriated funds.[77] Much has been made of the point that United States taxpayers have not been asked to pay for the awards rendered by the Foreign Claims Settlement Commission under past claims programs, and tech-

---

[73] On the importance to claimants of "the first phase of the process of lump sum settlements," see Soubbotitch, Book Review, 9 N.Y.L.F. 257, 262-63 (1963).

[74] See text at and accompanying notes 46-54 *supra*.

[75] Metzger, note 7 *supra*.

[76] The original draft bill which eventually became the Cuban Claims Act contained a section authorizing loans to claimants not to exceed 30% of their unpaid awards, this figure being upped to 80% if the claimant agreed to use his loan to carry out an acceptable project under the Alliance for Progress program. H.R. 10327, 88th Cong., 2d Sess. § 520 (1964).

[77] Great Britain has appropriated funds to provide additional compensation for Egyptian claimants who establish claims before the British Foreign Compensation Commission. 11 Eliz. 2, c. 12, § 1 (1962). True, the appropriation was made to supplement funds already received from Egypt, but this distinction is one of fact more than principle.

nically this assertion is correct. The fact remains, however, that the United States, when it utilized certain economic lures to achieve a settlement with Poland in 1960, used the money of taxpayers in part to effect a settlement for the benefit of Polish claimants.[78] If claimants against one country are being assisted indirectly, the argument can be made that no reason exists why claimants against other countries should not receive similar assistance in a more direct and forthright manner.[79]

An expanded guaranty program, the preadjudication of claims as a routine matter, and the compensation of award holders from the public purse are all self-help measures to be sure. Yet their adoption need not undercut the international law standard asserted by the United States in this area any more than the indemnification of tuna fish boat owners for fines paid to foreign countries making exaggerated claims to the territorial sea represents a departure from the three-mile limit.[80] Indeed, the United States, by indemnifying its citizens rather than waiving a part of their claims, would be able to maintain its international law position, settle at the most favorable moment, and then as subrogee reimburse the Treasury against the earlier use of appropriated funds. The net loss incurred would be no more than that suffered under recent lump sum agreements, and it would be spread over all taxpayers and not limited to those who had lost property abroad.[81]

[78] LILLICH, *op. cit. supra* note 49, at 108.

[79] Congressman Fascell, arguing for the Cuban loans provision, note 76 *supra*, frankly stated that "all we are doing is laying the cards on the table and doing it in a direct route for the benefit of our own people." *Hearings Before the Subcommittee on Inter-American Affairs of the House Committee on Foreign Affairs*, 88th Cong., 2d Sess. 104 (1964). These hearings contain the best discussion to date of the pros and cons of the problem.

[80] See the Act to Protect the Rights of Vessels of the United States on the High Seas and in Territorial Waters of Foreign Countries, 68 Stat. 883 (1954), 22 U.S.C. §§ 1971-76 (1958). Owners are reimbursed only for fines actually paid. "Compensation for that part of the claim based upon the confiscation of . . . equipment can be obtained only by the successful espousal of a formal claim . . . through diplomatic channels." *Contemporary Practice of the United States Relating to International Law*, 57 AM. J. INT'L L. 894, 901-02 (1963). For a long list of incidents occurring from September 15, 1951, to June 28, 1963, see 109 CONG. REC. 21252-53 (1963), reprinted in 3 INT'L LEGAL MATERIALS 61-62 (1964).

[81] The argument that the foreign investor should not have to pay exclusively for foreign policy benefits achieved for the entire body politic by the waiver of claims was advanced fifteen years ago by Drucker, *Agreement with Jugoslavia*, 159 THE ECONOMIST 1490 (Dec. 31, 1949).

The above procedure, of course, might well be conditioned upon the submission of American investors to some measure of government regulation and even, in the words of Secretary of State Rusk, supervision "in terms of how they should conduct themselves, whether or not they should expand their facilities with this or that rate increase or not. . . ."[82] This prospect, supposedly so repugnant to American business that the Secretary used it as an argument against the adoption of the Hickenlooper Amendment in 1962, somehow seems less worrisome today. Tomorrow it may even be acceptable, for most American investors abroad are sufficiently sophisticated to know that they cannot have their cake and eat it too. In short, the protection of foreign investment in the foreseeable future requires both cooperation and concessions on the part of government and business. It has been the purpose of these procedural studies to point out possible ways in which the interest of both can be reconciled and the rule of international law strengthened in this turbulent area.

[82] *Hearings on a Draft Bill to Amend Further the Foreign Assistance Act of 1961, as Amended, and for Other Purposes Before the House Committee on Foreign Affairs*, 87th Cong., 2d Sess. 811 (1962). See text at note 64 *supra*.

APPENDIX A

The Proposed Ervin Amendment

S. 1894, 89TH CONG., 1ST SESS. (1965)

A Bill

To AMEND title 28, United States Code, to provide means of redress for the unlawful seizure of American property by foreign governments.

Be it enacted by the Senate and House of Representatives of the United States of America in Congress assembled,
That (a) section 1332, title 28, United States Code, is amended by—

> (1) redesignating subsections (c) and (d) thereof as subsections (d) and (e), respectively; and
> (2) inserting therein, immediately after subsection (b) thereof, the following new subsection:

"(c) If the matter in controversy in any such action involves, or arises out of, an act of a foreign state in violation of general principles of international law, or of a treaty to which the United States and the foreign state are signatories, it shall be no bar to the maintenance of the action that it is brought against a sovereign state, without its consent, or that it involves the validity of officials acts of such state."

(b) Section 1655, title 28, United States Code, is amended by adding at the end thereof the following new paragraph:

"In any such action by an American citizen or corporation, involving or arising out of an act of a foreign sovereign in violation of the general principles of international law, or of a treaty to which the United States and such foreign sovereign are signatories, it shall be no bar to the maintenance of the action that it is brought against a foreign state, without its consent, or that it involves the validity of official acts of such state."

Sec. 2. (a) Title 28, United States Code, is amended by inserting therein, immediately after section 1655 thereof, the following new section:
"§ 1655A. Lien enforcement; property of foreign states

"It shall be no objection to the issuance of mesne or final process with respect to property, as provided by rule 64 of the Rules of Civil Procedure promulgated under this title, that the property is owned by a foreign state, if it is used in or acquired from commercial activities by such foreign state, or has been acquired by it as a result of acts against an American citizen or corporation in violation of general principles of international law or of a treaty to which the United States and the foreign sovereign are signatories."

(b) The analysis of chapter 111, title 28, United States Code, is amended by adding thereto, immediately after the item relating to section 1655 thereof, the following new item: "1655A. Lien enforcement; property of foreign states."

APPENDIX B

The Sabbatino Amendment

SUBSECTION 301(D)(4) OF THE FOREIGN ASSISTANCE ACT OF 1964;
22 U.S.C.A. § 2370(E)(2) (SUPP. 1964).

NOTWITHSTANDING ANY other provision of law, no court in the United States shall decline on the ground of the federal act of state doctrine to make a determination on the merits giving effect to the principles of international law in a case in which a claim of title or other right is asserted by any party including a foreign state (or a party claiming through such state) based upon (or traced through) a confiscation or other taking after January 1, 1959, by an act of that state in violation of the principles of international law, including the principles of compensation and the other standards set out in this subsection: Provided, That this subparagraph shall not be applicable (1) in any case in which an act of a foreign state is not contrary to international law or with respect to a claim of title or other right acquired pursuant to an irrevocable letter of credit of not more than 180 days duration issued in good faith prior to the time of the confiscation or other taking, or (2) in any case with respect to which the President determines that application of the act of state doctrine is required in that particular case by the foreign policy interests of the United States and a suggestion to this effect is filed on his behalf in that case with the court, or (3) in any case in which the proceedings are commenced after January 1, 1966.

APPENDIX C

Executive Branch Comments to Conference Committee (September, 1964)

REQUIREMENT THAT COURTS IN UNITED STATES EXAMINE ACTS OF
FOREIGN STATES UNLESS THE PRESIDENT DETERMINES OTHERWISE

The Difference

The Senate version adds an amendment to the Act providing that no court in the United States shall decline, on the ground of the act of state doctrine, to examine the validity of acts of foreign states which have occurred after January 1, 1959 and which are alleged to be contrary to international law. The provision authorizes the President to invoke the act of state doctrine, and thereby prevent examination into the act of a foreign state, when he determines that this is required in a particular case by the foreign policy interests of the United States.

The House version contains no comparable provision.

Executive Branch Position

The Executive Branch strongly opposes inclusion of this amendment in the Foreign Assistance Act.

This amendment would seriously prejudice the President's conduct of foreign relations. The amendment would require the courts of the United States to determine the validity of acts of foreign states with respect to property located in their territories. Both the timing of the litigation and the decisions of courts would be beyond the control of the Executive Branch. Discretion in the President to waive application of the statute at the time the litigation is brought would not cure this problem, since a case could well extend over several years in changing international circumstances.

The Executive Branch position is consistent with the recent decision of the Supreme Court, by an 8 to 1 vote, in the *Sabbatino* case. The amendment would eliminate, or substantially modify, the act of state doctrine which has been part of U.S. law, as enunciated by the Supreme Court, at least since 1898. The *Sabbatino* decision was consistent also with the practice followed in a number of the principal trading countries of the Western world, including Great Britain, France and Japan.

Neither the Supreme Court decision in the *Sabbatino* case nor the Executive Branch position in any sense constitute support for the Castro regime in Cuba. Nor does the Executive Branch position constitute any departure from the traditional view of international law, including the right to prompt, adequate and effective compensation for expropriatory acts.

Since nationalization programs are typically undertaken as a result of deep-seated political, social and economic causes inherent in local conditions, the deterrent effect of the amendment on such programs of foreign countries would appear to be slight. It is unrealistic to expect that nationalization programs would be prevented by the prospects of later litigation in United States courts which might declare the actions unlawful and ineffective to pass title.

The ability of United States citizens to obtain compensation as a result of the amendment would depend on the coincidence of property which could be levied on coming to the United States. Thus, as in the *Sabbatino* case, the particular claimants might recover a portion of their assets, but the great majority of claimants would not be able to share equitably in distribution. On the other hand, adoption of the amendment could well make it more difficult for the United States to secure relief for its nationals in international adjudication or negotiation.

Finally, it should be noted that the *Sabbatino* case did not result in any gain for the Castro Government, since all Cuban assets in the United States have been frozen under Treasury Department regulations. Passage of the amendment would not therefore be in any way detrimental to the interests of the Castro Government.

APPENDIX D

The Hickenlooper Amendment

SECTION 301(E) OF THE FOREIGN ASSISTANCE ACT OF 1962, AS AMENDED; 22 U.S.C. § 2370(E) (SUPP. 1964).

THE PRESIDENT shall suspend assistance to the government of any country to which assistance is provided under this chapter or any other Act when the government of such country or any government agency or subdivision within such country on or after January 1, 1962—

(1) has nationalized or expropriated or seized ownership or control of property owned by any United States citizen or by any corporation, partnership, or association not less than 50 per centum beneficially owned by United States citizens, or

(2) has taken steps to repudiate or nullify existing contracts or agreements with any United States citizen or any corporation, partnership, or association not less than 50 per centum beneficially owned by United States citizens, or

(3) has imposed or enforced discriminatory taxes or other exactions, or restrictive maintenance or operational conditions, or has taken other actions, which have the effect of nationalizing, expropriating, or otherwise seizing ownership or control of property so owned, and such country, government agency, or government subdivision fails within a reasonable time (not more than six months after such action, or, in the event of a referral to the Foreign Claims Settlement Commission of the United States within such period as provided herein, not more than twenty days after the report of the Commission is received) to take appropriate steps, which may include arbitration, to discharge its obligation under international law toward such citizen or entity, including speedy compensation for such property in convertible foreign exchange, equivalent to the full value thereof, as required by international law, or fails to take steps designed to provide relief from such taxes, exactions, or conditions, as the case may be; and such suspension shall continue until the President is satisfied that appropriate steps are being taken, and no other provision of this chapter shall be construed to authorize the President to waive the provisions of this subsection.

Upon request of the President (within seventy days after such action referred to in paragraphs (1), (2), or (3) of this subsection), the Foreign Claims Settlement Commission of the United States (established pursuant to Reorganization Plan No. 1 of 1954, 68 Stat. 1279) is hereby authorized to evaluate expropriated property, determining the full value of any property nationalized, expropriated, or seized, or subjected to discriminatory or other actions as aforesaid, for purposes of this subsection and to render an advisory report to the President within ninety days after such request. Unless authorized by the President, the Commission shall not publish its advisory report except to the citizen or entity owning such property. There is hereby authorized to be appropriated such amount, to remain available until expended, as may be necessary from time to time to enable the Commission to carry out expeditiously its functions under this subsection.

APPENDIX E

Agency for International Development

OFFICE OF DEVELOPMENT FINANCE AND PRIVATE ENTERPRISE

Investment Guaranties Division
Washington, D.C. 20523

Countries Where Investment Guaranties Are Available—January 1, 1965

Convertibility	Expropriation	War Risk
Afghanistan	Afghanistan	Afghanistan
Argentina	Argentina	*Argentina
Bolivia	Bolivia	*Bolivia
Central African Republic	Central African Republic	*Central African Republic (Dec. 31, 1964)
Chile	Chile	*Chile
China, Republic of	China, Republic of	*China, Republic of
Colombia	Colombia	*Colombia
Congo (Brazzaville)	Congo (Brazzaville)	*Congo (Brazzaville)
Congo (Leopoldville)	Congo (Leopoldville)	*Congo (Leopoldville)
Costa Rica	Costa Rica	—
Cyprus	Cyprus	*Cyprus
Dominican Republic	Dominican Republic	*Dominican Republic
Ecuador	Ecuador	*Ecuador
El Salvador	El Salvador	—
Ethiopia	Ethiopia	—
Gabon	Gabon	*Gabon
Ghana	Ghana	—
Greece	Greece	*Greece
Guatemala	Guatemala	—
Guinea	Guinea	*Guinea
Haiti	Haiti	—
Honduras	Honduras	—
India	India	—
Iran	Iran	—
Israel	Israel	*Israel
Ivory Coast	Ivory Coast	*Ivory Coast
Jamaica	Jamaica	*Jamaica
Jordan	Jordan	*Jordan
Kenya	Kenya	*Kenya
Korea	Korea	Korea
Laos	Laos	*Laos (Dec. 29, 1964)
Liberia	Liberia	*Liberia

213

Convertibility	Expropriation	War Risk
Malagasy, Republic of	Malagasy, Republic of	*Malagasy, Republic of
Malaya, Fed. of	Malaya, Fed. of	—
Mali	Mali	*Mali
Mauritania	Mauritania	*Mauritania
Morocco	Morocco	*Morocco
Nepal	Nepal	*Nepal
Nicaragua	Nicaragua	Nicaragua
Niger	Niger	*Niger
Nigeria	Nigeria	—
Pakistan	Pakistan	—
Panama	Panama	Panama
Paraguay	Paraguay	—
Peru	—	—
Philippines	Philippines	—
Portugal	Portugal	—
Senegal	Senegal	*Senegal
Sierra Leone	Sierra Leone	*Sierra Leone
Somali Republic	Somali Republic	*Somali Republic
Spain	Spain	—
Sudan	Sudan	*Sudan
Tanzania	Tanzania	*Tanzania
Thailand	Thailand	Thailand
Togo	Togo	*Togo
Trinidad-Tobago	Trinidad-Tobago	*Trinidad-Tobago
Tunisia	Tunisia	*Tunisia
Turkey	Turkey	*Turkey
U.A.R. (Egypt)	U.A.R. (Egypt)	*U.A.R. (Egypt)
Uruguay[1]	Uruguay[1]	
Venezuela	Venezuela	*Venezuela
Vietnam	Vietnam	*Vietnam
Yugoslavia[2]	Yugoslavia[2]	—

[1] Although applications will be accepted for Uruguay, guaranties cannot be processed until agreement is ratified by the country's legislative body.

[2] Restricted availability.

* Including also guaranties against loss due to revolution & insurrection; also extended risk.

[AUTHOR'S NOTE: An AID list published April 23, 1965, indicates that all three specific risk guaranties are available for Dahomey and some will become available for Brazil.]

SELECTED BIBLIOGRAPHY

Chapter I

CARDOZO, MICHAEL H. *Judicial Deference to State Department Suggestions: Recognition of Prerogative or Abdication to Usurper?* 48 CORNELL LAW QUARTERLY 461 (1963).

FALK, RICHARD A. THE ROLE OF DOMESTIC COURTS IN THE INTERNATIONAL LEGAL ORDER. Ch. VII. Syracuse, N.Y.: Syracuse University Press, 1964.

FRANCK, THOMAS M. *The Courts, the State Department and National Policy: A Criterion for Judicial Abdication.* 44 MINNESOTA LAW REVIEW 1101 (1960).

JESSUP, PHILIP C. *Has the Supreme Court Abdicated One of Its Functions?* 40 AMERICAN JOURNAL OF INTERNATIONAL LAW 168 (1946).

SWEENEY, JOSEPH M. THE INTERNATIONAL LAW OF SOVEREIGN IMMUNITY. Washington, D.C.: United States Government Printing Office, 1963.

TIMBERG, SIGMUND. *Sovereign Immunity, State Trading, Socialism and Self-Deception,* IN ESSAYS ON INTERNATIONAL JURISDICTION. Columbus, Ohio: Ohio State University Press, 1961.

Chapter II

FALK, RICHARD A. THE ROLE OF DOMESTIC COURTS IN THE INTERNATIONAL LEGAL ORDER. Syracuse, N.Y.: Syracuse University Press, 1964.

————. *The Sabbatino Controversy,* IN THE AFTERMATH OF SABBATINO. New York, N.Y.: The Association of the Bar of the City of New York, 1965.

LAYLIN, JOHN G. *Holding Invalid Acts Contrary to International Law— A Force Toward Compliance.* 58 AMERICAN SOCIETY OF INTERNATIONAL LAW PROCEEDINGS 33 (1964).

LILLICH, RICHARD B. *A Pyrrhic Victory at Foley Square: The Second Circuit and Sabbatino.* 8 VILLANOVA LAW REVIEW 155 (1963).

METZGER, STANLEY D. *Act-of-State Doctrine Refined: The Sabbatino Case.* [1964] THE SUPREME COURT REVIEW 223.

STEVENSON, JOHN R. *The State Department and Sabbatino—"Ev'n Victors Are by Victories Undone."* 58 AMERICAN JOURNAL OF INTERNATIONAL LAW 707 (1964).

215

Chapter III

BROWN, WINTHROP G. *The Use of Foreign Aid as an Instrument to Secure Compliance with International Obligations*. 58 AMERICAN SOCIETY OF INTERNATIONAL LAW PROCEEDINGS 210 (1964).

CARDOZO, MICHAEL H. *Intervention: Benefaction as Justification*, IN ESSAYS ON INTERVENTION. Columbus, Ohio: Ohio State University Press, 1964.

LILLICH, RICHARD B. *The Protection of Foreign Investment and the Foreign Assistance Act of 1962*. 17 RUTGERS LAW REVIEW 405 (1963).

————. *The Protection of Foreign Investment and the Hickenlooper Amendment*. 112 UNIVERSITY OF PENNSYLVANIA LAW REVIEW 1116 (1964).

METZGER, STANLEY D. *Property in International Law*. 50 VIRGINIA LAW REVIEW 594 (1964).

OLMSTEAD, CECIL J. *Foreign Aid as an Effective Means of Persuasion*. 58 AMERICAN SOCIETY OF INTERNATIONAL LAW PROCEEDINGS 205 (1964).

Chapter IV

ASSOCIATION OF THE BAR OF THE CITY OF NEW YORK. COMMITTEE ON FOREIGN LAW. *The Guaranty Program of the International Cooperative Administration*. 14 THE RECORD 269 (1959).

BREWER, WILLIAM C., JR. *The Proposal for Investment Guarantees by an International Agency*. 58 AMERICAN JOURNAL OF INTERNATIONAL LAW 62 (1964).

CLUBB, BRUCE E., AND VANCE, VERNE W., JR. *Incentives to Private U.S. Investment Abroad Under the Foreign Assistance Program*. 72 YALE LAW JOURNAL 475 (1963).

FATOUROS, A. A. GOVERNMENT GUARANTEES TO FOREIGN INVESTORS. New York and London: Columbia University Press, 1962.

NOTE. *The Investment Guaranty Program: Problems of Administration*. 64 COLUMBIA LAW REVIEW 315 (1964).

WHITMAN, MARINA VON NEUMANN. THE UNITED STATES INVESTMENT GUARANTY PROGRAM AND PRIVATE FOREIGN INVESTMENT. Princeton, N.J.: Princeton Studies in International Finance No. 9, 1959.

Chapter V

BROOKS, E. A. S. *Registration of International Claims Under the Foreign Compensation Act, 1950*, IN 44 TRANSACTIONS OF THE GROTIUS SOCIETY 187 (1959).

CHRISTENSON, GORDON A. *The United States-Rumanian Claims Settlement Agreement of March 30, 1960.* 55 AMERICAN JOURNAL OF INTERNATIONAL LAW 617 (1961).

LILLICH, RICHARD B. *International Claims: A Comparative Study of American and British Postwar Practice.* 39 INDIANA LAW JOURNAL 465 (1964).

———. INTERNATIONAL CLAIMS: THEIR ADJUDICATION BY NATIONAL COMMISSIONS. Syracuse, N.Y.: Syracuse University Press, 1962.

———. *The United States-Bulgarian Claims Agreement of 1963.* 58 AMERICAN JOURNAL OF INTERNATIONAL LAW 686 (1964).

RE, EDWARD D. *Domestic Adjudication and Lump-Sum Settlement as an Enforcement Technique.* 58 AMERICAN SOCIETY OF INTERNATIONAL LAW PROCEEDINGS 39 (1964).

INDEX

Espousal of claims. *See* Department of State, espousal of claims; Diplomatic remedies

Exhaustion of local remedies, 138, 191

Ex parte Peru, 11, 19, 22, 29

Export-Import Bank, 124

Expropriations: Argentina, 140, 141; Brazil, 117-20 *passim*, 125, 140, 141, 142, 143, 196; Ceylon, 131, 140, 143; Chile, 140; Cuba, 45, 49-50, 51, 55, 61, 62, 65, 67, 69, 134, 135, 182; Honduras, 140; Indonesia, 129, 140, 144; Panama, 140; Peru, 140; compensation for, 8, 55, 59, 67, 68, 69, 81, 88, 103, 109, 118; retaliation, 67, 69; mentioned, 64, 67, 90

Falk, 16, 24, 31, 50n*26*, 51n*33*, 52n*36*, 53n*44*, 55, 58, 65, 66n*108*, 75n*166*, 76, 77, 78, 80, 82, 103n*304*, 106, 111, 112, 113

Fatouros, 137

Fifth Amendment, 20, 37, 108, 192

Fisher, Roger, 41

Food for Peace, 124

Foreign Assistance Act of 1961, 97, 124, 127, 150-51, 153-56

Foreign Assistance Act of 1962, 121, 146

Foreign Assistance Act of 1963, 148

Foreign Assistance Act of 1964, 97, 99, 103

Foreign Assistance Program, 109

Foreign Claims Settlement Commission: preadjudication, 170-74, 177, 180, 185, 195; investigation of Gut Dam claims, 174-76; mentioned, 181, 188, 197, 199n*55*, 202, 203

Foreign Compensation Act of 1950, 177

Foreign Compensation Commission, 177, 179

France, 46

Franck, 22, 36n*194*

Freezing of assets, 92

Friendship, Commerce and Navigation treaties, 117, 132, 190

General Assembly, resolution, 83

Geneva Convention on the Territorial Sea and the Contiguous Zone of 1958, 15, 26

Germany, 46

Government programs, problems of, 202-05

Gray v. United States, 193

Great Britain, 7, 46, 168, 177, 184

"Green light theory." *See Bernstein* exception

Gut Dam Claims Act, 175-81 *passim*, 184, 188

Hackworth, 3

Henkin, 94

Hickenlooper Amendment: history, 117-23; text, 121-23; analysis, 123-34; objections to, 135-38; consensus on, 139-40; mentioned, 87, 92, 105, 121-23

Holmes, 4

Honduras, 138n*91*, 140

Hughes Letter, 8

Hungarian claims, 173 & n*41*, 185

Hungary, 172, 178, 180, 185, 188n*117*

Indirect ownership, 129

Indonesia, 140, 145

International Bank for Reconstruction and Development, 190

International Claims Settlement Act of 1949, 169, 172, 173, 185, 197

International Joint Commission, 175

International law, violation of, 64, 66, 73, 75, 89

Investment Guaranty Program: history, 147-52; convertibility, 149, 158-60; expropriation and confiscation, 149, 155-58; all risks, 150, 151; housing projects, 150, 151; war, revolution, or insurrection, 150, 152; extended risk, 151; specific risk, 151, 152-60; evaluation, 160-64; Congo claims, 163

Jay Treaty of 1794, 167

Jay Treaty Commission, 168

Jessup, 15, 17, 27, 33, 44

"Judicial deference," 13, 16, 27

Judicial remedy, 95

Keating Resolution, 196-99, 203

DATE DUE

GAYLORD			PRINTED IN U.S.A.